Theory and the Practice of Education

Volume I

Theory, values and the classroom teacher

Theory and the Practice of Education

Volume I

Theory, values and the classroom teacher

edited by

ANTHONY HARTNETT

Lecturer in the Sociology of Education, School of Education,
University of Liverpool

and

MICHAEL NAISH

Lecturer in the Philosophy of Education, School of Education,
University of Liverpool

HEINEMANN EDUCATIONAL BOOKS LTD

Heinemann Educational Books Ltd
LONDON EDINBURGH MELBOURNE AUCKLAND TORONTO
HONG KONG SINGAPORE KUALA LUMPUR
IBADAN NAIROBI JOHANNESBURG
LUSAKA NEW DELHI

ISBN 0 435 80410 3

First published 1976

Published by
Heinemann Educational Books Ltd
48 Charles Street, London W1X 8AH

Photoset and printed by
Interprint (Malta) Ltd

To
Elizabeth,
Isobel,
and Vera

Quotations

Even in ancient Greece, the independent thinking of the great pre-Socratic philosophers evoked strong and anxious reactions. In late Medieval times, a few decades of confrontation with alien world-views and 'open' sceptical thinking tended to be succeeded by decades of persecution of those responsible for disturbing established orthodoxy and by a general 'closing-up' of thought. In present-day Nigeria, we seem to be seeing yet another example of the atrocious birth-pangs of the 'open' society.

Why should the transition be so painful? Well, a theme of this paper has been the way in which a developing awareness of alternative world-views erodes attitudes which attach an absolute validity to the established outlook. But this is a process that works over time—indeed over generations. Throughout the process there are bound to be many people on whom the confrontation has not yet worked its magic. These people still retain the old sense of the absolute validity of their belief-systems, with all the attendant anxieties about threats to them. For these people, the confrontation is still a threat of chaos of the most horrific kind – a threat which demands the most drastic measures. They respond in one of two ways: either by trying to blot out those responsible for the confrontation, often down to the last unborn child; or by trying to convert them to their own beliefs through fanatical missionary activity.

Again, as I said earlier, the moving, shifting thought-world produced by the 'open' predicament creates its own sense of insecurity. Many people find this shifting world intolerable. Some adjust to their fears by developing an inordinate faith in progress towards a future in which 'the Truth' will be finally known. But others long nostalgically for the fixed, unquestionable beliefs of the 'closed' culture. They call for authoritarian establishment and control of dogma, and for persecution of those who have managed to be at ease in a world of ever-shifting ideas. Clearly, the 'open' predicament is a precarious, fragile thing.

ROBIN HORTON
'African Traditional Thought
and Western Science' Part II, *Africa*,
Vol. 37 (1967), pp. 185–6.

... the practice of Communist states and, more logically, of Fascist states (since they openly deny and denounce the value of the rational question-and-answer method), is not at all the training of the critical, or solution-finding, powers of their citizens, nor yet the development in them of any capacity for special insights or intuitions regarded as likely to reveal the truth. It consists in something which any nineteenth century thinker with respect for the sciences would have regarded with genuine horror – the training of individuals incapable of being troubled by questions which, when raised and discussed, endanger the stability of the system; the building and elaboration of a strong framework of institutions, 'myths', habits of life and thought intended to preserve it from sudden shocks or slow decay. This is the intellectual outlook which attends the rise of totalitarian ideologies – the substance of the hair-raising satires of George Orwell and Aldous Huxley– the state of mind in which troublesome questions appear as a form of mental perturbation, noxious to the mental health of individuals and, when too widely discussed, to the health of societies. This is an attitude which looks on all inner conflict as an evil, or at best as a form of futile self-frustration; which considers the kind of friction, the moral or emotional or intellectual collisions, the particular kind of acute spiritual discomfort which rises to a condition of agony from which great works of the human intellect and imagination, inventions, philosophies, works of art, have sprung, as being no better than purely destructive diseases – neuroses, psychoses, mental derangements, genuinely requiring psychiatric aid; above all as being dangerous deviations from that line to which individuals and societies must adhere if they are to continue in a state of well-ordered, painless, contented, self-perpetuating equilibrium.

ISAIAH BERLIN
'Political Ideas in the
Twentieth Century', *Foreign Affairs*,
Vol. 28 (1950), p. 372.

No man need despair of gaining proselytes to the most extravagant hypothesis, who has art enough to represent it in any favourable colour. The victory is not gained by the men at arms, who manage the pike and sword, but by the trumpeters, drummers, and musicians of the army.

DAVID HUME

Those present must have long remembered the morning early in the war when German propaganda had got into a fearful tangle through the constantly repeated claims about the sinking of the *Ark Royal*, and the representative of the Navy, asked by Göebbels what should be done about it, replied, rather tartly: 'I am afraid I can't make any suggestion on this subject, Herr Reichsminister; after all the *Ark Royal* was sunk by the Ministry of Propaganda and not by us'.

HUGH GREENE
Review of *The Secret
Conferences of Dr. Goebbels
1939–43*, ed. W. A. Boelcke,
(Weidenfeld and Nicolson),
in *New Statesmen* 18 December 1970,
p. 840.

It was done in this way: gangs of some twenty workers were formed who had to accomplish a length, say, of five hundred yards of wall, while a similar gang built another stretch of the same length to meet the first. But after the junction had been made the construction of the wall was not carried on from the point, let us say, where this thousand yards ended; instead the two groups of workers were transferred to begin building again in quite different neighbourhoods. Naturally in this way many great gaps were left, which were only filled in gradually and bit by bit, some, indeed, not till after the official announcement that the wall was finished. In fact it is said that there are gaps which have never been filled in at all, an assertion, however, which is probably merely one of the many legends to which the building of the wall gave rise, and which cannot be verified, at least by any single man with his own eyes and judgement, on account of the extent of the structure.

FRANZ KAFKA
'The Great Wall of China',
in *Metamorphosis and Other
Stories* (Penguin Books, 1961),
p. 67.

Contents

Contents of volume II

Foreword

I once had a colleague who referred to the refectory menu as 'the theory'. Most Englishmen would probably have some sympathy with his usage. For what passes in England as common sense is an attitude according to which theory is something slightly suspect and slightly unnecessary. No Englishmen hold this view more deeply than teachers; at least, that is, when teachers are talking about education. Practice, they say, makes perfect: theory does not even make sense.

Engineers used to say much the same. Their folk heroes were people like James Brindley who, illiterate and all but innumerate, changed the face of England with roads and canals that worked. But the time came, a century or so ago, when people who believed in theory, such as the Germans, began to make things that in practice worked better. We all know the story of the Great Exhibitions and the beginnings of technical education in England, and we realize that practical engineers nowadays, while retaining some disdain for the mere theorist, have a healthy respect for 'theory'.

Why can we not say the same about teachers? The comparison with engineers may suggest why. 'Theory', to an engineer, is a recognizable body of knowledge based on sciences such as mechanics, metallurgy and electronics, whose relation to practice is in general terms demonstrable. If he strengthens his structure according to particular theoretical considerations, it will in fact, and almost invariably, carry the additional stresses that he intends. But 'theory' in education is, even to an educational theorist, a matter for debate, and its relation to practice is far from obvious. Even if, as is far from certain, some consensus can be achieved as to the types of subject-matter which constitute 'educational theory' – is it philosophy plus psychology plus sociology plus history plus curriculum development? – it may appear to have little value as a guide to action. It can, of course, posit some broad limits within which we must act, and can indicate that some developments are improbable, such as that a physically-handicapped docker's daughter is not very likely to become a Harley Street specialist. However, these limits and improbabilities themselves vary from time to time, and if we look for some area of relative reliability in educational theory, we may find ourselves unable to do more than offer a series of plausible explanations for what has happened, and a general schema such as Piaget's within which things may happen, instead of offering detailed guidance for what can, or should, happen. No amount of Bernstein or Peters will tell anyone just what to say to IIIB or how to say it effectively.

It is small wonder, then, if the place of theory in the training of teachers causes problems. What exercises the ingenuity of an experienced specialist for a lifetime has to be offered to the initiate in a hurry. It is scarcely surprising if the student teacher selects one aspect of it, according to inclination. After all, it is easier to take a political or clinical or pastoral stand, or just to teach reading, than to educate. Or he may reject it all in favour of the accumulated folklore of the teaching profession which appears to work, at least to the extent of keeping the children in their desks and producing CSE results that will not give rise to awkward questions. As behaviour by a beginner, this is understandable. Unfortunately, the structure of the teaching profession is such that the older a practising teacher becomes, the more cynical he tends to be about theory. Not only does he find it of little direct applicability, but he notes that those of his colleagues who take theory seriously tend not so much to illuminate the classroom as to withdraw from it. So he concludes that it is all a racket, and probably tells his junior colleagues so.

He is wrong. His attitude may be explicable, but he is nevertheless wrong. He is quite right to think that philosophers, or psychologists, or sociologists, who claim a monopoly or a decisive voice in education, are exceeding their function, but he is wrong if he thinks that theory is unimportant. He would be more justified if he emphasized its complexity than if he asserted its irrelevance. He would be even more justified if he claimed that its strength is his strength too, for he cannot do anything without acting implicitly on some theory, and conversely no theory can be built which is not in some way grounded in the experience of people like him. He may even end by finding that the making of theory is itself a kind of practice, a kind which he may well catch himself undertaking, in his homespun way, and much to his surprise.

Mr Hartnett and Mr Naish have written an unusual, stimulating, and necessary book. They take the ordinary student and the ordinary teacher and try to tease out how philosophy and sociology really do relate to their professional activities. They are quite honest and fearless in what they say and at the same time they contrive to show a real concern both for their disciplines and for teachers. Some of their writing is quite demanding: so much for the belief that books about education are beneath the intellectual appetite of the really educated. Our experienced practical colleague, if he is as intelligent and open-minded as he thinks he is, will find plenty here to extend his thinking and enliven his imagination as he goes about his practical affairs.

W. A. L. BLYTH
School of Education
University of Liverpool

Preface

This book arose out of our work at the School of Education, in the University of Liverpool, where between us we were teaching the philosophy of education, and the sociology of education, to three groups of students: experienced teachers attending full-time or part-time in-service courses for advanced diplomas; experienced teachers studying for the Master of Education degree; and graduates on a one-year, full-time, initial training course. During the course of our work, we came to reflect more and more on the issues that teaching such courses raised for our students, and for us.

Our students appeared to have diverse, and often incompatible views, both about what theory was in education, and about what it could offer them. They could, speculatively, be divided into the following groups, depending on their view of theory.

(*i*) Those who believed that all theory was irrelevant to good practice. For these students all that mattered was diverse experience in schools.

(*ii*) Those who thought that theory could resolve value disputes and problems about what roughly might be called educational ends, namely the aims, purposes, and point of education.

(*iii*) Those who did not see theory as impinging upon questions of ends, but solely on those of means. Theory, on this account, enabled people to be more effective in doing whatever they thought worth doing. Thus a teacher of science might see theory as telling him how to teach effectively, or more effectively, or how to use what is often called educational technology (visual aids and so on), where it is taken for granted that science should be taught, and that its nature is understood. Heads and aspiring heads might see theory as telling them how to run their schools more effectively, where some account of what education is, and of what is educationally valuable, is assumed. Students in this group, in particular, were inclined, when discussing theory, to deploy pairs of terms such as relevant and irrelevant, constructive and destructive, positive and negative, practical and academic, or practical and theoretical. In these pairs were embodied, it seemed to us, a number of implicit and unexamined views about the roles of teachers and others in the educational system; about our roles; and about education itself.

(*iv*) Those who saw theory as a source or corpus of officially approved views about what ought to go on in schools.

None of these views about theory seemed to us to be adequately grounded, and we were led to reflect on the whole problem of the relationships between theoretical activities (such as philosophy and sociology) and practical activities (such as teaching). We came to the conclusion that the connexion between theory and practice, which students of education are often expected to make for themselves, ought not to be left peripheral to or outside a course, but ought to be its central point. This book is a consequence of this conviction. We also decided that more light might be cast upon the problems of theory and practice in education if philosophy and sociology were together used to examine them.

The format of the book

Given these points, the question then arose about the sort of book which would best suit our purposes. We did not want to write a textbook, partly because we wished to include views other than our own. Nor did we feel that a book of readings, with a short introduction, would adequately cover the issues we wished to raise. All too frequently readers of such books are left to discover why the readings were included, how they relate to each other, and what sort of issues they give rise to.

Eventually, we decided on a compromise between a textbook, and a book of readings. Volume I contains seven readings, and is in two sections. Volume II contains six readings. Each reading is given an introduction in which we pick out the main points it makes *for our purposes*, and we say (where this is necessary) why it has been included in the book, and how it relates to education. Following the readings in each section of Volume I, and following those in Volume II, there are discussions entitled 'Some issues arising from the readings'. These discussions are meant to raise issues that might be further followed up, rather than to be considered contributions to the literature. Although each volume is self-contained and can be read without the other, the two volumes together are intended to constitute a unified argument about the role, and particularly about some of the limitations, of theory in education.

There is a final point about the format of this book and this concerns what might be taken to be our lavishness with footnotes and references to literature. Footnotes enable us to raise issues arising from points we make, without at the same time breaking the flow of the discussion. Citing literature enables us to indicate where points that we merely mention are more fully discussed. It is also a way of inviting students to look up things for themselves, and to see that very few things in philosophy and sociology are undisputed. This seems to us something that is very important to learn. Further, the amount and range of literature called upon in the philosophy and sociology of education seems to us lamentably small. The same references appear again and again, even though there is a considerable body of work in the main disciplines that remains unexploited. One useful exercise (in the sociology of knowledge) would be to see who cites whom, and what communality of viewpoint this indicates. One reason, therefore, for our citing such literature as we do is simply to bring it to people's notice and to indicate that the frontiers of the philosophy and sociology of education can be much wider than some discussions presuppose.

Using the book

The articles and discussions vary in difficulty. We found this hard to avoid, partly because of the nature of the issues themselves, partly because we did not wish to pass off as relatively simple issues those which were not, partly because we have preferred to choose readings for the quality of their discussion even if this meant excluding those which were of a lesser quality but which might be thought, on a conventional assessment, to be open to a more immediate understanding. In any case different readers, depending on their experience and background, are likely to find different parts of the book easy or difficult. One way into the readings and discussions may be: (*i*) to read our introductions to the readings and then the readings themselves; (*ii*) to re-read the introductions in the case of the more difficult articles; (*iii*) to look at the section entitled 'Some issues arising from the readings'. Introductory material to the area under discussion can often be found among our references to the literature.

The role of theory: our position

Our views about what theory can offer those who work in schools and elsewhere in the educational system, and about what we think the consequences of these views are for the way education should be conducted are, we hope, reasonably explicit in what we have ourselves written in this book, and in the quotations at the front of it. Our view on the place of theory is, briefly, one of what might be called a moderate scepticism, relative both to the claims for theory often made by those professionally engaged in the education of teachers, and to the claims that (to judge from the use they put it to) a number of policy makers, and others administering or otherwise working in the educational system, are currently prepared to make for it. In particular, it needs to be said that neither sociology nor philosophy is likely to make the often intractable problems faced by teachers, policy makers, and others any easier to solve. The contrary might often be true. For what these disciplines might do is to narrow the area of what is unquestioned in education. They might make teachers, policy-makers, and others more aware of their own values, more critical of what might be called 'official views', more aware of the values of those they teach, and more aware of what is not known, and so of what they do not know. Because it is important, in our view, that teachers and others have, as far as possible, a reasonably grounded and realistic view about what theory can offer (both in their own interests, and in those of the children and students with whose well-being they are concerned) this book is intended very much more as a discussion of the limitations of theory, than as a justification of philosophy and sociology in the education of teachers, though we do discuss this issue towards the end of the book. But to the extent to which the issues raised in this book are of importance to teachers, it might be said to be at least a contribution towards how philosophy and sociology are to be justified in the education to teachers, without being designed as one.

A possible criticism

One complaint that might be raised against this book is that it is neither sociological nor philosophical, but occupies a sort of no-man's-land beyond the trenches of academic and intellectual respectability. It needs to be emphasized that this book is concerned with a problem, or series of problems, centred on theory and practice, which we believe can be illuminated by the *joint use* of philosophy and sociology. Though we have been concerned to identify the sorts of question with which we had to deal (normative, conceptual, logical, empirical, etc.), it has been a matter of comparative indifference to us whether, on some conventional categorization, they are to be described, in particular cases, as philosophical or as sociological. Even so, parts of the book can be reasonably held to be more philosophical or sociological than others. In some parts the distinction may be harder to draw, and we do not regard this as a defect. But even where the distinction can be fairly sharply drawn, the responsibility for what is said there is joint. The choice of articles is joint, each read the work of the other as the book went through its numerous drafts, and we did not feel precluded from making comments or writing on topics that might reasonably be held to have fallen under the other's discipline, when we felt that this could be profitably done. Whether or not the journey to this no-man's-land has been worth while, we leave for the reader to judge.

Possible readership

We stated at the beginning of this preface that this book arose from our teaching with a number of different groups of students at Liverpool, and we hope that the book will appeal to those who are similarly placed and to others – that is, to experienced teachers on in-service courses who are studying philosophy and sociology of education; students studying for Masters degrees in education; students undergoing initial training in university departments of education, polytechnics, and colleges of education; as well as those who are professionally concerned with the training and education of teachers. Some parts of the book raise issues about how decisions may be made at the level of educational policy. Those who are interested in this area, whether as participants, researchers, or spectators may also find something of use.

Acknowledgements

A book of this sort consists of a large number of intellectual debts, many of which have been unconsciously incurred. We would, however, like to mention some of the people whom we know have influenced its final form, and contents.

We would like to thank those who have taught us in the recent past, especially Basil Bernstein, Brian Davies, Mrs Pamela Huby, and Michael Young.

We are indebted to Alan Blyth, Douglas Finlayson, Steve Ferguson, Derek Meakin, Hazel Sumner, Norton Tempest and David Thomas, and to other of our colleagues in the School of Education, including those involved in the Schools Council Project, 'History, Geography, and Social Science 8–13'. They have provided us with ideas, references, and stimulation; what they said at coffee, they may well now find in our book.

It can be inferred from the preface that perhaps our greatest debt is to the students who have attended our courses, especially those who took the Diploma in the Advanced Study of Education, the Diploma in Special Education, and the Master of Education degree, between 1969 and 1973. They have been confused and baffled by our early attempts to deal with some of the issues discussed in this book. We can only hope that the interest they have shown, the questions they have asked, and the criticisms they have made, have been taken adequate note of, and that now the issues seem a little clearer.

We would like to thank the children, staff, and headteachers of two primary schools – Cherryfield County Primary School and St Francis Xavier's Primary School – where we made some videotape recordings. We are also indebted to the director and staff of the Audio-visual Aids and Programmed Learning Unit of the University of Liverpool, who enabled us to make the recordings. It was during filming at these schools that we developed some of the ideas and issues with which the book deals.

It has been our delight to use one of the best education libraries in the country. We owe a great debt to John Vaughan (the tutor-librarian), to his assistant Geoffrey Smith, and to the library staff in general. They have helped us with inter-library loans with the purchase of books, with the photo-copying of material, and have given us a great deal of useful advice. Their tireless co-operation made this book possible.

We would like to thank those who have read part, or all, of the various drafts that this book has been through: David Aspin, Olive Banks, Alan Blyth, Leon Boucher, Brian Davies, Ray Derricot, Douglas Finlayson, F. H. Hilliard, Liz Hindess, Derek Meakin, Peter Renshaw, and Norton Tempest. They all took a great deal of care, often at busy times of the year, to make detailed and helpful comments. We would like to thank, too, Joan Carr who read the entire manuscript, and who kept a sharp eye on our English. We owe a great debt to Mrs Kath Moore, who, as if by magic, transformed our illegible, cut-up, corrected, manuscripts into clear, accurate, double-spaced typescripts. Without her help, neither of us would have been able to read what the other had written.

We are grateful to the copyright holders for permission to reproduce material included in the *Readings* Sections. Full details are given at the beginning of each reading.

We would, finally, like to thank Paul Richardson and Philippa Stratton, of Heinemann Educational Books, who waited for our vague ideas to be turned into a book, and who gave us encouragement and advice while they waited.

SCHOOL OF EDUCATION
UNIVERSITY OF LIVERPOOL
NOVEMBER 1975

1
Theory, practical problems, practical knowledge and education

Introduction to the readings

In this section we discuss one or two ways in which theory and practice can be distinguished, and some of the limitations of theory, as they bear on the work of teachers and others in the educational system.[1]

During the course of a day teachers are faced with innumerable problems about what to do. Some may be trivial, others not. Some may be solved routinely, others be more difficult. Problems about what to do are practical problems; problems not of this sort are theoretical problems. In the first reading, D. P. Gauthier discusses the distinction between practical and theoretical problems, and he makes a number of points

[1] Theory and practice can be distinguished in many ways and the issues (philosophical, sociological, historical, etc.) that the concepts give rise to are innumerable. The following will suggest some ways in which distinctions might be made: D. J. O'Connor, *An Introduction to the Philosophy of Education* (Routledge & Kegan Paul, 1957), Chapters 4 and 5; P. H. Hirst, 'Educational theory', in J. W. Tibble, ed., *The Study of Education* (Routledge & Kegan Paul, 1966), pp. 29–58; W. B. Gallie, 'The idea of practice', *Proceedings of the Aristotelian Society*, Vol. LXVIII (1967–68), pp. 63–86; S. L. Smith, 'The pattern of educational theory, 1968', *Australian Journal of Education*, Vol. 12 (1968), pp. 252–64; E. Nagel, 'Philosophy of science and educational theory', *Studies in Philosophy and Education*, Vol. 7 (Fall, 1969), pp. 5–27; J. C. Walker, 'Theory and practice in education', *Philosophy of Education Society of Australia, Proceedings*, Vol. I, No. 1 (June, 1972), pp. 62–80. Further literature is given in J. P. Powell, *Philosophy of Education: a Select Bibliography* (Manchester University Press, 2nd edn, 1970), pp. 9–12. For more general discussions see also N. Lobkowicz, *Theory and Practice: History of a Concept from Aristotle to Marx* (University of Notre Dame Press, 1967); R. Edgley, *Reason in Theory and Practice* (Hutchinson, 1969); B. Crick, 'Theory and practice', in B. Crick, *Political Theory and Practice* (Allen Lane, The Penguin Press, 1972), pp. 1–34.

1

about the solutions to practical problems. A distinction can be made, therefore, between theory and practice in terms of a distinction between practical and theoretical problems, and so between practical and theoretical reasoning and, as a consequence of this, between practical judgements (or statements) which will be the conclusions of practical reasoning and theoretical judgements (or statements) which will be those of theoretical reasoning.

Any discussion of theory and practice, particularly if it begins with the distinction between theoretical and practical problems, will eventually have to involve what is sometimes described as 'the fact-value problem'. This problem, raised by S. Hampshire (among other related ones) in the second reading, is implicit in Gauthier's discussion, and much of what Hampshire says can be seen as a continuation of the discussion of issues raised there. Many practical judgements are value judgements (for example, I ought to do this, this is the best thing to do, this is the right thing to do). The grounds adduced to justify such judgements will include factual statements (i.e. theoretical ones). Thus, a teacher might decide that he ought to abandon one teaching method for another on the grounds that with the second one his pupils will learn more quickly. The fact-value problem can, on one interpretation then, be seen as a problem about the way that theoretical statements can justifiably be used to support practical judgements. The question of how the empirical statements of psychology, sociology, or of common sense might justify practical judgements in education about teaching methods, classroom, school, and system organization, for example, is a special case of this more general problem. In so far as theoretical statements can be used to justify practical judgements, solutions to practical problems will depend to some extent on solutions to theoretical ones. Teachers, therefore, have an interest in problems of both these kinds.

Theory and practice have been distinguished so far in terms of inter-related distinctions between theoretical and practical problems, reasoning, and judgements or statements. But another general way of making a distinction between theory and practice is in terms of theory as theorizing (i.e. reasoning) and practice in the sense of doing (i.e. action). On this interpretation, important questions about theory and practice are, to give examples: what is the relationship between theorizing (reasoning) about what to do and how to do it, and actually doing it? and what is the role of the theory of activities or skills (understood as the rules, maxims, precepts, etc. governing them) in learning to perform the activities and skills in question, and in actually performing them? The third reading, an article by H. Entwistle, deals with issues of theory and practice of this sort. It also gives a good idea of their relevance to education. One particular issue discussed in his article is the relative roles of theory (maxims, precepts, and explanations) and practice (e.g. actually teaching) in the training and education of teachers.

It is a truism that teachers and others have to solve their practical problems and exercise their skills in organizational contexts. But this fact has considerable consequences for the sorts of solutions they can offer to their practical problems, and for the skills they can exercise. It is with important issues about the relationship of organizational contexts to individuals and to the work they do, that the fourth reading (taken from a book by Dorothy Emmet) is concerned. It can be said to be concerned with practice (what people do), though it does not, nor is it meant to, add to or elaborate on the distinctions between theory and practice noted prior to it. This reading can also be seen as a link between the three readings that precede it and Volume 1, Section 2, which contains a discussion, specific to education, about the organizational and wider contexts in which teachers have to do their work and about the tasks they undertake.

We now discuss each reading in turn.

D. P. Gauthier, 'Practical problems'[2]

Gauthier begins by distinguishing practical from theoretical problems. The former are problems 'about what to do' and their 'final solution is found only in doing something, in acting'. Problems not of this kind (for example, What is the relationship between social class and entry to higher education?) are theoretical problems. Gauthier goes on to suggest that practical problems are 'related to a particular context' and confront a 'certain person (or group) whose capacities, outlook and achievements limit his action' and 'must be met by action on a specified occasion or situation'. Thus a teacher might be faced with a practical problem about what to do about a pupil who is disrupting a particular lesson. If he fails to solve it at that time, the opportunity to solve it will have passed.[3] Theoretical problems, however, do 'not specify any occasion or situation' in which they must be solved and remain to be solved until they are.

Gauthier next makes various comments on practical reasoning – that is, on the reasoning involved in solving practical problems. Firstly, for a practical problem to arise at all for a person, he 'must be able to affect what happens by his action'. If, for example, in spite of everything a teacher can do, his class is very bored, then he has no practical problem about whether or how he ought to get the students interested, since he cannot. Secondly, if there are a number of things he can do in response to

[2] D. P. Gauthier, *Practical Reasoning* (Oxford University Press, 1963), Chapter 1.
[3] Cf. S. Hampshire, 'Logic and appreciation', in *Aesthetics and Language*, ed. W. Elton (Blackwell, 1954), p. 163, who writes: 'One can suspend judgement on theoretical questions and refuse either to affirm or to deny any particular solution: but no one can refuse to take one path or another in any situation which confronts him . . . . One cannot pass by a situation, one must pass through it in one way or another.'

this problem, and if he judges them to be equally desirable or undesirable, then he cannot think there is a point in considering the problem seriously, because he cannot think it matters which of them he does. Thirdly, practical problems are solved 'by doing the right thing, by performing the correct action' and a person must be able to decide what the right thing to do is 'under the limitations the context imposes'. As Gauthier points out, one of the limitations might be that a person lacks knowledge that he would like to have. In such a case, to justify a practical judgement (an answer to a practical question) what needs to be shown is that what was done was, *given the context*, what there were the strongest grounds for thinking was the right thing to do. This may well be very different from what in fact might have solved the practical problem with least cost.[4] Fourthly, since the contexts of practical problems are likely to be dynamic and not static, then 'general formulae for the solution of practical problems or for the justification of proposed solutions, which do not take account of the dynamic context' are of little use. The rigorous utilitarian calculation that Gauthier mentions is not practicable, because no one can stop the world and get off. Gauthier suggests that in practice many practical judgements might have to be justified by 'an appeal to a context of activity in which the general programme is already fixed'. Thus in education the inclusion of science in school curricula might be justified by reference to some general educational aim or programme. However, not all practical judgements can be justified in this way. One reason is that the practical question as to whether the general programme should be adopted can be raised, and not all programmes can be justified by reference to further programmes.[5] Further, where there are difficulties in justifying general programmes, there will be difficulties in justifying practical judgements which are to be justified by reference to them. Education seems to us to be an area not only where disputes about general programmes are likely to arise but one where they might be particularly

----

[4] For this point see D. Emmet's discussion of 'bounded rationality' on pp. 51–55 and our discussion on pp. 103–07.

[5] I. Scheffler, 'Justifying curriculum decisions', *School Review*, Vol. 66 (1958), pp. 461–72, is a discussion relevant to issues raised here. He distinguishes two kinds of justification – relative justification and non-relative (or general) justification. In the former, justification consists in showing that something is in accordance with some established practice or set of rules. In the latter, justification consists in showing that something is desirable or obligatory absolutely. He says (page 465), 'When we decide broad educational issues, we are often asking not merely what jibes with American practice, past and present, but what is generally justified, whether or not it is sanctioned by practice. The desire to evade this general question is understandable because it is difficult. But this evasion, I think, is responsible for much of the inadequacy of value-discussions in education. Two tendencies seem to develop. A move is defended on the grounds of its conformity with American practice, and the question of the justification of this practice is not considered at all. Or it is flatly asserted that it is the duty of the teacher to conform to the educational practices of his society, an assertion which, besides calling on a non-relative notion of duty that is itself uncriticised, seems to many schoolmen to be far from obvious.' ('Jibes' here is American usage and means 'is in accordance with'.)

intractable.[6] If this is so, then there may be less room in education than elsewhere for such contextual justification. Fifthly, the answer to a practical problem 'may determine in a general way an entire sequence of actions'. A decision to set up a system of comprehensive schools may involve other decisions about new buildings, redeployment of staff, and so on. Though these decisions may be justified by reference to the overall programme, they may also have a bearing on its justification, because its worth will depend, in part, on what has to be done to implement it. Sixthly, Gauthier notes that, though some problems might be confined within a simple hierarchy (he calls such problems 'procedural'), many are not. A person may adopt an objective and consider how to attain it and find that other objectives and activities are affected by it. A teacher, for example, may be able to keep some classes particularly well motivated if he uses tapes, slides, filmstrips, displays, and so on. Yet because setting these up may involve using breaks, lunch hours and time after school, he may have little informal contact with his colleagues, and so perhaps have very little influence on decisions about policy in the school.

Gauthier now makes a number of comments specifically about the solution of practical problems. His examples are easily adapted to educational contexts and we will, using his numbering, discuss a practical question, 'Ought I to unstream?', that might face a headmaster.[7]

(*i*) Here, after thinking what to do, I judge that I ought to unstream and do so, and I consider that I have solved the problem satisfactorily.

(*ii*) Here, after thinking what to do, I judge that I ought to unstream and do so. But on reflection and without any additional information, I reconsider the matter, and judge that I ought to have retained streaming and, in consequence, that I made a mistake in solving my problem. I might, for example, have misinterpreted relevant psychological data or perhaps have given incorrect weighting to a number of important factors. To make this sort of mistake is to make a mistake in one's practical reasoning.

(*iii*) Here, after thinking what to do, I judge that I ought to unstream and do so. But on reflection and taking into account additional information that I could not reasonably be expected to have had at the time of my original decision, I think that I ought to have retained streaming. Now I think that I solved my problem as far as was possible at the time, and yet that the solution has proved unsatisfactory. To admit this is not to admit that my practical reasoning was in any way defective, since what I decided to do was, given the context, what there were the strongest grounds for thinking was the best thing to do.

(*iv*) Here, after thinking what to do, I can only judge that I most probably ought to unstream. I consider that I have solved my problem as far as possible but not fully, because even though I have done my best, I have

[6]See the discussions on pp. 73–94 and pp. 100–03.
[7]See pp. 21–22.

not been able to come to any conclusion to which I can give wholehearted consent. To make this admission is not to admit that my practical reasoning was in any way defective. It is rather to imply that, given the information to hand, there was no way of making a clear decision about what to do.

(v) Here, after thinking what to do but not very extensively, I judge that I ought to unstream. I consider that I have made a tentative solution to my problem. This case differs from (iv) in that there, after full deliberation, I can only judge what I most probably ought to do. Here I might, on further reflection, have been able to make a fairly certain judgement about what to do. My solution is tentative in that I believe that I might have had to change it, had I made more effort or taken more time.

(vi) Here I make no effort at all to determine what to do, but more or less plump for unstreaming. I might on reflection decide that I ought to have unstreamed, and thus that I did the right thing. But I do not hold that I solved my problem satisfactorily, because I did not solve it all, even though I did the right thing. Gauthier's discussion of solving an equation shows that this is possible. As Ryle says,[8] one can perfectly well 'ascribe a success partly or wholly to luck' and 'arrive at true conclusions without weighing the evidence'.

There are further points which can be drawn from Gauthier's discussion about solutions to practical problems. From a comparison of (i) with (iii) it can be seen that I can justifiably say that a solution is satisfactory only if I have grounds for thinking that with the advent of further information I would not have done something else. To know this, I would need to know the consequences of implementing my decision. To take an example, in order to know whether punishing someone is a satisfactory solution to a practical problem about discipline, one of the things I need to know is the effects of such punishment on the rest of the group. In so far as I know this, I can have some idea about whether the solution is satisfactory or not. But in education, foreknowledge of outcomes is hard to come by, and at best I may be able to say only that the solution I propose is the best possible, given the circumstances and the knowledge available, but that even so it might turn out to be unsatisfactory. From looking at (ii) again, it can be seen that the sort of error involved there might, for example, mean doing something that was morally unjustified. I might decide to punish a whole class because of a misdemeanour of one unknown person. On reflection, I might judge that, even if such an action is morally justifiable in some circumstances, it is not in these. Gauthier's example (iv) suggests that there may be no conclusive answer to at least some practical problems. This might be so particularly in the case of

[8] G. Ryle, *The Concept of Mind* (Hutchinson, 1949), p. 150. Cf. also A. Kolnai, 'Deliberation is of ends', *Proceedings of the Aristotelian Society*, Vol. LXII, (1961–62), p. 214, who writes, 'Nor ... is wise choice identified with one that actually happens to lead to success and beneficial results – the lucky hit as it were.'

moral judgements (which are central to education) where issues might be raised about criteria of evaluation or about the reliability of what are taken to be relevant empirical data.[9] In (v) Gauthier describes a case that is likely to be common in education. For in many cases there may be no time for extensive deliberation about what to do. I may consciously decide that, given the circumstances, action is imperative, and that a quick decision is all that there is time for.[10] In such a case, at least two things might happen. Firstly, I might be unsure whether the solution is satisfactory, because I may suspect or know that information is available which, had I consulted it, might well have altered what I decided to do. Secondly, the very haste of my decision may make me unsure that, even given the information I did use, I did not make a mistake – that I did not, as in (ii), err in solving the problem.

Gauthier next makes a distinction between 'resolving' and 'solving' a practical problem and concludes by discussing its bearing in cases where one person is subject to the authority of another. He says that where a superior decides what an inferior shall do to meet a practical problem, the superior resolves the problem in that he reflects upon it and *decides* what shall be done, and the inferior solves it in that he *performs* whatever is resolved.[11] It can be seen that teachers and others may, on one

---

[9] For these points see pp. 100–07.

[10] A. Kolnai, op. cit. (page 214), notes that 'hesitancy and overdeliberation as well as thoughtlessness and haste and audacity may adversely affect practice'. See also J. Rawls, *A Theory of Justice* (Oxford University Press, 1972), page 418, who writes, 'Rational deliberation is itself an activity like any other, and the extent to which one should engage in it is subject to rational decision. The formal rule is that we should deliberate up to the point where the likely benefits from improving our plans are just worth the time and effort of reflection. Once we take the costs of deliberation into account, it is unreasonable to worry about finding the best plan, the one that we should choose had we complete information.'

[11] It should be noted that Gauthier's points about resolving and solving practical problems are logical ones. It is an empirical matter to discover, for example, (i) who is empowered in organizations to resolve practical problems and to instruct others to carry out what he has decided should be done; (ii) who *in fact* resolves them and issues instructions; (iii) what area of discretion is left to the person instructed. All this is likely to vary from problem to problem and from organization to organization. There is no necessary connexion between being empowered to decide what should be done and affecting what is done. A person may simply ignore or modify what another has decided he shall do. The distinction between who is resolving and who is solving a practical problem (where these are separated) might, in some circumstances, be left implicit. For to insist on it might generate hostility, by making differences in power and authority within an organization explicit, and this may make decisions more difficult to implement, particularly if those who are merely to solve the problem see themselves as at all autonomous. The discussion, mentioned in *The Politics of Education*, edited by M. Kogan (Penguin Books, 1971), page 184, and described by Crosland as 'important', about whether in Circular 10/65 local authorities should be 'requested' or 'required' to 'produce comprehensive plans' (i.e. plans for comprehensive schools) can be seen in part as a discussion about whether it was prudent to make explicit to the authorities the extent to which they were to solve but not to resolve practical problems about how to reorganize secondary education.

occasion, both resolve and solve a practical problem and, on another, do one without the other.[12]

S. Hampshire, 'Fallacies in moral philosophy'[13]

We begin by indicating some of the more important reasons for including this article by Hampshire. First, it contains a discussion of the relationship between theoretical judgements (what Hampshire also calls 'statements of fact' or 'descriptive statements', and included in these are empirical statements) and practical judgements. As such, it continues the discussion of theory and practice. Secondly, it is concerned with how theoretical judgements might justify practical judgements, above all those that are also moral judgements. Since moral judgements are central to education, their justification is a matter in which educators have an interest.[14] As O'Connor suggests, 'The nature of value judgements and the logic of their justification is ... the most important and

[12]A number of issues arise in cases where practical problems are resolved by one person or group of persons, and are to be solved by another. One issue is about feasibility. For example, can teachers and schools in fact achieve the goals governments and others might set for them? See pp. 190–204 on this point. Another issue concerns the often difficult moral problems that arise for those who, in solving practical problems resolved by superiors, are instructed to do what they believe is wrong.

[13]*Mind*, Vol. LVIII (1949), pp. 466–82. Beginners to philosophy may find this article more difficult than others in this book. But in our view its relevance, quality, and range outweigh what might be taken to be its disadvantage, as far as this book is concerned. For background reading, see R. S. Peters, *Ethics and Education* (Allen & Unwin, 1966), Chapter 3, and G. Warnock, *Contemporary Moral Philosophy* (Macmillan, 1967). For elementary discussions of the thesis of 'logical independence' discussed by Hampshire, see the references to the discussion of naturalism by Ewing, Hospers, and Atkinson on page 95 of this book. Hampshire's article can be usefully read in conjunction with the discussion between B. Williams and B. Magee on moral philosophy printed in *The Listener*, Vol. 85, No. 2184, 4 February 1971, pp. 136–40 and reprinted in *Modern British Philosophy*, ed. B. Magee (Secker & Warburg, 1971). Williams, twenty-two years later, makes a number of points similar to Hampshire's. He suggests, for example, that the form the fact/value distinction has taken seems 'to have distorted the whole nature of the debate' in moral philosophy.

[14]Cf. T. F. Daveney, *Education – a Moral Concept* (University of Exeter Press, 1970), page 22, who writes, 'Education whether we like it or not is a moral concept, and educational discussions of a non-technical kind are logically moral discussions.' Cf. R. M. Hare, 'The practical relevance of philosophy', in R. M. Hare, *Essays on Philosophical Method*, (Macmillan, 1971), pages 100–1, who writes, 'In the same way, if we take almost at random any field of domestic policy – say that concerning education – another crop of moral problems arises. There is for example the question of equality in education: is it right to devote equal resources to the education of each child, irrespective of ability; or ought we, as some advocate, to devote more resources to educating abler children; or, as others urge, devote more resources to educating less able children, in order to compensate for their handicap? Arguments of a moral sort can be adduced for each of these three courses .... Then there are all the questions about moral education itself: to what extent is it legitimate for one generation to try and influence the moral attitudes of the next generation, and by what means? What is the difference between moral education,

obvious point of contact between philosophy and education ....'[15]
Thirdly, Hampshire raises a number of issues about practical reasoning.
Fourthly, he outlines two different conceptions of moral philosophy, and
his comments on them have a bearing on issues raised in Volume II.

Hampshire's article is divided into seven sections and we number our
discussion of it accordingly.

1. Hampshire distinguishes two conceptions of moral philosophy –
one represented by Aristotle and the other derived from Kant. Aristotle
is concerned primarily with what Hampshire takes to be 'the typical
moral problem' – namely, that of the moral *agent* (that is, of a person
faced with a practical problem of a moral kind). Post-Kantian philosophers, who take 'the logical independence' of statements of fact and
value judgements (above all moral judgements) as defining 'the main
problem of ethics', are mainly concerned with 'the problems of the
moral *judge* or critic' and have been led away from 'the primary and proper question of moral philosophy'.[16] The difference between the two
parties can be seen in the way each compares ethics and aesthetics.

The thesis about logical independence is that value judgements are
neither deducible from nor definable by statements of fact. It follows that
practical judgements of a moral kind are neither deducible from nor
definable by theoretical ones and that, for example, the answer to the
practical problem about unstreaming (discussed on pages 5–7) cannot
be simply read off from empirical data, even if all that were needed were
to hand.[17]

(Ftn. 14 cont.)
which most of us applaud, and indoctrination, which most of us condemn? What is a
morally educated man? What, in general, ought parents, teachers, and others to be trying
to do to the young?' See also D. J. O'Connor, 'The nature of educational theory', *Proceedings of the Philosophy of Education Society of Great Britain*, Vol. VI, No. 1 (January 1972),
page 108, who writes, 'Of course, there are moral problems central to education as there
are to any large scale social institution like marriage, or the law, or the political framework. And there are day to day moral decisions called for in teaching and administering
the system as there are in medicine or in politics or in marriage.'

[15] D. J. O'Connor, *An Introduction to the Philosophy of Education* (Routledge & Kegan
Paul, 1957), p. 13.

[16] For a discussion of the relation between moral agents and moral judges see P. W.
Taylor, 'Prescribing and evaluating', *Mind*, Vol. LXXI (1962), pp. 213–30.

[17] For the relevance and use made of the thesis of logical independence by philosophers
of education see E. Best, 'The suppressed premiss in educational psychology', *Universities
Quarterly*, Vol. 16 (1962), pp. 283–95; E. Best, 'A failure in communication', *Studies in
Philosophy and Education*, Vol. 13 (1964), pp. 163–84; E. Best, 'Common confusions in
educational theory', in R. D. Archambault, ed., *Philosophical Analysis and Education*
(Routledge & Kegan Paul, 1965), pp. 39–56; P. H. Hirst, 'Morals, religion, and the
maintained school', *British Journal of Educational Studies*, Vol. 14 (1965), pp. 5–18;
C. D. Hardie, 'Description and evaluation in education', *Australian Journal of Higher
Education*, Vol. 2 (1965), pp. 119–24; R. F. Dearden, *The Philosophy of Primary Education*
(Routledge & Kegan Paul, 1968), Chapter 2; J. P. White, 'The concept of curriculum
evaluation', *Journal of Curriculum Studies*, Vol. 3 (1971), pp. 101–12.

2. In this section, Hampshire briefly outlines and rejects accounts of practical (moral) judgements which have been defended, at one time or another, by some twentieth-century philosophers. He goes on to say that the procedure of practical reasoning can be rational, even though it might not be described in logical textbooks. For they do not discuss all the patterns of rational argument.

3. Hampshire here begins by discussing why post-Kantian philosophers have not realized that practical judgements are established 'by familiar patterns of argument' and why they believe that practical reasoning is 'irrelevant to the real problem'. Such philosophers, he suggests, hold that all rational argument must be deductive argument. He argues that this is not so, that practical (moral) judgements are established 'by arguments consisting of factual judgements of a particular range' without being deducible (in a strict logical sense) from them, and that they are not thereby removed from the sphere of rational discussion. In order to illustrate his argument, Hampshire discusses a specific moral problem (about suicide). He says that though the disputants may agree on 'the facts of a particular situation' and 'disagree in their moral judgement', further rational argument is not thereby precluded. For facts or beliefs about the world which are not strictly facts about the particular situation in question may be relevant to the argument. As examples, he cites Christian beliefs about life after death and the logical and empirical issues they give rise to. He notes how advances in knowledge (for example, in academic disciplines) may show previous moral judgements to be groundless.

The educational relevance of Hampshire's general point here can be seen from the issue as to whether religious assemblies and periods of religious instruction (of a Christian sort, say) should be permitted in schools. Two disputants might agree on the empirical issues about the consequences, in the specific circumstances, of including them in school timetables, and disagree about whether they should be permitted. But both might admit that additional wider issues are relevant, for example, about the existence of God, the nature or possibility of religious knowledge, the connexion between religion and morality, or the historical role of Christianity in the formation of British society.[18]

Hampshire goes on to say that in the light of argument about such wider issues a person might change his mind about what to do.[19] He comments on the importance of pointing out further known facts in moral argument, and says that the situations in which we have to act do not come to us ready labelled. Determining the facts of a situation, he sug-

---

[18] The article of Dumont and Wax on the Cherokee Indians reprinted on pages 158–73 gives rise to a number of these wider issues – for example, philosophical ones about the justification and value of different modes of life and about moral relativism.

[19] Cf. the examples Hampshire cites with those listed on pp. 5–7 of this book.

gests in a footnote, is a 'matter of analysing and interpreting the situation'. He quotes a phrase from Aristotle's Nicomachean Ethics (1109^b 23) to the effect that what we decide to do will depend on how we see the situation.[20]

He concludes from his preceding discussion that 'the logical divorce between so-called judgements of value and factual judgements is misleading', because practical (moral) judgements are 'corrigible by experience and observation'.

4. Hampshire now discusses ultimate moral disagreement (that which survives agreement about all matters of fact) and compares it with ultimate disagreement about a theoretical judgement. He goes on to say that people can only argue about conflicting moral judgements 'if they can agree on some common criteria of rightness' but no argument can show that one party *must* adopt the criteria of the other and that between consistently applied terminologies, whether in theoretical or moral matters, 'ultimately we must simply choose'.[21]

5. Hampshire says that thinking about what to do cannot be analysed without constant reference to specific cases and he comments on the distinction (within practical problems) between moral and technical problems.[22] The latter are about choice of means to an already determined end but the former require a choice of an action or policy as a whole.[23]

The importance of the moral/technical distinction for education can be seen, for example, from an article by J. P. White, who distinguishes two

---

[20] See the reading by D. Emmet (pages 51–72). She suggests (page 54) that in institutions and organizations, in particular, people may see situations in different ways depending on their social and intellectual backgrounds, and on their role in the organization. The Cherokee Indians, for example, are unlikely to see their situation in the same way as their mentors. One important question is 'Given competing definitions of the situation, whose is to count?' For some further relevant material see the article by Smith and Stockman in Volume II, pp. 39–55.

[21] Section 4 of Hampshire's article raises, in a short space, a number of important philosophical issues about meaning, contradiction, the propriety of imperatives as models for practical judgements, and about whether the adoption of ultimate criteria is simply a matter of choice. These are all matters of current dispute.

[22] For the reference that Hampshire here makes to Kant see H. J. Paton, *The Moral Law*, Paperback edn. (Hutchinson University Library, 1966), pp. 78–80. This is an edition and translation of Kant's *Groundwork of the Metaphysic of Morals*.

[23] The impossibility of reducing moral problems to technical ones (discussed by Hampshire in Section 3 of his article also) is closely related to the fact/value issue, as he makes clear. This issue is discussed further on pp. 94–99 of this book and our comment here should be read in the light of that. Two immediate objections to any proposed reduction of moral to technical problems are: (i) that the issue of the value of the end (irrespective of the means) is not raised in a technical problem but is in a moral one; (ii) that no order of priority between ends can be derived from technical judgements about how to realize them, when the ends are independent of each other and cannot be realized at the same time and to the same extent.

general kinds of curriculum evaluation – empirical and non-empirical.[24] One of the two sorts of empirical evaluation he mentions is concerned with whether a curriculum is attaining its objectives. This is a technical issue about whether by doing X, we achieve Y, and resolving this issue does not answer the moral problem as to whether the curriculum should be adopted. The distinction between these two sorts of problem is sometimes obscured where educational schemes, methods, and policies are described as 'successful'. It is often unclear which of three things is meant: (*i*) that the scheme has attained its objectives; (*ii*) that the scheme ought to be generally adopted; (*iii*) both that the scheme has attained its objectives and that it ought to be generally adopted, together.

6. Another reason, Hampshire suggests, why philosophers misunderstood the nature of practical judgements was because they believed that literally meaningful sentences had to correspond to or describe something. As a result, practical judgements were classified by some not as prescriptions for actions but as descriptions.[25]

7. Hampshire argues here that moral philosophy is likely to be unenlightening, if it is taken simply as a matter of *defining* moral terms. An informative treatise on ethics would consist of examples of the different kinds of moral decisions made and an account of the considerations adduced in support of them.[26] The article ends with a summary.

H. Entwistle, 'Practical and theoretical learning'[27]

The readings by Gauthier and Hampshire have enabled us to distinguish theory and practice in terms of a distinction between theoretical and practical problems. Entwistle's article enables us to distinguish theory and practice in another way and that is in terms of a (general) distinction between (*i*) 'theorizing' meaning 'reasoning' and (*ii*) 'practice' meaning

[24] J. P. White, op. cit. (1971), p. 102. For a discussion of some technical judgements see B. J. Diggs, 'A technical ought', *Mind*, Vol. LXIX (1960), pp. 301–17.

[25] For a discussion of some of the issues raised in section 6 of Hampshire's article, see R. F. Atkinson and A. C. Montefiore, ' "Ought" and "Is" ', *Philosophy*, Vol. XXXIII (1958), pp. 29–49.

[26] It might be held that the programme for moral philosophy that Hampshire proposes may lead to moral philosophy sanctioning the existing paradigms of moral reasoning of a particular group, society, or culture. Whether this is in fact so is not clear. The programme would have to be given in more detail. However, A. O. Rorty, 'Naturalism, paradigms, and ideology', *Review of Metaphysics*, Vol. XXIV (1971), p. 646, states that 'The characteristic paradigms of normal moral discourse at any particular period will be reflected in the ethical theories of that period.' See also the references to Montefiore, Schneewind, and MacIntyre, given on page 647 of that article. For a further relevant discussion by Hampshire, see his *Thought and Action* (Chatto and Windus, 1959), particularly page 260 onwards.

[27] *British Journal of Educational Studies*, Vol. 17, No. 2 (July, 1969), pp. 117–28.

'performing actions'.[28] This somewhat rough and ready distinction can be illustrated further by saying that to succeed in (*i*) is to come to some justifiable conclusion or other, and to succeed in (*ii*) is to effect some desired or justifiable change. Thus a teacher might be said to be engaged in theorizing when he is thinking about what to do and how to do it, and to be engaged in practice when he is actually doing it. It is with the relationships between thinking what to do and how to do it, and doing it that Entwistle is concerned, particularly as they relate to skills.[29]

Entwistle notes that there has been a tradition in education which emphasizes learning by doing as opposed to learning from 'theoretical teaching'. This emphasis seems to have been supported by the work of some philosophers. Entwistle mentions, among others, G. Ryle who questions whether theorizing is necessary for intelligent practice. He takes Ryle's point but says that Ryle deploys his argument in such a way as to discredit theorizing undeservedly and to play down the fact that some skills are 'a complex of several activities', some of them theoretical, others practical in character. He takes as an example playing cricket (analogies can easily be made here with teaching) and Entwistle concludes this part of his discussion by saying that theorizing can be 'an essential part of the intelligent practice of skill' and that the view that 'educational theory is useless and that teaching practice is all that matters' may be hard to justify.

[28]This distinction, often colloquially expressed in terms of thinking and doing, is probably the basic distinction between theory and practice, in that other ways of making the distinction are derived from it. For the closely related distinction between theoretical and practical activities, and for education as a practical activity, see G. Langford, *Philosophy and Education* (Macmillan, 1968), Chapter 1. It can be seen that 'theorizing' in the sense of 'reasoning' can be used to describe both the reasoning involved in solving theoretical problems (theoretical reasoning) and that involved in solving practical ones (practical reasoning).

[29]One difficulty in discussing distinctions between theory and practice is that they frequently seem to overlap. Thus, G. Ryle, in *The Concept of Mind* (Hutchinson, 1949), page 26, says that 'theorizing is one practice among others'. Given this, it might be argued that the distinction we are here discussing (between thinking about what and how to do something, and doing it) is not a distinction between theory and practice but is rather one within the concept of practice itself. Again, K. Baier, in *The Moral Point of View*, abridged edn. (Random House, 1965), page 49, makes a point substantially reflecting the distinction we are here discussing. He says, 'When we deliberate, we are therefore attempting to accomplish two quite different tasks, a theoretical and a practical task. The theoretical is completed when we have answered the theoretical question "Which course of action is the best?" The practical task is simply to act in accordance with the outcome of the theoretical.' But what he calls 'the theoretical question' (which he takes to be more or less equivalent to 'What shall I do?') is, in Gauthier's and our terminology, a practical question, even though in attempting to answer it a person will be engaged in theorizing. Baier's terminology is not, however, consistent because on page 91 of his book the questions 'What shall I do?' and 'What should be done?' are described as 'practical questions'. Even in this article by Entwistle each of the terms 'theory', 'theorizing' and 'theoretical' has more than one use though which one can be usually determined from the context.

He next discusses the role of theory in acquiring skills and argues that though, because of their 'tacit component', there is a sense in which skills can be acquired only by practice, prior acquaintance with theory can facilitate their acquisition.[30] He goes on to defend the importance of what he calls 'information' both for learning skills and for understanding everyday life. The article ends with a summary.

D. Emmet, 'Living with organization man'[31]

Emmet begins by arguing that 'moralists would do well to look at sociological studies' of social situations, particularly studies of organizations. A consequence she draws from her discussion is that Max Weber's account of 'rational bureaucracy' is too simple. He defines rationality for subordinates, for example, as 'acting according to the book of rules'. He does not define it for 'the top people' but for them it is usually taken to be that of 'economic man' who maximizes interests, of the organization in this case, with least risk of loss. Simon, from whom Emmet takes her account, describes economic man as follows: 'This man is assumed to have knowledge of the relevant aspects of his environment which, if not absolutely complete, is at least impressively clear and voluminous. He is also assumed to have a well organised and stable system of preferences, and a skill in computation that enables him to calculate, for the alternative courses of action that are available to him, which of these will permit him to reach the highest attainable point on his preference scale.'[32] Simon elsewhere implies that such a man has 'virtual omniscience and unlimited computational power'.[33]

Those who work in organizations, not least in educational ones, are unlikely to be in the situation of economic man. The theoretical knowledge about alternatives and consequences is not available: further it is unlikely that there will be either the time or resources to undertake the necessary calculations, even if any of the various kinds of educational problem allowed of such calculation; nor is it clear that there could be one stable and well-organized set of values in education, which could be shown to be preferable to all other ones.[34] Those who take decisions in organizations are likely to have to work with what Simon calls 'bounded

[30] This and other issues raised by Entwistle's article are discussed further on pages 107–19.
[31] D. Emmet, *Rules, Roles, and Relations* (Macmillan 1966), Chapter 9.
[32] H. A. Simon, *Models of Man* (New York: John Wiley, 1957), p. 241.
[33] Ibid., p. 202.
[34] For some relevant points see our discussion on pp. 100–03. See also J. M. Collins, 'The Labour Party and public schools: a conflict of principles', *British Journal of Educational Studies*, Vol. 17, (1969), pp. 301–11. Collins suggests (page 301) that the difficulty of the problem as to whether the public schools should be abolished arises 'from a clash of principles – between equality and freedom, the pursuit of each being capable of demanding our rational support in a democratic society', where one principle has to be

rationality' and Emmet gives some reasons why this is so. To take decisions on the basis of bounded rationality is to take them on the basis of 'a simplification of the actual facts of the real world'; the situation is interpreted in terms of 'relevant' or 'strategic' factors.[35] Some facts may be unknown or ignored and give rise to unforeseen consequences. Bounded rationality will certainly involve looking for viable as opposed to ideal solutions and seeing that imperfect decisions may be better than none but it is not to be seen as a degenerate form of rationality proper, however that is defined. For given a choice between acting with bounded rationality on the one hand, and not acting without complete knowledge and objective rationality on the other, it will almost always be rational to choose the former.[36] This choice itself will necessarily be made with bounded rationality because the complete consequences of acting on one or other of the alternatives are unknown.[37]

In the light of her discussion so far, Emmet comments on the relationship between rational and ethical behaviour. She then goes on to say that bounded rationality is not only due to ignorance of fact but to people's different perceptions of a situation which arise from differences in 'social and intellectual background', role, and role-priority, and she argues that these and other factors complicate practical problems (moral and otherwise) in organizations.[38] With references to work of W. H. Whyte, of G.

(Ftn. 34 cont.)
given priority over the other. It is by no means clear whether such priorities can be decided in advance of specific cases. If they cannot there is no possibility of computing answers to moral questions, in education and elsewhere. For such computation would require that the priorities be decided in advance. Further, conflicts about educational aims might make such computation even more unlikely. For some points of general relevance see A. P. Griffiths, 'Justifying moral principles', *Proceedings of the Aristotelian Society*, Vol. LVIII (1957–58), particularly page 119 onwards.

[35] For some of the vocabulary used to identify strategic or relevant factors in education see the discussion of educational categories in Volume I, Section 2, pages 179–83. The simplification that Emmet mentions may come in part from such vocabulary, which may obscure relevant differences between individuals who are, even so, held to fall under the same category. This is particularly likely where the criteria for inclusion in the categories are varied or indeterminate and possibly both. Educational categories of one sort or another may be necessary if educational problems are to be tractable but the simplification they involve should not be ignored. See also Florence Hollis, 'Principles and assumptions underlying casework practice', particularly pages 34–8, in *Social Work and Social Values: Readings in Social Work*, Vol. III, ed. E. Younghusband (Allen and Unwin, 1967).

[36] For 'objective rationality' and other points relevant here see the reference to Rawls and Hospers, cited on page 105.

[37] The general point is that the choice we are discussing could not be presented to us were we able to act with objective rationality. If, therefore, it is presented to us, it must be made under bounded rationality.

[38] Differences in perceptions arise in educational organizations, as elsewhere. We have already mentioned the education of the Cherokee Indians (see page 11 and pages 158–73 of this book and Hampshire's comments on 'the facts of the situation' on page 33). Such differences are likely to be seen in the UK, for example, between pupils' and teachers' per-

Homans, a reviewer of Whyte, and of M. Dalton, she comments parti-cularly on the moral issues (and to a lesser extent on the factual ones) which arise from the relationships between individual and organizational values.

The numerous other important issues that Emmet raises in her discussion do not require as much detailed comment, as far as this introduction goes, and we merely give a brief outline of them. Citing a study by A. W. Gouldner, Emmet discusses a problem to which there was no ideal solution and where the solution brought other problems with it. Citing work of T. Burns and G. M. Stalker, and of M. P. Follet, she draws attention to some of the problems connected with 'organic' (as opposed to 'mechanistic') kinds of organization. She notes the importance of diagnosing unintended consequences of decisions, in part by a reference to a study by P. Selznick, and of appraising 'the problems of implementing unanalysed abstractions.'[39] She suggests that analysis of such abstractions may be discouraged where they have an ideological role and that sometimes they are the front for decisions 'determined opportunistically by immediate exigency.'[40] She argues that moral judgements in organizations call for 'moral intelligence of high order' and that where it is missing 'manipulation' may take its place. She comments on the problems that the divorce between power and responsibility, and the notions of 'loyalty' and 'commitment' to organizations give rise to. She draws attention to a distinction, suggested by Talcott Parsons, between organizations whose purposes are 'specific' and those whose purposes are 'diffuse', and to the implications of the distinction for the ways that organizations might be run.[41] She discusses issues arising from the recognition of the complexity of moral problems in organizations and concludes by emphasizing the importance of having an understanding of large organizations (among

---

(Ftn. 38 cont.)
ceptions of what school is doing for pupils; or between Christian and atheist teachers' perceptions of religious assemblies in schools. All Emmet's points about loyalty, efficiency, degrees of commitment, rate for the job, etc. apply to education.

[39] For 'unintended consequences' see pp. 190–204.

[40] For 'ideology' see Volume II, pages 55–117 and for some unanalysed abstractions see pages 63–64. Some common examples are 'equality of opportunity', 'freedom of choice', 'the needs of the child', and 'the needs of society'.

[41] Educational organizations are likely, in our view, to have 'diffuse' purposes. For a distinction related to that of Emmet between 'diffuse' and 'specific', see A. P. Griffiths, 'A deduction of universities', in *Philosophical Analysis and Education*, ed. R. D. Archambault (Routledge & Kegan Paul, 1966), pages 187–207. Griffiths distinguishes 'open' institutions and those (page 188) 'whose "end" is limited by articles, such as a project to build a war memorial or to prevent a road running through a park, having clear and definite criteria for deciding when their activities are successful or unsuccessful, complete or incomplete . . .'

them, schools).[42] The issues raised in this area, Emmet suggests, are ones which sociologists and philosophers can fruitfully co-operate in exploring.[43]

[42] Emmet's comments here on the dangers of 'the ideological pursuit of a single ideal or principle without realistic appraisal of its implications in a particular setting' are usefully read together with P. King's comments on the context-free nature of ideologies in P. King, 'An ideological fallacy', in *Politics and Experience, Essays Presented to Michael Oakeshott on the Occasion of his Retirement* ed. P. King and B. C. Parekh (Cambridge University Press, 1968), pages 341–94. See particularly pages 390–4.

[43] Emmet's book, as a whole, provides a good example, in our view, of how philosophy and sociology can be used jointly to explore an area.

Readings

1 Practical problems D. P. GAUTHIER
(D. P. Gauthier, *Practical Reasoning*, Oxford
University Press, 1963, Chapter 1)

A practical problem is a problem about what to do. In saying this we are using the word 'practical' more widely than in everyday discourse, to characterize all problems, individual and social, prudential and moral, whose final solution is found only in doing something, in acting. Practical problems may be contrasted with theoretical problems, whose solution is found in knowing something, in understanding.

Each of us is continually faced with practical problems – some trivial, others important, some easily met, others admitting no satisfactory solution. Examples will suggest their variety:

I've put tab A in slit A ; what do I do next?
How can I convince her that I love her?
Which of these suits shall I buy?
For which candidate ought I to vote?
Should I read for the law, or consider some other profession?
Ought I to engage in civil disobedience, in support of nuclear
    disarmament?
What shall I do this evening?
What shall I do, now that George is dead?
I ought to visit my aunt this afternoon, but shall I?
I could make a tidy sum speculating against sterling, but should I?

1.1. Context

A practical problem is related to a particular context. It confronts a certain person (or group) whose capacities, outlook, and achievements limit his actions. It usually arises out of his particular circumstances, and must be met by action on a specified occasion or situation. On the occasion the person concerned must be able to affect what happens by his action, and, if he is to consider the problem seriously, must judge one possible effect to be more desirable than another.

Theoretical problems do not display this same relation to context. A theoretical problem may arise for a particular person, whose ability to solve it is limited, but the solution is not itself thereby limited. And it may arise out of particular circumstances – one wants to explain why the bathroom pipes froze last night – but it does not specify any occasion or situation in which it must be solved. What to do about a theoretical problem may be a practical problem, dependent on the person concerned and his situation, but the theoretical question may be separated from this context.

A practical problem is met by action in a situation, or at a certain time. What shall we serve when the Smiths come to dinner? What shall we do this afternoon? When the situation arises, or the time comes, we must do something – even if we do nothing. But what we do need not solve the problem. For we may well do the wrong thing. When I ask 'What am I to do?', I do not want to know what I *shall* do, but what I *should* do.

Practical problems are solved by doing something – but only by doing the right thing, by performing the correct action. Once the action, whatever it may be, is performed, the possibility of solving the problem is past – if it has not then been solved, it can never be solved. The problem specifies the occasion of its *possible* solution – it demands resolution at this time, but may not receive it.

The relation of practical problems to their context is of the first importance in considering the methods of practical reasoning. These methods must enable us to solve a problem under the limitations which the context imposes. If we are not able to determine what to do, but only what, had we but known, we should have done, we are not able to solve our practical problems. Thus it is quite mistaken to employ ideal standards in justifying practical judgements; the standards must relate to the judgement or decision as contributing to the solution of the actual problem.

The *dynamic* aspect of the context of practical problems also affects the methods of practical reasoning Although we consider what to do before we act, yet we act in the light of what we are already doing, of what is presently happening, and of what we propose to do, of what we expect to happen. When confronted with a practical problem, we do not and cannot bring ourselves and our world to rest, and then set everything once more in motion by our actions. This possibility is perhaps most nearly realized if the course of a man's life is brought to a sudden halt – his family is killed, or his business is ruined – and he must consider what to do to begin anew. But such extreme situations are fortunately rare.

General formulae for the solution of practical problems, or for the justification of proposed solutions, which do not take account of the dynamic context, can offer little practical guidance to the agent. A rigorous nineteenth-century utilitarian would insist that any question about what to do ought to be answered by considering what action would provide the greatest happiness for the greatest number, or would satisfy some subordinate principles derived from this supreme criterion. But in practice the answer to a practical question must depend, not only on an appeal to a hierarchy of principles, but far more on an appeal to a context of activity, in which the general programme of action is already fixed. Practical reasoning often consists in showing that an action fits into such a context.

Rather than a hierarchy of principles, a hierarchy of problems confronts us in practical reasoning. Suppose, for example, that I am undecided about what to do this morning. After reflecting on several alternatives, I decide to work in my garden. I then consider what I shall do there, and settle on weeding the lawn. And after making all preparations, I may hesitate just for a moment, and ask myself where to begin.

The subdivision of problems suggested in this example is by no means necessary. I might equally well, on first considering what to do, have settled immediately on weeding the lawn. On the other hand, I might merely have elected to work at home, rather than to go to the university to continue a philosophical paper, or to the railway to watch trains.

The individuation of problems within a hierarchy depends on the questions the person concerned actually considers. There is no simple correspondence between actions and problems. One problem may determine, in a general way, an entire sequence of actions (as in the example), or it may – should one decide to do nothing about some matter – determine no actions whatever. One action may be intended to contribute to the solution of quite independent problems (as those who insist that business may be combined with pleasure assure us) or – as a random or reflex action – to the solution of no problem at all.

Problems which belong entirely within a hierarchy, although common, are of little interest in the study of practical reasoning. The arguments used to resolve them, or to justify a solution adopted, do not present considerations of importance. Only when, through failure satisfactorily to solve them, we are forced to reconsider the context within which they arise, do they give rise to more interesting patterns of reasoning. Most frequently we find, not only a satisfactory, but a definite, conclusive answer to questions such as 'How do I weed my garden?' or 'What do I do after putting tab A in slit A'?' Problems of this type may be termed *procedural*.

But many of our problems, even if they begin as procedural, cannot be confined to a simple hierarchy. Having adopted an objective, I consider how to attain it, but, in so doing, issues relevant to other activities in which I am engaged, or objectives which I seek, may arise. Again, such problems may raise quite different issues, such as the effect of my actions upon the

activities of other persons, which introduce questions extending beyond
my entire range of objectives.

When we are faced with problems which cannot be treated as procedural, our reasons for acting are not fully established in advance. Only
as we consider what we can do or not do, can we determine what wants
and desires, aims and ends, may be affected by our action. As a result of
this inquiry we establish practical judgements.

1.2. Solution

To clarify the role of practical judgements, it is necessary to consider
more fully the nature of the solution to a practical problem. Certain terminological distinctions will prove useful here. The verbal formulation
of a practical problem I shall call a *practical question*. Thus the exemplification of practical problems at the beginning of this chapter consisted
of a series of practical questions. An action, or set of actions, performed
by the person in the situation specified in the problem, I shall call the
solution. A decision taken by the person concerning what to do in
the situation, I shall call the *resolution*. A judgement about what to do
in the situation or an injunction to do something, I shall call the *answer*
to the practical question. Whether these three are completely distinct,
and whether each is always present, will have to be considered, as will
the distinction between judgement and injunction.

1.2.1. Action

However resolved we may be on what to do, however certain we may be
of what we should do, unless we do in fact perform the action decided
upon, we do not satisfactorily meet our practical problem. The answers
to practical questions are intended, not merely to increase our knowledge, but to guide our actions. Decisions, although they end our deliberations and hence our practical worries, are intended only to determine
our actions. I may know how to convince her that I love her, but unless I
put my knowledge into practice, I shall not convince her, and hence I
shall not achieve the objective which sets my problem. Thus it is reasonable to use 'solution' to refer to the action, rather than the decision or
judgement, provided it be recognized that the solution is, or may be,
but a part of our response to a practical problem.

We have seen that not all actions that could be performed in the situation envisaged solve a practical problem. If, when I enter the polling-
booth, I mark my ballot-paper at random, I have in no way solved the
problem of how I ought to vote (unless, for some unlikely reason, I
judge that I ought to mark the ballot-paper quite at random). I have voted,
but I have not taken any step towards voting as I should, voting for the
best candidate, or the candidate of the best political party. The problem,

at least as a practical problem, no longer exists because the situation has passed, but I have not met the problem by solving it.

One may fail to solve a practical problem fully and satisfactorily in any of several ways. Examples will suggest the most important:

(*i*) I judge that I ought to vote for Jones, and do so. In this case, I consider that I have solved my problem, and solved it satisfactorily.

(*ii*) I judge that I ought to vote for Jones, and do so. Later, however, I reflect on my judgement, and decide that I was mistaken; I ought to have voted for Smith. I now consider that I erred in solving my problem.

(*iii*) I judge that I ought to vote for Jones, and do so. Later, I come into possession of information, which I could not reasonably have known at the time of voting, that leads me to conclude that I ought rather to have voted for Smith. I now consider that, although I did solve my problem, so far as was possible at the time, yet the solution has proved unsatisfactory.

(*iv*) I am unable to determine conclusively how I ought to vote, despite my best efforts to do so. I judge, however, that most probably I ought to vote for Jones. I consider that I have solved my problem as far as possible, but not fully.

(*v*) I make no extensive effort to determine how I ought to vote, but judge that, on the face of it, I ought to vote for Jones. I consider that I have reached a tentative solution to my problem.

(*vi*) I make no effort to determine how I ought to vote, but merely mark my ballot-paper for Jones. I do not consider that I have in any way solved my problem. If I later decide that indeed I ought to have voted for Jones, I do not suppose that in fact I solved my problem satisfactorily, but only that I did the right thing.

Compare this last case with a mathematical problem. A man, confronted with an algebraic equation, writes down, as a pure guess, the answer '$x = 6$'. Finding this to be the right answer does not lead him to suppose that he has solved the equation. To do the right thing, to get the right answer, is of course achieved by the person who solves his problem satisfactorily, but it may be achieved without solving it at all.

1.2.2. Decision

A practical problem is *resolved* when the person confronted with it decides, or is decided about, what to do. Decision, although it does not in itself solve our practical problems, terminates our consideration of them; once we have decided, the problem no longer presents itself as a problem. If asked what we shall do, we have a ready answer.

Resolution need not involve the *making* of a decision. We need not suppose that, to be decided about what to do, we need have come consciously to a decision; it is not unusual simply to *find* oneself decided. But the process of decision-making is not our concern; it is only the result – the decision itself – which enters our argument.

When we are decided, we know what we shall do. It is important to distinguish this knowledge from that which rests upon *prediction*. If, for example, I know that I shall go to a party, because I know that I shall not have the will-power to refuse, I cannot suppose either that I have decided to go, or not to go. If I have decided to go, I need not predict that I shall go; if I have really decided not to go, I cannot predict that nevertheless I shall.

When we are decided, we know what we shall do, but do we know what to do? I decide to vote for Jones, not because I know him to be the candidate for whom I ought to vote, but simply to settle the matter. I terminate consideration of my problem, but without satisfactorily answering the question it raises. Resolution would seem not to imply a prospective solution.

But is my decision a true resolution of my problem? Perhaps it is more reasonable to say that, just as I must, in some cases, act without my action constituting a solution to my problem, so here I decide without my decision constituting a resolution. Although my problem concerns what to do, it is resolved only by deciding to do that which I should do, just as it is solved only by doing that which I should do. Thus the initial statement of this section demands qualification; a practical problem is resolved when the person confronted with it decides, or is decided, to do what he considers will best solve his problem.

A resolution, just as a solution, may prove unsatisfactory, and in the same ways. But in addition, it is worth noting the case in which one is unable to do what one decides to do, so that one's supposed resolution does not in fact provide a solution – satisfactory or unsatisfactory – to the practical problem.

The connexion between practical solution and resolution is quite straightforward. If I perform an action, considering it to be the solution to some practical problem, then I must have reflected on what to do and decided upon that action – that is, I must have resolved my problem. If I have not resolved my problem, then, however much I may hope that what I do will prove right, I cannot suppose it to be the solution.

Many actions are, of course, performed without prior decision. Frequently I glance at my watch to determine the time without having considered whether to do so; I may rise and dress in the morning without taking thought about the matter. In such cases I should not say that I had decided to perform the action or set of actions, although I should not mean that I was undecided whether to perform them. To act without consideration is to act without the possibility either of decision or indecision. Such action, although it may in fact meet a practical problem, is not performed *as* a solution to it.

Note that the connexion between decison and action may be complicated if one person is subject to the authority of another. A soldier is expected to act on the order of his superior officer; it is insubordination for him to consider whether or not to carry them out. It is the officer who decides what the soldier is to do, expressing his decision in his order. The soldier's actions may then be intended by the officer to meet some practical problem; the officer resolves the problem, the soldier solves it.

In such a case, the problem 'belongs' to the person who resolves it. In so far as what is to be done is *my* problem, it is for me to decide. And only if I decide, does what is done count as a solution to my problem.

2 Fallacies in moral philosophy   S. HAMPSHIRE
(*Mind*, Vol. LVIII, 1949, pp. 466–82)

1. In 1912 there appeared in Mind an article by the late Professor Prichard entitled 'Does Moral Philosophy Rest on a Mistake?' I wish to ask the same question about contemporary moral philosophy, but to suggest different reasons for an affirmative answer. Most recent academic discussions of moral philosophy have directly or indirectly reflected the conception of the subject-matter of moral philosophy which is stated or implied in Professor Prichard's article; and this conception of the subject was in turn directly derived from Kant. Kant's influence has been so great, that it is now difficult to realise how revolutionary it was; yet I think that his main thesis, now generally accepted without question by philosophers as the starting-point of moral philosophy, had not been advocated, or even seriously entertained, by any philosopher who preceded him. I shall suggest that the *unbridgeable* separation between moral judgements and factual judgements, which Kant introduced, has had the effect, in association with certain logical assumptions, of leading philosophers away from the primary and proper questions of moral philosophy.[1]

What I shall summarily call the post-Kantian thesis, now so widely accepted without question, is: there is an unbridgeable logical gulf between sentences which express statements of fact and sentences which express judgements of value and particularly moral judgements; this absolute logical independence, ignored or not clearly stated by Aristotle, must be the starting-point of moral philosophy, and constitutes its peculiar problem. Post-Kantian philosophers of different logical persuasions have, of course, given very different accounts of the logic and use of value judgements; but they have generally agreed in regarding the logical independence of moral and empirical beliefs as defining the main problem of ethics.

If one reads the Nicomachean Ethics after reading the works of (for

---

[1] Hume never denied that our moral judgments are based on arguments about matters of fact; he only showed that these arguments are not logically conclusive or deductive arguments.

example) Professor G. E. Moore or Sir David Ross or Professor Stevenson, one has the impression of confronting a wholly different subject. The first point of difference can be tentatively expressed by saying that Aristotle is almost entirely concerned to analyse the problems of the moral *agent*, while most contemporary moral philosophers seem to be primarily concerned to analyse the problems of the moral *judge* or critic. Aristotle describes and analyses the processes of thought, or types of argument, which lead up to the *choice* of one course of action, or way of life, in preference to another, while most contemporary philosophers describe the arguments (or lack of arguments) which lead up to the acceptance or rejection of a moral *judgement about actions*. Aristotle's Ethics incidentally mentions the kind of arguments we use as spectators in justifying sentences which express moral praise and blame of actions already performed, while many contemporary moral philosophers scarcely mention any other kind of argument. Aristotle's principal question is – What sort of arguments do we use in practical deliberation about policies and courses of action and in choosing one kind of life in preference to another? What are the characteristic differences between moral and theoretical problems? The question posed by most contemporary moral philosophers seems to be – What do we mean by, and how (if at all) do we establish the truth of, sentences used to express moral judgements about our own or other people's actions?

The difference between these two approaches to the problems of moral philosophy emerges most clearly from the analogy between aesthetics and ethics to which allusion is made both in Aristotle's Ethics and also in most modern discussions of so-called value judgements (e.g. by Sir David Ross in 'The Right and the Good' and by Professor Ayer in 'Language, Truth and Logic'). For Aristotle (as for Plato) the aesthetic analogy which illuminates the problem of moral philosophy is the analogy between the artist's or craftsman's characteristic procedures in designing and executing his work and the similar, but also different, procedures which we all use in designing and executing practical policies in ordinary life. For contemporary moral philosophers, largely preoccupied with elucidating sentences which express moral praise or blame (moral 'judgements' in the sense in which a judge gives judgements), the relevant analogy is between sentences expressing moral praise or condemnation and sentences expressing aesthetic praise or condemnation. As aesthetics has become the study of the logic and language of aesthetic *criticism*, so moral philosophy has become largely the study of the logic and language of moral criticism.

No one will be inclined to dispute that the processes of thought which are characteristic of the artist or craftsman in conceiving and executing his designs, are essentially different from the processes of the critic who passes judgement on the artist's work; it is notorious that the processes involved in, and the gifts and training required for, the actual making of a work of art are different from those which are required for the competent appraisal of the work; the artist's problem is not the critic's problem. An aesthetician may choose – and in fact most modern aestheticians have chosen – to confine himself to an analysis of the characteristic arguments involved in arriving at a judgement about a work of art (theories of a special aesthetic emotion, of objective standards of taste, etc.). Alternatively he may analyse and characterise the creative process itself (theories of imagination, the relation of technique of conception, the formation of style, the nature of inspiration, etc.). He may decide that the two inquiries, though certainly distinguishable and separable, are in some respects complementary, or at least that there are some questions contained within the first which cannot be answered without a prior answer to the second. But, however complementary they may be, the first inquiry certainly does not include the second. Those who wish to distinguish more clearly the peculiar characteristics of artistic activity, will learn little or nothing from the typical aestheticians' discussions of the objective and subjective interpretations of critical aesthetic judgements. But it seems now to be generally assumed that to ask whether sentences expressing moral praise or blame are to be classified as true or false statements, or alternatively as mere expressions of feeling, is somehow a substitute for the analysis of the processes of thought by which as moral agents we decide what we ought to do and how we ought to behave. Unless this is the underlying assumption, it is difficult to understand why moral philosophers should concentrate attention primarily on the analysis of ethical terms as they are used in sentences expressing moral praise and blame; for we are not primarily interested in moral criticism, or even self-criticism, except in so far as it is directly or indirectly an aid to the solution of practical problems, to deciding what we ought to do in particular situations or types of situation; we do not normally perplex ourselves deeply in moral appraisal for its own sake, in allotting moral marks to ourselves or to other people. The typical moral problem is not a spectator's problem or a problem of classifying or describing conduct, but a problem of practical choice and decision.

But the aesthetic analogy may be misleading, in that the relation of the value judgements of the art critic to the characteristic problems of the artist or craftsman cannot be assumed to be the same as the relation of the sentences expressing moral praise or blame to the problems of the moral agent.[2] To press the analogy would be question-begging, although

---

[2] In so far as we now distinguish between the creative artist and the mere craftsman, a work of art by definition is not the answer to any problem; the artist is only said to have problems when conceived as a craftsman, that is, as having technical problems of devising means towards a given or presumed end. Where there is no problem posed, there can be no question of a right or wrong solution of it. Therefore the critic of poetry cannot be expected

the validity of the analogy between the problems of ethics and aesthetics is so often assumed. Leaving aside the analogy, the issue is – Is the answer to the question 'What are the distinguishing characteristics of sentences expressing moral praise or blame?' necessarily the same as the answer to the question 'What are the distinguishing characteristics of moral problems as they present themselves to us as practical agents?'? Unless these two questions are identical, or unless the first includes the second, much of contemporary moral philosophy is concerned with a relatively trivial side-issue, or is at the very least incomplete. My thesis is that the answer to the second question must contain the answer to the first, but that, if one tries to answer the first question without approaching it as part of the second, the answer will tend to be, not only incomplete, but positively misleading; and that the now most widely accepted philosophical interpretations of moral judgments, their logical status and peculiarities, are radically misleading for this reason. They purport to be logical characterisations of moral judgments and of the distinguishing features of moral arguments, but in these characterisations the *primary* use of moral judgments (= decisions) is largely or even entirely ignored.

2. Suppose (what probably occurs occasionally in most people's experience) one is confronted with a difficult and untrivial situation in which one is in doubt what one ought to do, and then, after full consideration of the issues involved, one arrives at a conclusion. One's conclusion, reached after deliberation, expressed in the sentence '*x* is the best thing to do in these circumstances', is a pure or primary moral judgment (the solution of a practical problem). It is misleading to the point of absurdity to describe this sentence, as used in such a context, as meaningful only in the sense in which an exclamation is meaningful, or as having no literal significance, or as having the function merely of expressing and evoking feeling. It is also misleading to describe it as a statement about the agent's feeling or attitude; for such a description suggests that the judgement would be defended, if attacked, primarily by an appeal to introspection. It is surely misleading to describe the procedure by which such a judgment or decision is established as right as one of comparing degrees of moral emotion towards alternative courses of action. I am supposing (what is normal in such cases) that the agent has reasoned and argued about the alternatives, and am asserting that he would then justify his conclusion, if it were attacked, by reference to these arguments; and a statement about his own moral feelings or attitudes would not be, within

---

(Ftn. 2 cont.)

to show how the poem should be re-written; he describes, but he does not prescribe or make a practical judgment, as does the critic of conduct or technique. So the aesthetic analogy misleads in at least this respect; the valued critic of art excels in description and classification; he is not the artist's adviser, while, moral or technical criticism is necessarily the giving of practical advice.

the ordinary use of language, either a necessary or sufficient justification. Therefore the characterisation of such judgments as purely, or even
largely, reports of feelings or attitudes is at the least incomplete and
misleadingly incomplete, because in this characterisation the typical
procedures of deliberation on which the judgment is based are suppressed
or ignored. It is also paradoxical and misleading to introduce the word
'intuition', as another group of post-Kantian philosophers have done,
in describing the procedure by which such a judgment is arrived at, or by
which it is justified and defended; for the force of the word 'intuition' is
to suggest that the conclusion is not established by any recognised form
of argument, by any ratiocinative process involving a succession of steps
which are logically criticisable; the word 'intuition' carries the suggestion
that we do not, or even cannot, deliberate and calculate in deciding what
we ought to do; but we always can and often actually do deliberate and
calculate.

If the procedure of practical deliberation does not conform, either in
its intermediate steps or in the form of its conclusions, with any forms of
argument acknowledged as respectable in logical text-books, this is a
deficiency of the logical text-books. Or rather it is a mistake in the *interpretation* of text-books of logic to assume that they provide, or that they
are intended to provide, patterns of all forms of reasoning or argument
which can properly be described as rational argument. Arguments may
be, in the ordinary and wider-sense, rational, without being included
among the types of argument which are ordinarily studied by logicians,
since logicians are generally concerned exclusively with the types of
argument which are characteristic of the *a priori* and empirical sciences.
There are other patterns of argument habitually used outside the sciences,
which may be described as more or less rational in the sense that they
are more or less strictly governed by recognised (though not necessarily
formulated) rules of relevance. If one criticises a sequence of sentences
by saying that assertion or denial of the earlier members of the sequence
is irrelevant to acceptance or rejection of their successors, then this
sequence is being regarded as constituting an argument. Aristotle at least
remarks that not all arguments are theoretical arguments, terminating in
a conclusion which is intended as a statement, either factual or logically
true; there are also practical arguments – he naturally says 'syllogisms' –
the form of which is similar in many respects to some types of theoretical
arguments, but which are also characteristically different in their form;
in particular they differ in the form of their conclusion, which is not a
theoretical or true-or-false statement, but has the distinctive form of a
practical judgment, e.g. 'this is the right action' or 'this is the best thing
to do', or 'this ought to be done'.

Even when sentences containing moral terms are used by spectators
(not agents) in contexts in which they seem to be in fact associated with

a purely emotional reaction to a decision or action, it is misleadingly incomplete to characterise them as having the logical force only, or largely, of expressions of, or statements about, the speaker's or writer's feelings or attitudes. If a purely critical and apparently emotional moral judgment of this kind is challenged and needs to be defended and justified, it will be justified by the same kind of arguments which one would have used as an agent in practical deliberation. If I am not prepared to produce such practical arguments, pointing to what ought to have been done, I shall admit that I am not making a genuine moral judgment, but merely expressing or reporting my own feelings; and I shall admit that it was misleading to use the form of sentence ordinarily associated with moral judgments, and not with expressions of feeling. Doubtless many sentences containing moral terms are ambiguous, and may be normally used both as expressions of practical judgments and as expressions of feeling; but the important point is that, if challenged about our intentions, we are required to *distinguish* between such uses; and our languages, by providing the distinctive quasi-imperative form of the practical judgment, enable us to distinguish. But moral philosophers, tacitly assuming that moral judgments must be descriptive statements, have represented a moral problem as a critic's or spectator's problem of proper classification and description.

If, following Aristotle, one begins by describing how moral problems differ both from technical and theoretical problems, one will have begun to answer the question about the distinctive nature of moral judgments, even in their purely critical use. But if one begins by separating them from their context in practical deliberation, and considers them as quasi-theoretical[1] expressions of moral praise and condemnation, the resulting characterisation of them must be misleadingly incomplete.

3. The fact that moral judgments, in spite of the peculiarity of their form as practical judgments, are established by familiar patterns of argument, has been under-emphasised by post-Kantian moral philosophers as a consequence of three connected logical doctrines: (a) the doctrine that so-called value judgments cannot be derived from factual judgments: (b) the doctrine that, although we deliberate and argue about the facts of moral situations (e.g. about the probable consequences of various possible actions), no further argument is possible when once the facts of the situation have been determined; we are thus left in every case of practical deliberation with (c) an ultimate moral judgment, which cannot be replaced by any statement of fact, or by an empirical statement of any kind, and which cannot itself be defended by further argument. From no

---

[1] To pose the problem of ethics as the problem of 'ethical predicates' or 'non-natural characteristics', is at the outset to suggest that moral judgments are to be interpreted as a peculiar kind of descriptive statement.

consideration of facts, or accumulation of factual knowledge, can we ever deduce a moral judgment of the form 'this ought to be done' or 'this is the right action in these circumstances'. Therefore all appeal to the procedure of deliberation is irrelevant to the real problem, which is the analysis or characterisation of these *ultimate* moral judgments.

The fallacy in this position, as I have stated it, emerges in the words 'derive' and 'deduce'. It is only in limiting cases that, in describing the logic of any class of sentences of ordinary discourse, one can reasonably expect to find another class of sentences from which the problem-sentences are logically deducible. Statements about physical things cannot be deduced, or logically derived, from statements about sensations; statements about people's character or dispositions cannot be deduced, or logically derived from, statements about their behaviour; yet in both cases the truth of the first kind of statement is established exclusively by reference to the second kind. In general, one kind of sentence may be established and defended exclusively by reference to another kind, without the first kind being deducible, or logically derivable, from the second. When as philosophers we ask how a particular kind of sentence is to be categorised or described, we are asking ourselves by what sort of arguments it is established and how we justify its use if it is disputed; to explain its logic and meaning is generally to describe and illustrate by examples the kind of sentences which are conventionally accepted as sufficient grounds for its assertion or rejection. So we may properly elucidate moral or practical judgments by saying that they are established and supported by arguments consisting of factual judgments of a particular range, while admitting that they are never strictly deducible, or in this sense logically derivable, from any set of factual judgments.

Certainly no practical judgment is logically deducible from any set of statements of fact; for if practical judgments were so deducible, they would be redundant; we could confine ourselves simply to factual or theoretical judgments; this is in effect what strict Utilitarians, such as Bentham, proposed that we should do. Bentham recommended the removal of distinctively moral terms from the language, so that moral problems would be replaced by technical problems, or problems of applied science. He made this proposal quite self-consciously and deliberately, wishing to introduce a science of morals, in which all moral problems would be experimentally decidable as technical problems. The distinctive form in which moral problems are posed and moral conclusions expressed disappears in his usage, precisely because he makes arguments about matters of fact *logically conclusive* in settling moral problems; and it is to this *replacement* of moral terms that critics of strict Utilitarians have always objected (e.g. Professor G. E. Moore in *Principia Ethica*); they have argued that Utilitarians confuse the reasons on which moral judgments may be based with those judgments themselves; and this confusion arises from supposing that the reasons must be logically conclusive reasons, so that to accept the empirical premisses and to deny the moral conclusion is self-contradictory. But it does not follow from the fact that moral or practical judgments are not in their normal use so deducible that they must be described as ultimate, mysterious, and removed from the sphere of rational discussion. All argument is not deduction, and giving reasons in support of a judgment or statement is not necessarily, or even generally, giving logically conclusive reasons.

Once this assumption is removed, it is possible to reconsider, without philosophical prejudice, what is the difference and the relation between ordinary empirical statements and moral judgments as we actually use them when we are arguing with ourselves, or with others, about what we ought to do. It is important to consider examples of practical or moral problems which are neither trivial in themselves nor abstractly described; for it is only by reflecting on our procedure when confronted with what would ordinarily be called a genuine moral problem that the characteristic types of argument can be seen clearly deployed. A simplified variant of the situation presented in a recent novel[4] may serve the purpose. Suppose that I am convinced that if I continue to live, I cannot avoid inflicting great and indefinitely prolonged unhappiness on one or both of two people, and at the same time on myself; by committing suicide without detection I can avoid this accumulation of unhappiness; I therefore decide, after careful deliberation, that the right or best thing to do is to commit suicide. This is a moral judgment of the primary kind. (Having reached this conclusion, I may of course in any particular case fail to act in accordance with it; as Aristotle points out, deciding *that* x is the best thing to do and deciding *to* do x are both distinguishable and separable.) Suppose that in this case the moral judgment, which is the conclusion of my deliberation, is challenged by someone who at the same time agrees with me in my assessment of all the facts of the situation; that is, he agrees with me about the probable consequences of all the possible courses of action, but does not agree with my conclusion that it is right to commit suicide. An argument develops; we each give our reasons for saying that suicide under these circumstances is right or wrong. However the argument may develop in detail, it will generally exhibit the following features. (1) Although it is assumed that my disputant agrees with me about the facts of this particular situation (probable consequences of various actions etc.), he will in his argument appeal to other facts or beliefs about the world, which are not strictly describable as beliefs about the facts of this particular situation. For instance, we might both recognise as relevant a dispute, partly empirical and partly logical, about whether there is life after death, and whether the Christian dogmas on this subject are true or significant; or we may become involved in a largely historical

---

[4] *The Heart of the Matter*, by Graham Greene.

argument about the social effects of suicide; and it would be recognised as pertinent to produce psychological arguments to the effect that intense unhappiness is often preferred to mere loneliness and *therefore* (and this 'therefore' is not the sign of an entailment) it would be better not to desert the other two people involved. *The point is that it does not follow from the fact that two people are in agreement about the facts of a particular situation, but disagree in their moral judgment, that their disagreement is ultimate and admits of no further rational argument;* hence (2) our disagreement about the moral or practical conclusion, which is not a disagreement about the facts of the particular situation, is nevertheless, a disagreement to which empirical arguments, beliefs about an indefinitely wide range of matters of fact, are recognised to be relevant. If we are deliberating or arguing about whether suicide is right or wrong in these particular circumstances (or in any circumstances), then our psychological, historical and religious beliefs are always taken to be relevant parts of the argument. By representing so-called value judgments as ultimate and logically divorced from ordinary factual judgments, philosophers have implicitly or explicitly suggested that such sentences as 'suicide is always wrong' or 'suicide is wrong in these circumstances' cannot be defended or refuted by appeals to facts or to the empirical sciences. This paradox is a legacy of Kant's anxiety to underline as strongly as possible the difference between practical problems which are moral problems and those which are purely technical problems. Almost all previous philosophers – and most people without Kantian or other philosophical prejudices – have assumed accumulating knowledge, or changing beliefs arising out of the study of history, psychology, anthropology and other empirical sciences, to be relevant to their moral judgments; to be relevant, not in the sense that the falsity of moral judgments previously accepted as true can be *deduced* from some empirical propositions of history, psychology or any natural science, but in the sense in which (for example) propositions about somebody's conduct are relevant to propositions about his character; that is, previous moral judgments are shown to be groundless, the empirical propositions on which they were based having been contradicted as scientific or historical knowledge increases. The conflicting moral conclusions of a Marxist and a Christian Fundamentalist, or the differences which may arise even between two contemporary and similarly educated liberal unbelievers, will generally (but not always or necessarily) be shown in argument to rest on different empirical or at least corrigible beliefs about the constitution of the universe. Whenever we argue about any moral question which is not trivial, our beliefs and assumptions, however rudimentary and half-formulated, about psychological, sociological and probably theological questions are recognised as relevant, as logically involved in the nature of the dispute.

The result of the supposed argument about my judgment that suicide is the right policy in this particular circumstance might be that I am convinced that my judgement was wrong, and am persuaded that suicide is not the right policy. I might be persuaded to withdraw my original judgement, either because I have been made to recognise a fault in the logic of my previous argument, or because I have been persuaded to abandon admittedly relevant beliefs about matters of fact, or because my attention has been directed to new facts as being relevant to the decision, facts which I had known but the relevance of which I had previously overlooked. To direct attention to further known facts as relevant to a judgment is perhaps the most important effect and function of moral arguments or practical deliberation (e.g. of giving practical advice). It is misleading to speak of 'the facts of a situation' in such a way as to suggest that there must be a closed set of propositions which, once established, precisely determine the situation.[5] The situations in which we must act or abstain from acting, are 'open' in the sense that they cannot be uniquely described and finally circumscribed. Situations do not present themselves with their labels attached to them; if they did, practical problems would be conclusively soluble theoretical problems, the philosopher's dream; but ἐν τῇ αἰσθήσει ἡ κρίσις – the crux is in the labelling, or the decision depends on how we see the situation.

For these reasons the logical divorce between so-called judgements of value and factual judgements is misleading; for arguments about practical conclusions are arguments about facts. Our moral or practical judgements – 'x is the right or best course of action (in these or in all circumstances)' – are corrigible by experience and observation; we feel certain about some, and very doubtful about others.

4. Certainly there may (logically) be cases in which we cannot attribute conflicting solutions of practical moral problems to conflicting beliefs about matters of fact; that is, two disputants, in giving their reasons for conflicting moral judgements, may be unable to find among their reasons any empirical proposition which is accepted by one of them and rejected by the other. It is logically possible that A and B should agree entirely e.g. about the effects of capital punishment, and furthermore should find no relevant differences in their general psychological or sociological or other beliefs, and yet disagree as to whether capital punishment should or should not now be abolished. However rare such situations may be (and I believe them to be much more rare than is commonly allowed) such so-called 'ultimate' moral differences may occur. Both A and B,

---

[5] The word 'fact', here as always, is treacherous, involving the old confusion between the actual situation and the description of it; the situation is given, but not 'the facts of the situation'; to state the facts is to analyse and interpret the situation. And just this is the characteristic difficulty of actual practical decisions, which disappears in the text-book cases, where the 'relevant facts' are pre-selected. So the determining arguments are cut out of the text-book, and the gap is filled by 'intuition' or feeling.

if they can claim to be making a moral judgement and not merely expressing their own feelings about, or attitudes towards, capital punishment, will be able to give the reasons which seem to them sufficient to justify their conclusion; but what is accepted by A as a sufficient reason for a practical conclusion is not accepted by B as a sufficient reason and *vice versa*. They may then argue further to ensure that each does recognise the reason which he is claiming to be sufficient in this case as sufficient in other cases; but, when this consistency of use is once established, the argument must terminate. How is such an 'ultimate' or irresoluble difference about a moral judgement properly described?

Compare this ultimate difference about the practical judgment with a similar ultimate difference about a theoretical judgement: if A and B were to disagree about whether somebody is intelligent, and yet find that they did not disagree about the facts (actual behaviour) or probabilities (how he is likely to behave under hypothetical conditions) on which their judgement is based, they would describe their difference as a difference in the use of the word 'intelligent'; they would say 'you use a different criterion of intelligence, and so do not mean by "intelligent" exactly what I mean'.[6] Similarly when it has been shown that A and B generally apply wholly or largely different tests in deciding whether something ought or ought not to be done, they might properly describe their so-called ultimate difference by saying that they do not both mean the same, or exactly the same, thing when they say that something ought or ought not to be done; and in most such cases of ultimate or irresoluble moral differences this is in fact what we do say – that different societies (and even different individuals within the same society) may have more or less different moral terminologies, which are not mutually translatable. But of practical judgments one cannot say that differences which are in principle irresoluble are *simply* terminological misunderstandings and in *no* sense genuine contradictions; for it is the distinguishing characteristic of practical judgements that they have a prescriptive or quasi-imperative force as part of their meaning. There is therefore one sense in which, when A says that capital punishment ought to be abolished and B says that it ought not, they are contradicting each other; their judgements contradict each other in the sense in which two conflicting commands or recommendations may be said to contradict each other. They can only argue about which of their prescriptions is right if they can agree on some common criteria of rightness. A, following the practice

---

[6] 'What do you mean by saying that he is intelligent?' is ordinarily interpreted as the same question as 'What are your reasons for saying or why do you say, that he is intelligent?' Similarly, 'What do you mean by saying that that was a wrong decision?' is the same question as '*Why* do you say that that was a wrong decision?' To find the different reasons in different cases is to find the meaning of 'wrong', although no *one* set of reasons is *the* meaning.

of all reforming moralists and many moral philosophers, may try to influence B's actions by giving moral reasons for preferring his own criteria of use to B's use; but in his advocacy of his own use of moral terms, he will be using his moral terms in his own way. The argument might have shown B that his conclusion was wrong in A's sense of 'wrong' or even in his own sense of 'wrong'; but no argument can show that B *must* use the criteria which A uses and so must attach the same meaning (in this sense) to moral terms as A. Between two consistently applied terminologies, whether in theoretical science or in moral decision, ultimately we must simply choose; we can give reasons for our choice, but not reasons for reasons for ... *ad infinitum*.

5. We may find that many people do not deliberate and so can scarcely be said to make moral judgements, but simply act as they have been conditioned to act, and, when challenged, repeat the moral sentences which they have been taught to repeat or merely state or express personal feelings or attitudes. A second, and much smaller class, act generally, and even wholly, on impulse, in the sense that they do not propose practical problems to themselves or choose policies, but simply do whatever they feel inclined to do – and such people are to be distinguished from those who have *decided that* to act on impulse, or to do what one feels inclined to do, is the right policy; for this is to make a moral judgement. But the great majority of people for some part of their lives are thinking about what is the best thing to do, sometimes reaching a conclusion and failing to act on it, sometimes reaching a conclusion which, in the light of corrections of their empirical beliefs or their logic, they later recognise to have been a wrong conclusion, and sometimes reaching a conclusion which they are prepared to defend by argument and acting in accordance with it.

'Thinking what is the best thing to do' describes a procedure which it is unprofitable, if not impossible, to analyse, or find a paraphrase for, in general terms without constant reference to specific cases. Aristotle begins by describing it as calculating means to a vaguely conceived end (happiness or well-doing), the nature of the end being more precisely determined by the means chosen as involved in its realisation. But he progressively qualifies and complicates this schematic account in such a way as to suggest that to make a moral decision is not to choose means to an already decided end, but to choose a policy of means-to-end which is judged right or wrong as a whole. Practical problems are (as Kant emphasised and over-emphasised) sub-divisible into moral and purely technical problems; the choice of the most efficient means to an already determined end is not called a moral choice. It is the defining characteristic of a moral problem, that it requires an unconditional decision, the choice of an action or policy as a whole.

6. There is another and related logical fallacy, often implicitly assumed and not explicitly stated, which has led philosophers to describe moral or

practical judgments as expressions or reports of feeling or as established by *a priori* intuitions, and to neglect their normal occurrence as the corrigible conclusions of arguments involving the facts of a particular situation and our general beliefs about the world; this is the fallacy of assuming that all literally significant sentences must correspond to something, or describe something. As ordinary empirical statements were said to correspond to facts, so some philosophers have introduced the word 'values' in order that there should be something to which moral (and aesthetic) judgements can be said to correspond; we are said to 'intuit' or to 'apprehend' these values, these words being used to suggest an analogy with sense-perception. Other philosophers, wishing to define the world as the totality of facts, or as the objects of sense and introspection, have inferred that, as moral judgements cannot be said to correspond to anything in the external world, they must either correspond to something in the internal world (i.e. to feelings) or, failing that, that they cannot be admitted to be literally significant. The question 'what do moral judgements correspond to?' or 'what do they describe?' suggests itself particularly to those who are preoccupied with the critical use of these judgements as expressions of retrospective praise or blame; in so far as we relate them to practical deliberations and decisions, we come to recognise them as not descriptions of, but prescriptions for, actions. Practical judgements, no less than theoretical or descriptive statements, are in the natural sense of the words, literally significant, although they do not in the normal sense describe. If I say 'this is (or would have been) the right action in these circumstances', this judgement can be significantly denied; but, as it is not a descriptive statement or statement of fact, the denial is not normally expressed in the form 'it is *false* that this is the best action in these circumstances'; 'true' and 'false' are more naturally used with theoretical judgements and statements of fact.[7] Of course this distinction between true or false descriptive statements and right or wrong practical judgements is not absolute and clear; many sentences are partly descriptive and are partly expressions of practical judgements. But there is a distinction which emerges clearly in simple cases of pure moral judgements and purely descriptive statements. One *can* describe somebody's behaviour or character without making any moral judgement (i.e. prescription), even if in fact prescriptions and descriptions are often almost inextricably combined.

7. There is (I think) a widespread impression that the concentration of academic moral philosophers on the attempt to *define* ethical expressions – 'good', 'right', 'ought', etc., – as being the principal problem of

---

[7]Although we can speak of believing that this is the right action we cannot speak of evidence that it is right. 'Evidence' is tied to statements which are true or false.

moral philosophy has tended to make the subject sterile and unenlightening. One is inclined to say that it does not *matter* whether 'right', as ordinarily used, is definable in terms of 'good' or not. There is the feeling that the clarifications which one expects from the moral philosopher cannot be answered by verbal definitions or the discovery of paraphrases. And I think this apparently philistine impatience with the search for verbal definitions or equivalences has good logical grounds. If we wish to clarify our own or somebody else's use of moral terms, the discovery of verbal equivalences or paraphrases among these terms is not an answer, but, at the most, a preliminary step towards an answer. I can become clear about what somebody means by saying 'this is the right action in these circumstances' only by finding out under what conditions he makes this judgement, and what reasons (and there may be many) he regards as sufficient to justify it. What we want to know, in clarifications of differences in our use of moral (or aesthetic) terms, is – What makes me (in the logical, not the causal sense) decide that this is the right action? There is no reason to expect a simple answer in terms of a single formula, e.g. 'it is likely to increase happiness'. But to search only for definitions or verbal equivalences is to assume that there must be a single sufficient reason from which I always and necessarily derive my judgment. This is another expression of the fundamental fallacy of thinking of analysis or clarification of the standard use of words or sentences as necessarily a matter of exhibiting deducibilities or entailments. If I am asked what I mean by saying of someone that he is intelligent, I explain my use of the word by describing specimens of the type of behaviour to which I apply the word; I give some specimens of the types of statements about his behaviour which would be taken as sufficient grounds for asserting or denying that he is intelligent. Similarly, one can only clarify the use of the principal moral (or aesthetic) terms – 'good', 'right', 'ought', etc. – by describing specimens of conduct to which they are applied, that is, by quoting the different characteristics of actions which are normally and generally taken to be sufficient grounds for deciding that they are the right actions. The type of analysis which consists in defining, or finding synonyms for the moral terms of a particular language cannot illuminate the nature of moral decisions or practical problems; it is no more than local dictionary-making, or the elimination of redundant terms, which is useful only as a preliminary to the study of typical moral arguments. An informative treatise on ethics – or on the ethics of a particular society or person – would contain an accumulation of examples selected to illustrate the kind of decisions which are said to be right in various circumstances, and the reasons given and the arguments used in concluding that they are right. An uninformative treatise on ethics consists of specimens of moral sentences, separated from actual or imaginable contexts of argument about particular practical problems, and treated as text for the definition of moral terms; and many academic text-books follow this pattern.

Summary – The four logically related fallacies underlying the typical post-Kantian approach to moral philosophy are (*a*) The assimilation of moral or practical judgments to descriptive statements, which is associated with concentration on the use of moral terms in sentences expressing a spectator's praise or blame; (*b*) the inference from the fact that moral or practical judgements cannot be logically derived from statements of fact that they cannot be based on, or established exclusively by reference to, beliefs about matters of fact; hence theories that moral judgements must be ultimate and irrational, that they are established by intuition or are not literally significant; (*c*) the assumption that all literally significant sentences must correspond to or describe something; moral decisions do not correspond to or describe anything, but they may, nevertheless, be said to be rational or irrational, right or wrong.[8] (*d*) The confusion between clarifying the use of ethical terms with discovering definitions of, or verbal equivalences between, these terms; the search for definitions is another expression of the old obsession of philosophers with entailment and deducibility as the only admissible relation between sentences in rational argument. To interpret 'rational argument' so narrowly is, although misleading, not in itself fallacious; but if, on the basis of this arbitrary restriction, moral judgements are relegated to a logical limbo, labelled 'emotive', the study of the characteristic logic of these sentences, and of the types of argument in which they occur, is obscured and suppressed.

3 Practical and theoretical learning   H. ENTWISTLE
(*British Journal of Educational Studies*, Vol. 17, No. 2, July 1969, pp. 117–28)

There is an educational tradition which stresses the importance of learning by doing, in a way which puts a premium upon the learner's own first hand experience at the expense of theoretical teaching. At best, theorizing (and especially listening to the theoretical explanations of teachers) is something which follows a period of self-help. This reversal of the roles traditionally ascribed to theoretical and practical activity in schools finds some support from philosophers having an anti-Cartesian conception of mind. The intellectualist, theory-biased schools of

---

[8] 'I decided that x was the right thing to do' is a descriptive statement, true or false; but 'x was the right thing to do' is a practical or moral judgment, right or wrong.

Western Europe appear to reflect the Cartesian orientation of Western thought: they seem living exemplars of Descartes' 'I think, therefore I am'. They reflect the assumption that thought is the primary category of experience and that efficient practice is the step-child of intelligent theorizing. Since thinking is the guarantee of personal identity, experience begins and is centred in thought and this is where schooling ought to begin.

Against this assumption of the fundamental place of reflection in human experience some contemporary philosophers have stressed the primacy of practical experience. For example, MacMurray has written of his intention 'to exhibit the primacy of the practical in human experience' and of 'the need to transfer the centre of gravity in philosophy from thought to action ... we should substitute the "I do" for the "I think" as our starting point and centre of reference.'[9] On this view, theorizing is at best a middling, instrumental activity. In relation to life's fundamental practical activity, theorizing has no independent status and much of Ryle's *The Concept of Mind* is concerned to question whether theorizing is at all necessary to intelligent practice. Indeed, Ryle casts doubt upon many of the purely cognitive activities which occur in our schools: 'In ordinary life as well as in the special business of teaching, we are more concerned with people's competences than with their cognitive repertoires. Indeed, even when we are concerned with their intellectual excellencies and deficiencies, we are interested less in the stocks of truths they acquire and retain than in their capacities to find out truths for themselves and their ability to organize and exploit them when discovered.'[10]

Ryle's argument depends upon his assumption that performing a task intelligently does not mean doing two things – thinking what one is doing and doing it – but only one. In his view, it is unnecessary to recall and recite to oneself factual information when one performs intelligently and skilfully. He suggests that playing chess or swimming the breast stroke does not require conscious recall of the rules every time a move is made or an awareness of the principles of hydrology at every stroke. Polanyi makes a similar point: 'A well known scientist, who in his youth had to support himself by giving swimming lessons, told me how puzzled he was when he tried to discover what made him swim: whatever he did in the water, he always kept afloat.'[11] It seems that we are often incapable of giving any sort of explanation of how we do things. Facts, theories which explain the skills we perform, elude us. Nor is this merely a feature

[9] J. MacMurray, *The Self as Agent*, Faber & Faber, 1961, Ch. IV.
[10] G. Ryle, *The Concept of Mind*, Hutchinson's University Library, 1949, Ch. II.
[11] M. Polanyi, *Personal Knowledge*, Routledge & Kegan Paul, 1958, p. 49.

of unsubtle animal skills like swimming. Polanyi goes on to indicate how one can practise diagnostic medical skill without reference to statements of matters of fact. 'While the correct use of medical terms cannot be achieved in itself without a knowledge of medicine, a great deal of medicine can be remembered even after one has forgotten the use of medical terms. Having changed my profession and moved from Hungary to England, I have forgotten most of the medical terms I learned in Hungary and have acquired no others in place of them; yet I shall never again view, for example, a pulmonary radiograph in such a totally uncomprehending manner as I did before I was trained in radiology. The knowledge of medicine is retained, just as the message of a letter is remembered, even after the text which has conveyed either kind of knowledge has passed beyond recall.'[12]

Ryle's expressed intention is to discredit the Cartesian dualism which, on his account of it, separates bodily from mental functions, and implies an interior monologue going on behind physical acts. There is not, he avers, a ghostly decision to act behind each human action. There are merely acts of reasoning, fishing, playing chess, swimming, clowning (to use his own examples), all of which can be effected more or less stupidly or intelligently. The point is taken. But the argument is presented in a way which discredits theorizing and plays down the importance of the fact that many activities are a complex in which theorizing, planning, reference to information and reflection upon the results of actions, all play a part along with overt physical performance itself. To argue this is not to fall back upon the notion of the ghost in the machine, a covert monologue which accompanies theorizing, planning, searching for information, making the move and evaluating the consequences of an action. Each of these activities is one thing and not two. But it makes sense to claim that all these can be related actions, part of a whole whose manifestation is only one of them (the stroke of the swimmer, the cricketer's shot, the clown's tumble); a sequence of single events, separate in time, but none the less part of a complex total performance.

What Ryle does not sufficiently allow is that some skills are thus a complex of several activities, some of them essentially theoretical, others practical in character. For example, it may be true that in cricket, making a stroke, delivering a ball, stumping or catching an opponent are all single activities and not tandem operations of hitting, bowling, taking the bails or a catch and *reminding* oneself that one is doing any of these things and that one ought to do it in a particular kind of way. There is no ghostly operation of this kind accompanying any of these skilled movements. But each of these activities takes place within the strategy of the

---

[12] *Ibid.*, p. 102.

game, its immediate tactics and, more immediate still, in relation to circumstances like how the field is disposed, what the batsman did with the last ball or what he failed to do if he played and missed. The batsman who goes on making hook shots to the square leg boundary when a fielder is posted there is not performing intelligently, however perfect in execution the shot itself is as a piece of stroke play. The shot which gets him caught on the boundary is no less copybook in execution than the earlier strokes which scored. As a display of knowing how to time a stroke the performance may be first class: the sort of model which would be an excellent example to the schoolboy during a coaching session in the nets. But so far as there is failure to respond to knowledge that (or even a failure to know that) the field has changed, the performance is unintelligent: 'One of the criteria of a performance being intelligent is that the performer will vary it in accordance with changes in the situation'.[13] A good batsman knows *that* the field is disposed in a particular way and it is in the context of this information that he decides *how* he will deal with each ball. But on the field of play the other kind of sportsman is not unknown: the one highly competent in the performance of isolated skills but unable to 'read the game', such a reading involving an appraisal which takes account of matters of fact and theorizes on this basis. The bowler who reads the game has a complex skill which consists of observing how a given batsman has been dealing with his bowling, knowing that he has certain weaknesses, knowing that there is a patch of rough in a fortuitous position, deciding that he will attempt to pitch there, motioning in a fielder for the anticipated catch – doing all this on his way back to his mark – and then turning and running in to bowl. His delivery must be judged skilful or not within the context of what he has made his mind up to do. Though the actual delivery of the ball is not a tandem operation consisting of a ghostly recital to himself of what he is doing as well as doing it, it has to be judged intelligent or not in the light of the sequence of decisions which led up to it and the consequences which follow from it. Spectators will pronounce stupid or mistaken the strokes or balls which are impeccable executions of intentions which, in the strategy of the game and in order to be judged intelligent at that point, ought to have been something else. Ryle appears to want to deal with this problem of how far a single, simple activity like bowling, stumping or hooking may be a complex of operations, by saying that the performance itself, though simple, requires a complex description: 'Only one thing is done, yet to say what is done requires a sentence containing, at least, both a main clause and a subordinate clause.'[14] Thus, the complex description of a bowler taking a wicket with a well thought out delivery would be: 'Jones, remembering

[13] R. S. Peters, *The Concept of Motivation,* Routledge & Kegan Paul, 1958, p. 91.
[14] Ryle, *op. cit.,* p. 30.

that Brown was vulnerable to leg spin and noticing a patch of rough just to the right of the popping crease at the other end, motioned in Black and bowled.' From this complex description of a simple motor activity, it is clear that to perform a skill intelligently may be to become involved in a theoretical as well as a practical activity. Bowling an over (or a 'spell' of overs) intelligently is to perform a series of manual operations punctuated by critical evaluations (theorizing) aimed at producing the sort of ball which will best exploit the batsman's limitations and such environmental conditions as may currently favour the bowler's art. In this sense, bowling intelligently *is* a tandem operation of reflective activity prior to the overt manifestation of the bowling (the run up, the swing of the arm etc.) followed by the actual delivery of the ball. It is not a tandem operation in the sense that concurrent with the physical action of bowling, the bowler is involved in reciting to himself exactly what he is doing in his run up, swinging his arm, spinning his fingers etc. For example, he has his run up worked out before he begins to bowl and should he reflect, whilst running, where exactly he is putting his feet, how many paces he has taken, he will be as likely as not to trip himself up or check himself in mid-delivery in the knowledge that his timing (an essentially tacit component of his skill) has gone awry.

Thus, in relation to the practice of bowling, two essentially different kinds of performance may be identified. First, there is the physical activity of bowling: once launched into this, the action is performed unreflectingly, tacitly; to reflect at this point is to be caught in two minds – a condition usually fatal to skilled performance. Secondly, there is the contextual reflection which prompts a decision to deliver a particular kind of ball. This theorizing involves knowing that certain things are the case; partly a matter of having information about the present state of the game, the condition of the pitch, the form of the batsman and so on; partly the possession of knowledge which wider experience of the game has taught the bowler about the idiosyncrasies of this particular ground, this individual opponent and the strengths and weaknesses of his colleagues. If intelligent activity does not depend upon the agent's reminding himself of what he ought to be doing whilst he is actually performing an activity, nevertheless, what he has actually *chosen* to do, if it is an intelligent choice, will have followed from a consideration of alternatives in the light of pertinent information. Once launched into an operation, a surgeon's activity may be 'unthinking' in that his manual skill is largely tacit, much like the bowler's unreflective running and delivery once he is launched into an actual delivery. But the surgeon's decision to operate at a particular time and in a particular way is the result of reflection which relates what he knows about the patient – the nature of his complaint (e.g. as revealed in X-rays), his general state of health, his age etc. – to what he knows about anatomy and physiology and the information he possesses about the diseased condition in question. Diagnosis, as distinct from surgery, is essentially a theoretical activity. But skilful surgery, an essentially practical activity, is partly a matter of accurate diagnosis.

It is evident that much of what we do professionally or in the general business of daily life is done intelligently, not merely in virtue of the technique or manual dexterity we have in actually performing a skill, but also by reference to the cognitive repertoires at our command. And this fact that intelligent performance depends upon an ability to 'read' a skill or technique into an appropriate context is the answer to those who would argue that technical or professional training is largely a matter of picking up a skill in a practice situation. In teacher training there is an insistent mythology which claims that educational theory is useless and that teaching practice is all that really matters. This account of teacher training might be adequate if trainees were likely to spend a professional lifetime in that particular school in which they did their teaching practice, if such a school left nothing to be desired in terms of the educational opportunities it provided for children, if one class of children were much like any other (or if individual differences hardly existed between children) and if novel subject matter or teaching methods were unlikely to evolve in the forty years or so of a professional lifetime. No doubt a purely practical training based on a few rules of thumb would produce teachers who could perform prescribed routines efficiently in familiar situations, but who would be unable to analyse their work in such a way that their competence would develop in response to changed situations. The teacher who has the resource to adapt himself to novel circumstances is probably the one who has sufficient appetite for theorizing to ask himself occasionally why he is doing what he does, and this seems likely to follow from some study of educational theory as well as from mastering teaching techniques in practical situations.

However, this justification of theorizing as an essential part of the intelligent practice of skill has referred mainly to that contextual theory and information which underpins the activities of planning and evaluating the performance of a particular skill: that is, we have considered the sort of knowledge which might contribute to skilled performance by helping to answer questions like, 'What should I do (e.g. with the next ball, with this patient, with 3B next time I take them)?', or, 'Did I do the sensible thing (with that googly, in prescribing that drug, in sending Jones to the headmaster)?' But so far, nothing has been said about the role of theory, if any, in actually learning, or mastering the skill of bowling a googly, manipulating a surgical probe, writing on the blackboard, disciplining an insolent child or a reluctant learner, delivering a lesson narrative or asking appropriate questions at the right moment in a lesson. How far, for example, does one learn these specific classroom skills by reference to theory, how far by simply picking up tricks through the experience of actually teaching children in a classroom? Teachers of educational theory might be quite successful in communicating helpful contextual theory and information through courses in child development, or philosophy, sociology and history of education; but one suspects that the preference which most student teachers display for school practice indicates that we are much less successful in actually teaching other people how to teach. Trainees (and this is probably also true of occupations other than teaching) seem to believe that their practical skills can only be learned in practice situations.

There is an important sense in which it is probably true that skills can only be learned through practice. The valid emphasis upon learning by doing relates to the fact that there is a tacit dimension of most skills which eludes articulation. Thus, unless the learner practises there is no guarantee (to himself as well as to his teachers) that he understands what is really required in the performance of a skill. Something is inevitably excluded from even the best of descriptions and demonstrations, and to have learned merely to recite the procedures involved in completing a given task is not necessarily to have learned how to perform the task itself. In a workshop situation an apprentice or pupil may notice all the overtly physical movements which a craftsman or teacher performs when practising a skill, but there are some things he cannot know until he tries himself; the sharpness of tools, the resistance or plasticity of materials, for example. The teacher may use words like 'hard', 'soft', 'sharp', 'greasy', 'heavy'. But these are relative terms and their meaning in a particular context can only be understood in practice. Even with the same tool at different times, and with similar materials on different occasions, there are slight differences which constitute an unexpected and, therefore, an unspecifiable element. However specific a practitioner may be in his analyses and explanations of a skill, there remains always what Polanyi calls 'a tacit component'.[15] At the heart of every skill there is something unspecifiable; some particulars remain ineffable. And this is as true of skills of social life like tact or of political skills like the 'art of exercising public liberty',[16] as it is of motor skills like sawing wood or firing a rifle, and of diagnostic skills like recognizing an epileptic seizure. In motor skills the tacit component is mainly a matter of 'touch'. Whether it is playing the piano, making a cover drive or manhandling a bale of cotton, skilled performance is, ultimately, a matter of the adjustment of the organism to the resistance of the object: partly a matter of pressure (literally 'touch'), partly a matter of timing. It is having the 'knack' and this, familiarly, is incommunicable. It is the mystery at the heart of the craft which the learner must discover for himself. In the end, making a skill one's own, performing economically, comfortably, powerfully,

---

[15] Polanyi, *op. cit.*, 102–3.
[16] MacMurray, *op. cit.*, pp. 87–8.

'perfectly', depends upon practice, upon first hand experience, upon doing. And this problem of timing, the nice adjustment of the performer to the objective conditions as he finds them, is equally necessary for those whose skills are intellectual or professional rather than manual. The experienced teacher's success in using those same disciplinary devices which are a broken reed in the hand of the novice is attributable, in part, to the precise timing and subtle emphasis which he employs in dealing with the unique classroom occasion. Generalizations about discipline often strike the trainee teacher as particularly unhelpful in throwing light on his own peculiar classroom problems. For the explanation of why the experienced teacher succeeded in disciplining a particular child or class will refer primarily to his experience and not to the intrinsic merits of one disciplinary device rather than another. Such explanation must omit a great deal of pertinent information; in particular, the peculiar knowledge he has of his own class or school or of a particular child's background. It is the unformulated, tacitly held knowledge of a class or a child, acquired through a multitude of daily encounters, which is the crucial factor in his success.

It is a danger, of course, that this element of mystery at the core of a skill can be overplayed and used as an excuse for neglect of theory and precept. Though something crucial to a skill may elude specification, efficient technical and professional education depends upon as much analysis and formulation of principle as possible. Because mastery of a skill depends ultimately upon practice, this does not mean that theoretical explanation cannot assist in learning and mastering it. Ultimately, the question is not one of the value of theory as against practice, but a matter of where and when the theorizing most profitably takes place. Perhaps the value of theorizing is diminished when carried on apart from the practice of a skill. It is questionable whether an instructor or a tutor can do very much more than coach performance (even in teaching sophisticated skills like surgery and teaching) in piecemeal fashion. It may be unhelpful to teach the theory of a skill ceremoniously in lecture courses apart from practical situations. It is arguable that theorizing is most helpful to practise when it is an *ad hoc* kind of activity carried in close association with practice: when the learner tries and the theorist warns, approves, corrects and initiates discussion of the practice immediately following the event. On this view, theories are not prescriptions which pupils learn and then go away to apply, so much as advice which is offered after or alongside practice in relation to his own peculiar strengths and limitations. Indeed, Ryle does seem to take this view of the role of theory in relation to skill: 'We learn *how* by practice, schooled indeed by criticism and example, but often unaided by any lessons in the theory.'[17] Here, 'lessons in the theory' should probably be understood

[17] Ryle, *op. cit.*, p. 41.

as referring to the sort of ceremonial schooling in theory which takes place in formal lecture periods.

It is probably true, particularly in professional education, that too little importance is attached to *ad hoc* theorizing of the kind implied in the quotation from Ryle and too much claimed for the efficacy of formalized explanations of skills. For example, when teacher trainees claim that teaching practice is the most valuable part of their course of training, they are unlikely always to be making the point that they are really self-taught thus, implicitly, making teacher training redundant. Rather, they are probably implying that the principles they learn by exemplification in the concrete situation, the advice offered by tutors or teachers as a result of seeing them at work, have more meaning for them than prescriptions offered in lecture courses. That is, they especially value the theoretical advice they receive through coaching following their mistakes and successes in classroom management, use of visual materials, treatment of a topic, disciplining a particular child or class and so on. Thus, in terms of the development of particular teaching skills or techniques which are the manifestation of the teacher visibly at work in the classroom, it may be that theory has most meaning when drawn out of practical situations than when offered ceremoniously in the lecture room prior to the event. For, logically, practice *is* prior to theory. It is not possible to formulate theoretical maxims pertinent to a skill aside from prior existence of the skill in fact or in imagination. Ryle makes this point with reference to the work of great innovators in different fields of human activity. For example,[18] he claims that Aristotle and Izaak Walton found themselves and others reasoning intelligently or fishing effectively before they formulated the principles underlying the efficient performance of these skills. Neither of these constructed complete theoretical frameworks before anybody ever fished or reasoned intelligently. No doubt both of them reflected upon their activities from the beginning. Though an activity like angling is logically prior to reflection on the practice, becoming skilled – searching for mastery of the art – involves reflection; doing the thinking after doing some fishing but before the next act of fishing. Some kinds of bait succeed; others fail as do different ways of casting, playing etc. One is making and refining maxims all the time in the intelligent pursuit of an activity. But the *systematization* of maxims by Aristotle and Walton followed a great deal of reasoning and fishing: Walton was only able to systematize his theory when he had become *The Compleat Angler*.

However, if the learner, like the innovator, is only able to develop a systematic theory of his craft or profession following considerable practical experience nourished by piecemeal *ad hoc* reflection, this is not to say that he can derive no benefit from familiarity with theory in

---

[18] *Ibid.*, p. 30.

advance of practice. Psychologically, the initiate may need the security of knowing some principles of procedure in advance of practice. This would seem particularly true of a student teacher facing a class of children for the first time. If a disorderly outcome is to be avoided, the intending teacher needs some plan of action, some idea of what he would do should certain fairly predictable contingencies arise. Some theoretical knowledge in advance of practice is also prudential in the interests of safety or economy. If a man is going to plant or prune roses, it may be costly (in terms of loss of his plants) to discover after the event that certain planting procedures are not conducive to a plant's taking root or that too rigorous a pruning may destroy points of growth. Again, prudence dictates a minimal familiarity with theory in advance of learning to drive a car. It would be disastrous to himself and other road users, as well as detrimental to the vehicle, to let the learner-driver pick things up as he went along. In this skill, close attention to some theory in advance of practice is absolutely essential. The learner needs to know in advance what some road signs mean. And though a knowledge of the principles of the internal combustion engine and its powering of a car is unnecessary to knowing how to operate clutch, gears and accelerator, the motoring teacher's instructions make much more sense if he knows how these parts function. Attempts to pick up a skill without prior resort to theory may also result in the formation of bad habits which have subsequently to be unlearned and which may, indeed, prove fatal to any subsequent attempt to learn to perform efficiently. Most people who learn to type without benefit of lessons in theory, live to regret the limitations upon speed imposed by their two-fingered 'sight' typing. This limitation of practical experience is, indeed, one reason for institutionalizing learning in schools. Skills and disciplines are there analysed by experts in terms of the epistemological priorities involved in learning them and their communication becomes somewhat less haphazard (though not entirely so) than if they were picked up from life itself.

However, Ryle's and Polanyi's reminders that much skilled performance is habitual, performed without conscious reference to information, helps to put into perspective a fact which constantly disturbs teachers and which is sometimes used to justify abolition of examinations: that is, whilst we usually remember how to perform the skills we have learned (especially so long as we continue to practise them), we often forget the pertinent theoretical explanations or the items of information which assisted in teaching the skill. Indeed, when performance becomes skilled, conscious thought about skill may be a hindrance. Information about the skill may be 'forgotten' and its conscious recall may inhibit skilled performance. This is obviously true, for example, of driving a car. Conscious attention to the mechanics of the vehicle or to the details of the Highway Code only inhibit the skilled driver: confusion and loss of efficiency results. More than this, the experienced driver is sometimes startled on reaching his destination and appalled at how little conscious he has been of traffic signs and signals which, from previous experience, he knows he must have observed on the way. And if a reading of the game of cricket is essential to intelligent stroke-play, once committed to a stroke a batsman is only confused by thinking about what he is doing. His touch, his timing, would go awry: he might even change his mind in mid-stroke in a way which could cost him his wicket.

It is important that teachers should remember this purely behavioural aspect of skilled performance when they are apt to wonder what has happened to the facts or theories they have taught. Because they appear to be forgotten in the sense that they cannot be recalled without prompting, this does not mean that it was a waste of time to teach them in the first place. As with Ryle's unsophisticated chess player who is unable to formulate the rules despite playing in accordance with them, unremembered facts and theories may nevertheless be assimilated within the educand's behaviour. Depending always on the intention and the context within which they were taught, they may have assisted in modifications of behaviour, the formation of new attitudes, tastes, dispositions and concepts, as well as the more overtly motor skills. For example, we use the concept *laisser-faire* appropriately in political discussion or everyday conversation, without recalling all the historical examples of *laisser-faire* which we learned from our study of history and which probably contributed, concretely, to our mastery of the concept. And this is true of many of the cultural concepts – scientific, religious, social, artistic – which we employ every day and which we acquired through the study of concrete exemplar situations in the academic disciplines. There is a sense in which the memory of the facts and theories we have learned persists in dispositions to behave appropriately in different life situations. The cultural product for which we look as a result of the teaching of facts and principles is not merely the capacity to reproduce information (to practise our cognitive repertoires): equally important are the dispositions which constitute much of our experience. One criterion for using information in the classroom is that it will assist in the forming of skills, attitudes and concepts.

Realizing that memory is thus manifest in skill saves us from the frustration which teachers often experience when they discover that children have forgotten the information they have been taught. It also saves us from flying to the other extreme and pretending that there is really no point in teaching information at all. Once we are persuaded that 'forgotten' information may have helped to cultivate a disposition to behave in a certain kind of way, it is not even a good argument against examinations that one soon forgets what one has learned in preparing for them. If there has never been acquaintanceship with information it is not available to memory in any of its senses; and though examinations may not be the only or the best way of securing a wide coverage of information, they are one way of ensuring that the learner attends to information which he might be disinclined to study if left to his own devices, but which is essential to the mastery and adaptation of skill. It is also useful to remember that dispositional memory is often manifest in an ability to recognize if not to recall (unprompted) items of information. This recognitional aspect of memory is, indeed, a justification for those of our testing practices which acknowledge an intermediate condition between complete loss of recall and the ability to reproduce information immediately upon demand. Those types of objective test which provide multiple choice items in which the correct response is given amongst incorrect alternatives, legislate for the fact that much of the information we acquire remains at the level of recognition memory rather than at recall. And experience testifies to the value of these items of information which, though we might not be able to reproduce them in response to direct questions, are recognizable in context. In a real sense these latent items of knowledge are an important part of our intellectual capital: our reading, for example, is profuse in items of this kind, our power of understanding what we read depending upon our 'store' of recognition items. We follow a narrative or an argument because we *know* what is referred to, even though in a prior test we might have shown up badly in recalling what we now recognize in context and which brings meaning to what we read.

Thus, whilst it is important to recognize that much of the information which is acquired in educational situations has primarily an instrumental value (assisting in the development of skill or providing 'scaffolding' for the building of conceptual structures), we need not also commit ourselves to the popular educational myth that information (knowledge *that*) has no intrinsic value apart from its value in learning skills, concepts and principles. In the passage quoted earlier, Ryle implies that learning *that* something is the case (acquiring cognitive repertoires) is of less importance than acquisition of skills or competences. In particular, he appears to subscribe to the widely held view that the chief product of an education is the capacity to discover information for onself and make appropriate use of it. No doubt this capacity for 'research' is an important acquirement, valuable even in the ordinary everyday business of living. But the notion that having stocks of truths is of less importance has some very odd implications. The fact that one has learned how and where to look up information does not render memorizing it any less important. The cricketer may keep his card index of what he knows of the idiosyncrasies of other players or the various county grounds, but unless he also memorizes a good deal of this contextual information it can be of little help to him in the heat of the game. And even odder than the sportsman who could only make use of his knowledge following repeated visits to the pavilion to consult his file, would be the person who could not make sense of a newspaper or an evening watching television without an encyclopaedia in his lap. To read or watch even the mass media with meaning depends on having a considerable cognitive repertoire; upon remembering (either at the level of recognition or recall) a great deal of information. To watch an evening's television is to be bombarded with a vast array of information whose significance one must understand to make sense of even the simplest of programmes. The news, for example, is often presented in terms of oblique geographical reference: Peking snubs Moscow, Moscow warns Prague, Paris mistrusts London, Washington faces Hanoi across the table and so on. Not only are items of a geographical, scientific, historical or literary nature the meat of the mass media, but these concepts are often used metaphorically requiring some cognitive sophistication from even the modestly educated viewer or reader. Either one already knows what is being referred to in a television programme or one completely misses the point. An entire accessible library of works of reference is of little relevance to the problem of having in mind the information which is essential to following a play or television documentary, or to reading a newspaper without constant interruption. And it is not an unfamiliar experience that one misses the opportunity of getting the most from a visit to a strange place because one lacks relevant background information. Being in a position to seize unexpected opportunities before they pass requires that one has a considerable repertoire of information which is sometimes a condition not merely for extracting the most from an experience, but for having the experience at all. Knowledge of this kind, which contributes towards the quality of living in a modern community, has often been dismissed by educationists as of little importance through their too ready characterization of it as 'inert ideas'. The research-oriented conception of education as a kind of intellectual banking system, in which one merely learns how to draw cheques upon reference libraries, ignores our common experience that the cognitive coinage of daily life must often be ready to hand. As with our financial resources, some of our cognitive assets must be liquid if we are to make the most of life's fortuitous encounters with the environment.

Our conclusion is that the tacit component at the heart of all skills makes learning by practice an essential condition of mastery. It also signals caution against claiming too much for the role of theoretical explanations in teaching technical and professional skills. On the other hand, reasons have been advanced for believing that theorizing may helpfully precede and accompany practical learning and for the view that knowing how to do something intelligently often depends upon reference to theoretical knowledge about the contexts in which a skill is practised. Similarly, a proper understanding of the contingent experiences of daily life depends upon the acquisition of a considerable cognitive repertoire.

4 Living with organization man[19] D. EMMET
(D. Emmet, *Rules, Roles and Relations,* Macmillan 1966, Chapter 9)

We started from the not very controversial observation that ethics and sociology are both concerned with social relations in social situations, and went on to say that sociologists do well to look at ways in which moral values can be involved both theoretically in the definition of a 'social situation' and practically in the methods chosen to study it. We have also said that moral judgments are made in *social* situations. That moralists would do well to look at sociological studies of these has been stated in general rather than by particular illustration. It needs substantiating by examples rather than precept; I shall now try to do this by calling attention to some recent sociological work in the study of organizations. There are some obvious reasons for this choice.

1. Large organizations are probably the most characteristic feature of contemporary society, at any rate western society, and they increasingly impinge on the ways we live our lives. These organizations are both public and private: government departments, business corporations, professional organizations, educational organizations, recreational organizations and so on and so on. That life is increasingly lived in and with the help of these is, I believe, a much more important feature of contemporary society than are controversies between socialist collectivism and individual enterprise. Large organizations can only be wished away if we can be content with a much more rudimentary standard of goods and services than we have come to take for granted, and if fewer people are to have claims on these. Those of us who live and work in universities are having to adjust ourselves to the change from the ways of a fairly informal and not very large community to those of a big organization; and those whose hearts, like the author's, are in the horse and buggy era of the university rather than the era of Organization Man, do not find the change in our ways easy. Nor do we want to make it uncritically.

2. The study of organizations is concerned with social units whose boundaries it is relatively possible to draw, though what goes on within them is of course also affected by what is happening in the wider social environment. Thus they form reasonably recognizable units, partly planned and self-contained, but also *milieux* for unplanned and competing relations. They can therefore provide manageable units of study which

---

[19]The title might lead some readers to expect a description of what it is like to be the mistress of the General Manager. I hasten to assure them there is no such *double entendre*.

are streamlined versions of some of the problems, including moral problems, of interlocking human relations in society in the wider sense.

3. Large organizations are networks of relationships between people acting and reacting on each other, sometimes in accordance with intended ways of furthering the purpose of the organization; sometimes in ways which are intended, though not in terms of the official purpose; and sometimes in ways not intended by anyone. These by-activities may either help to fortify the official purpose or to frustrate it. In either case decisions, both administrative and policy decisions, including the moral judgments which can come into these, can be made more intelligently if there is some realistic awareness of this complexity. A corollary of this is that even official policy is subject to considerations other than those deducible from the formal relationships within the organization, and account has to be taken of this in trying to set up criteria of its 'rationality'.

4. The theory of organizations includes questions of 'operational research'. This is concerned with trying to bridge the gulf between un-analysed abstractions, such as 'efficiency', or 'public service', or 'modernization', and actual decisions. It can thus provide a context for studying how such abstractions can function if one wants neither to be Utopian about them (i.e. idealistically indifferent about the hard facts of practice) nor to be cynical (i.e. using them emotively for persuasive purposes, while regarding them as vacuous). Such operational research may provide object lessons in thinking about the functions of similar abstractions in ethical and political thinking.

5. Sophisticated contemporary studies of organizations recognize conflict and tensions as facts of life. This is partly because participants in organizations have multiple roles and role sets, unofficial as well as official, within the organization, and roles such as political ones which have ramifications outside it. This can raise questions of an ethical kind, concerning, for instance, the degree of loyalty due to the organization and how to reconcile this with other claims. The organization cannot therefore be seen as a harmonious self-contained unit, in which problems can even in principle always be solved according to the rules. The 'solution' of one problem may bring others in its train; and wisdom may lie in being able to decide which problem to live with at any given time.

This means that the classical description of 'rational bureaucracy' as given by Max Weber is seen to be too simple, though indeed Weber must be acknowledged as the pioneer in seeing the growing importance of 'bureaucratic' types of organization and authority in modern society. I shall follow the excellent summary of his definitions given by Tom Burns and G. M. Stalker.[20]

---

[20] *The Management of Innovation* (Tavistock Publications, 1961), pp. 105–6. Cf. also M. Weber, *The Theory of Social and Economic Organization* (tr. Henderson and Parsons). W. Hodge, 1947, pp. 329–34 (Free Press, Glencoe, Ill., 1947).

(1) The organization operates according to a body of laws or rules, which are consistent and have normally been intentionally established.

(2) Every official is subject to an impersonal order by which he guides his actions. In turn his instructions have authority only in so far as they conform with this generally understood body of rules; obedience is due to his office, not to him as an individual.

(3) Each incumbent of an office has a specified sphere of competence, with obligations, authority, and powers to compel obedience strictly defined.

(4) The organization of offices follows the principle of hierarchy; that is, each lower office is under the control and supervision of a higher one.

(5) The supreme head of the organization, and only he, occupies his position by appropriation, by election, or by being designated as successor. Other offices are filled, in principle, by free selection, and candidates are selected on the basis of 'technical' qualifications. They are appointed, not elected.

(6) The system also serves as a career ladder. There is promotion according to seniority or achievement. Promotion is dependent on the judgement of superiors.

(7) The official who, in principle, is excluded from any ownership rights in the concern, or in his position, is subject to discipline and control in the conduct of his office.

This can now be seen to work on too simple a model of bureaucracy, as well as of 'rationality'. It shows rationality for the person in a subordinate role as simply acting according to the book of rules; for the top people rationality is not defined by Weber. Here the model has been that of classical economic man, where rationality consists in always doing what would maximize interests, in this case those of the organization. This assumes there is an optimum solution, which administrative man seeks if he is rational; it is an essentially Benthamite notion, which has reappeared in modern dress in Games Theory where rationality consists in 'mini-maxing', seeking to maximize advantage and minimize risks of loss by choosing the optimum utility among the alternatives. The assumption here is that the alternatives are calculable, and their consequences can be forecast. Such a model of rational optimum decision can have its uses in situations where there are a finite number of variables; where alternatives are known and limited, and where there can be a preference ranking among them.

In contrast, administrative decisions and policy decisions for organizations are likely to have to make do with what H. A. Simon calls 'bounded rationality'[21]. This works on a more complex theory of knowledge, where the 'situation' as perceived is recognized to be only a simplification of the actual facts of the real world. The 'situation' does not come ready packaged; it is interpreted in terms of 'relevant' or 'strategic' factors; but what

[21] Cf. H. A. Simon, *Models of Man* (New York, 1957), pt. iv, pp. 196 ff., 'Administrative Rationality and Decision Making'; also his *Administrative Behaviour*, and Simon and March, *Organizations* (New York, 1958), pp. 137 ff.

is not realized or is ignored may take revenge for its omission in the unforeseen consequences of a decision. For 'the capacity of the human mind for formulating and solving complex problems is very small compared with the size of the problems whose solution is required for objectively rational behaviour in the real world'.[22] The range of the human mind can be extended by collaborative collection of information, 'data processing' by computer, and so on, but the essential point of selectivity remains. Also, collaboration for extending powers of thought and action beyond those of the individual produces its problems as well as its advantages. 'It is only because individual human beings are limited in knowledge, foresight, skill and time that organizations are useful instruments for the achievement of human purpose; and it is only because organized groups of human beings are limited in ability to agree on goals, to communicate, and to cooperate that organizing becomes for them a "problem".'[23] This does not mean that decisions made in such a context cannot be 'rational'; it means that rationality will involve taking account of its own 'boundedness'. It will involve looking for viable solutions rather than ideal solutions (in Simon's terminology 'satisficing' rather than 'optimicing'), and seeing that there may be critical times at which an imperfect decision is better than none.

Rational behaviour is not of course the same as ethical behaviour; it may be concerned with questions of policy, interest, advantage, which are not directly ethical (though in a context of complex human relations these may well have ethical implications and there may indeed be a moral obligation to take account of them). On the views that I have argued earlier, ethical behaviour, while not exhaustive of rational behaviour, need not be irrational behaviour. Indeed, the rationality characteristic of at any rate the more difficult and interesting moral judgments may well be 'bounded rationality' in situations of uncertainty, where neither action by rule nor clear perception of consequences has a self-evident last word.

'Bounded rationality', whether in moral decisions or decisions on questions of, e.g., efficiency, is not only due to ignorance of fact. It is also due to the ways in which people see the facts of a situation as coloured by their own role in regard to it. This may be particularly the case in interpreting situations in organizations and institutions, where how a person sees a situation may not only depend on his own social and intellectual background, but on his role in the organization, or on which of his multiple roles he puts first. Tom Burns has a good illustration of this in a paper 'The Directions of Activity and Communication in a Departmental Executive Group'.[24] This is a study of how four executives in an engineer-

[22] *Models of Man*, p. 198.
[23] *Ibid.*, p. 199.
[24] *Human Relations* (1954), vol. VII, pp. 73–97.

ing firm reported that they spent their time when away from their desks. There was general agreement that they spent their time talking to people;[25] but when the accounts of what each executive said he talked about to the other executives were compared, they revealed significant discrepancies. There was fair agreement over how much time was spent in talking about 'Research and Developments'; but not so over 'Production Matters' and 'Personnel'. Burns' conclusion is not that the executives were inaccurate in their reports, still less that they were lying, but that they distorted the content of what they thought they were talking about in terms of what they were interested in through their special roles.[26]

The moral is that one cannot be sure that different participants in a situation are concerning themselves with the same 'image' of the situation; there is a problem of communication here if attempts at co-operation or agreed decisions are not to be at cross purposes. Moreover, the participants in an organization do not simply play their complementary roles within the organization. They are also human beings, adaptive and non-adaptive, anxious, ambitious, loyal, suspicious, generous. So there will be conflicts of interests and loyalties not only between different groups within the organization, but in the minds of each of its members from the top to the bottom.

To realize this makes for an approach to problems, both moral and practical, more complex than is allowed for in taking account of simple alternatives of efficiency and inefficiency, loyalty and disloyalty, rate for the job and exploitation. Indeed, what is thought to constitute any of these will depend on a context of moral assumptions, which will vary at different times and cannot just be taken as constant. The notion of the 'rate for the job', for instance, if it is not just left to the mechanisms of the market, will be discussed and bargained for with assumptions about acceptable standards of living in the wider community. There are other still more 'value laden' issues; for instance, terms on which people will collaborate with the goals of the organization and the degree of commitment that can properly be expected of them. This is a region where personal value judgments are bound to enter in, for though 'terms on which people will collaborate' could seem to be something just to be ascertained as a question of fact, it connects with the degree of commitment which can 'properly' be expected, and implies a decision on what ought or ought not to be asked. A statement to the effect that every organization will exact as much commitment as it can could not only be questioned as a matter of fact, but also it might be said that on ethical grounds members should try to prevent it from extracting a total commitment.

[25] i.e. talking to people as part of the job; what they talked about as coffee gossip was not counted.
[26] See the article by Tom Burns reprinted in Volume II of this book pp. 23–39 (Eds.).

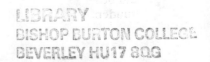

That there is indeed an argument here not only about the facts of organizations, but also about their ethics, has been abundantly shown by W. H. Whyte's onslaught on one view of the ethos of 'Organization Man'.[27] The burden of his attack is that those concerned with personal relations and loyalties within organizations, along with their sociological advisers, assume a culture based on the ethos of the organization as an essentially harmonious and indeed beneficent unity, where the needs of the individual are met by adapting to the needs of the group, and where tensions can be removed by better scientific understanding and social engineering. Whyte attacks these comfortable assumptions not only because he thinks people ought sometimes to take a stand and fight the organization, but also because he cares that they should have personal lives, political lives, intellectual lives, which are not only lived in its terms. His predilections are forcibly shared by one of his reviewers, Professor George Homans.[28]

> 'On top of all this, the organization takes such good care of its men that they may come to look on its ways not as habits to be put up with if they want to keep out of trouble but as virtues to be loved for themselves alone. In America, we were ready to love them anyway. Americans were never quite the rugged individualists they professed themselves to be. Rather, their easy associativeness was both their glory and their danger. When all three forces – American culture, corporate bureaucracy, and social science – work in line, the pressure may squash out qualities that give the life to men and nations. *The Organization Man* ends with an old plea in a new form, a plea that we render to the organization only what is the organization's – our service, not our souls.
>
> With this I heartily agree. The individualist is a pretty tough man. In the loosely knit societies of the past, there were plenty of places where he could hole up and glare out at us. And we could trust him to do it. Today the holes are getting fewer. We may need to take some thought how to make the world safe for him, for the world's sake as well as his own.'

There is little doubt that this candid avowal has stirred up a lively discussion of ethical assumptions that were slipping into the study of organizations. These assumptions encouraged the belief that techniques could be related to 'a finite achievable harmony'; that conflicts are due to misunderstandings and breakdowns in communication which should be capable of being eliminated by applying the methods of science to human relations; and that the needs of the individual could be met in terms of the needs of the organization. On the question of the facts as distinct from the ethics of conformity, Whyte has been taken up by Melville

---

[27] *The Organization Man* (New York and London, 1957).
[28] 'Bureaucracy as Big Brother', *The Listener*, Nov. 7, 1957; reprinted in *Sentiments and Activities* (Free Press, Ill., 1962), pp. 125–26. Quoted with permission.

Dalton in *Men who Manage*, a sociological study largely devoted to showing how scepticism and manipulation can go on under a public image of conformity. He suggests that those who mistake surface conformity in organizations for total conformity and the death of originality should study the ingenuity and evasion that actually goes on, and 'the ethics of protective coloration among thinking animals'.[29] Whyte himself is not in fact altogether innocent of this awareness; what he is after is to question some of the assumptions of a social ethos which he sees creeping into official literature and especially that of training schemes. He would no doubt welcome Dalton's well-documented argument that 'perpetual harmony is alien to all life', that, though areas of conflict may shift, it is unlikely that they can be eliminated entirely.

Another study, which shows how some problems in an organization can be met at the cost of producing others, is that of Alvin W. Gouldner,[30] describing a kind of situation in which there is no ideal solution. Where this is so the cost of a policy has to be measured against its success, 'cost' here not meaning monetary cost (people have always known about this), but the respects in which one problem within an organization is relieved by measures which will exacerbate others. Gouldner showed this in his study of a gypsum plant called 'Oscar Centre', Lakeport, near the Great Lakes in Wisconsin, where a popular lenient management had been replaced by a stricter and more efficient one. The old regime was mixed up with kinship links outside the factory, and other established community relations. There was indulgence, for instance, towards workers taking materials home from the factory for their own purposes. A new manager came with instructions to tighten things up; he tried to be impartial and act through official channels and not through the informal ties (such as the old lieutenants). This produced its tensions, culminating in a 'wildcat strike', which Gouldner judged to be only ostensibly about wage demands, on which grievances, due to the contravention of established expectations based on the older more informal code, had got displaced. (He suggests also that a strike on wages could be made to appear more acceptable to the wives.) The method of trying to resolve this conflict was to make the rules clearer. But insistence on rules encouraged a 'work to rule' mentality (called by Gouldner 'bureaucratic sabotage'). So there was need for closer supervision, and this in turn reinforced the emphasis on rules. Hence a vicious circle with mutual reinforcement, viz.

---

[29] *Men who Manage* (New York, 1959), p. 272. Melville Dalton calls the capacity to cope with this complexity a capacity to 'live with ambiguity'. It gave me pleasure to find his book catalogued in a great University Library in the section 'Useful Arts'.

[30] See especially his *Patterns of Industrial Democracy* and *Wildcat Strike* (London, 1955).

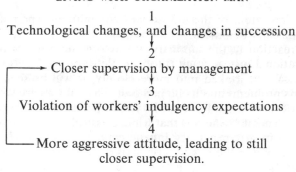

1
Technological changes, and changes in succession

2
Closer supervision by management

3
Violation of workers' indulgency expectations

4
More aggressive attitude, leading to still
closer supervision.

After the strike, an agreement was reached providing procedures for settling grievances at the cost of more bureaucratic rules. This relieved tensions due to informal actions, and enabled disputes to be passed up for higher consideration, but it increased supervision still further. Thus the settlement of the strike included a more centralized bureaucratic direction and definition of rights and obligations, which reduced some tensions, but meant there was less chance of informal communication between workers and supervisors, so that supervisors became even less aware of workers' 'indulgency expectations'.[31] The top management and union officials thus reached a solution in accordance with the interests of their own status and authority, but at the expense of curtailing the initiative of those below them on either side.

One way of meeting this, in so far as it is due to lack of 'participation' in decisions, is to develop an 'organic' system instead of the mechanistic form. The terms 'mechanistic' and 'organic' are taken from *The Management of Innovation* by Tom Burns and G. M. Stalker. The mechanistic form approximates most closely to the Weberian rules of rational bureaucracy; it is said to be appropriate in stable conditions. The most significant element for our purpose in the summary of its characteristics is that it is a hierarchic system of control, authority and communication, which is reinforced 'by the location of knowledge of actualities exclusively at the top of the hierarchy, while the final reconciliation of distinct tasks and assessment of relevance is made'.[32] In contrast, in the 'organic' form (which is said to be appropriate to changing conditions), there is 'adjustment and continual re-definition of individual tasks through interaction with others', and 'a lateral rather than a vertical direction of communication through the organization, communication between people of different rank, also, resembling consultation rather than

---

[31] Gouldner has shown that, not only in conflict situations, *succession* tends to weaken informal structures, and so at any rate temporarily to strengthen bureaucratic organization. (Cf. 'Succession and Bureaucracy' in *Studies in Leadership* (New York, 1950), pp. 644–59.)
[32] *Op. cit.*, p. 120.

demand'. The extent of the individual's commitment and responsibility is also less clearly delimited.[33]

A first reaction to the summary of the 'organic' form is that, just as Weber's rational bureaucracy is too simple to be true, this is too good to be true. When looked into more closely, it will be seen that it too produces its problems and its human cost. The authors are well aware of this, unlike Mary Parker Follett, who was a pioneer in this way of thinking about management.[34] She saw that while classical economic theory made participation in group activity instrumental to other satisfactions (e.g. being paid money), there were also satisfactions (and otherwise) in the actual process of the group activity itself. She could be starry-eyed as well as sophisticated about this, on paper at least, though not, I believe, in actual negotiations. One question is whether the continual need for discussion and communication will mean that people become more interested in the procedures by which decisions are reached and in having a share in reaching them than in getting on with the actual job for which the organization exists. While these procedures may lead to a more widespread sense of participation, no one can say that they are not time-consuming. They also depend on a widely shared intuitive morality and shared attitude, beyond the specific obligations of role and function. Therefore, alike in moral effort, time, and thought, the commitment of members to the organization is much more diffuse and unlimited than the 'nine to five' commitment to a limited role with limited responsibilities under a hierarchic system of authority. This again may be as it should be; but the cost must be reckoned (the loss to other roles, such as those of private life; the possibility of 'possessing one's soul' apart from the organization; and the preoccupation with methods and procedures). It is also useless to think that such more 'democratic' procedures in fact relieve those at the top of responsibility and lighten their load. It is arguable that the 'boss' in a hierarchic organization, whose decisions have to be accepted, has a less exacting time than the head of an 'organic' body who needs to consult and allow discussion at every level. Indeed one of the major problems in modern organizations (not just firms, but, e.g., government departments and increasingly universities as they are now developing) is the demand they make on the people at the top. Contrary to popular belief, these get greater and not less with attempts to make the organization more 'democratic'.

An instance of this is the effect of the combination of the official organization with its official purpose and the organization as a field within which people seek to pursue careers.[35] In the older kind of mechanistic

---

[33] *Ibid.*, p. 121.

[34] Cf. especially *Dynamic Administration: The Collected Papers of Mary Parker Follett*, edited by M. C. Metcalfe and L. Urwick (Management Publications Trust, London, 1941).

[35] Burns and Stalker (*The Management of Innovation*, pt. II, Chapter VII) have drawn attention to this double aspect of life in organizations.

hierarchical organization, promotion could be decided by superiors by considerations of seniority or technical competence in a clearly defined sphere. It is tempting to look for a formula, and so produce an impersonal (and obviously universalizable) basis for decision. But fairness in the sense of equity does not consist in operating with one formula alone. In the 'organic' kind of organization a larger and less specific range of competence and capacity for a more difficult kind of shared authority becomes relevant. This again may be as it should be; but judgments will be more difficult to make, and there will be bound to be people with claims of an obviously definable sort, such as seniority, who will complain that they are being passed over in favour of people whose claims are less definable. In order that justice may be seen to be done, there may be suggestions for relieving the tension between an organization as a community with a common purpose and an organization as a field within which people hope to have a career, by asking for more formalized procedures for review and promotion. Here again, there will be a need to be able to look with a critical eye at unintended consequences of *prima facie* plausible proposals. For instance, to take an example from the modern university world, the suggestion has been put forward that all university teachers below the rank of professor should have their status and claims to promotion reviewed every year. Apart from the question of how much this is going to add to the pressures on the time of the people at the top, it again raises questions of whether disadvantages might outweigh advantages. They may not; what is being said here is that they should be diagnosed and taken into consideration with open eyes. For if the object of the exercise is to cause the board concerned with promotions to have to take account at regular intervals of evidence other than that brought forward on the initiative of the head of a department, it is difficult to see how this could be collected apart from some means of monitoring which would surely take away from the wide freedom at present enjoyed by university teachers to do their own work in their own way with the minimum of supervision. Again, people may be prepared to stomach this change; but if so, they must know the implications of what they are asking for. It is also at least arguable that to know one is constantly under judgment may add to status anxiety rather than relieve it; it does not mean that there will not be an area of conflict, but that it will be shifted. Some cases of injustice would no doubt be met; but at the expense of heightening the emphasis on the organization as a field for careers, along with the amount of time and thought given to this aspect of it. Time and thought are scarce resources; the point is that choices of how to use them have to be made.

This is an instance of the cost of choices in unwanted consequences as well as wanted ones. The capacity to diagnose unintended consequences and so to make us more aware of the cost of the choices before us need not be an exclusive skill of sociologists. It might be said to be a matter merely of exercising a bit of realistic imagination. But, for all that, it is not a common skill; perhaps because of the fact already noted in considering 'bounded rationality', that a situation as diagnosed is in any case only a simplified version of the total situation, and, besides this, that the factors people take into account in reading the situation may be affected by how they see their roles in relation to it. A sociologist may manage to divest himself more easily of some of these reasons for selective interpretation, even if he can never reach the total view of omniscience or be the complete 'impartial spectator'. Moreover, he has trained himself to think in terms of reactions of multiple relationships on one another rather than of single strands of cause and effect. He has meditated on the simple but often neglected truth that a relation of A and B is also a relation of B to A; and probably also involves relations to C, D, E . . . and their relations back to each other and to A and B as well.

The problem of unintended consequences, and especially unintended consequences of what may seem eminently desirable aims, is the theme of Philip Selznick's *T. V.A. and the Grass Roots*.[36] This was a study made in the mid-1940s of the Tennessee Valley Authority, a public corporation set up by Congress in 1933 for the operation of electricity, fertilizer plants, irrigation, and flood control in the development of a depressed region. It was set up with a 'grass roots' policy of working with and through local associations, both statutory and voluntary. Such a policy of local 'democratic participation' meant that the Authority was caught up in the tensions of bodies on the spot; it had difficulty (but succeeded) in resisting colour discrimination in appointments. Moreover, it was found that the practical needs of the organization drove it towards alliances with certain well-organized local interests, above all the agriculturalists. Interpreting unanalysed abstractions such as 'institutions near to the people' in context meant that the Authority had to adapt itself not so much to the people in general as to the actually existing institutions which had the power to smooth or block its way, with all the problems for a liberal outlook which this involved. Alvin Gouldner takes Selznick to task over this study for fastening on the organizational and structural tendencies which militate against democratic practices, instead of those that support and encourage them.[37] This is hard; it is clear that Selznick's own sympathies are with the ideals of the T.V.A., and that he gives the emphasis he does because he thinks believers in such ideals are more likely to be unrealistically optimist than pessimist. (This applies also to Dr. Reinhold Niebuhr, who is often unjustly charged with cynicism and pessimism in his political writings

---

[36] *T. V.A. and the Grass Roots: A Study in the Sociology of Formal Organization* (University of California Press, 1949).

[37] A. W. Gouldner, 'Metaphysical Pathos and the Theory of Bureaucracy', *American Political Science Quarterly* (1955), vol. 49, pp. 496–507.

for the same reason.[38]) 'For the things which are important in the analysis of democracy are those which bind the hands of good men.'[39] Failure to appraise the problems of implementing unanalysed abstractions may well lead to a swing from idealism to cynicism and from Utopianism to disillusion. Selznick has diagnosed some of the problems in the T.V.A. context without falling for either of these. 'Where such analysis is considered destructive, it is usually because doctrine, assuming an ideological role, is not meant to be analysed. In extreme cases, unanalysed doctrine ceases to operate in action at all, and the real criteria of decision are hidden in a shadowland of unrecognized discretion, determined opportunistically by immediate exigency.'[40]

In discussing moral judgement in Chapter IV, I tried to put forward a view that this was neither simply deduction from principles nor simply calculation of consequences, and that it operates with what we may now call 'bounded rationality' in situations where there may be no simple answer, and where perhaps the only final betrayal may be to refuse to try to come to a decision. Abstractions expressing general aims, such as 'self-realization', 'love of God and one's neighbour', 'the greatest happiness of the greatest number', we saw were not the kind of objective which could be made operational in a straightforward way through clear-cut means to a specific end. They supply, rather, a general orientation for a policy for living, which can be partially, though never entirely, specified through moral principles. The analogy with the working of abstractions such as 'democratic participation' is apparent, though the operational meaning of the ultimate ethical abstractions can be even more elusive. Yet they can supply an orientation which prevents moral judgement from being just *ad hoc* and there are some kinds of behaviour they would exclude on any count. In so far as there is an intention to make moral judgment rational, we saw that it could also be guided by the general requirement to avoid special pleading in our own favour. I suggest that, even more evidently than in personal ethics, this is the sort of view of moral judgments which best fits the complexities of moral situations in institutional and organizational life. Far from calling for a simple morality of rule and rote, the pressures of different claims and interests call for moral intelligence of a high order; where this seems too difficult, demanding also too much moral toughness, we may find instead an amoral ingenuity (the favourite word in the literature is 'manipulation', with its suggestion of fixing things). I have already noted how Chester

---

[38] Dr. Niebuhr's books, based on his understanding of Christian morality, have been a sustained polemic against Utopianism, and especially self-righteous Utopianism. See, e.g., *An Interpretation of Christian Ethics* (New York and London, 1935).

[39] *T.V.A. and the Grass Roots*, p. 266.

[40] *Ibid.*, p. 69. (See also his remarks on Utopianism and opportunism in *Leadership and Administration*, pp. 143 ff.)

Barnard, whose books are a mine of wisdom on these questions, speaks of the need for *intelligence* as well as a high sense of responsibility, especially in the moral judgments which high executives have to make. Without the former, the complex morality needed may lead to personal breakdown; without the latter, there may be 'the hopeless confusion of inconsistent expediencies so often described as "incompetence"'.[41] In spite of a popular theological view, here surely is a sphere of moral decisions in which 'love' is not enough, even if it be enough (as I doubt) in the sphere of purely personal relations.

One feature of this complexity is that, in the morality of institutional action, the relations between the personal and impersonal kinds of responsibility come to a head. We have seen that perhaps by definition, but also by direction of interest, personalist discussions of morality in face-to-face relations have had little to say about this. We have also seen that the ethics of role (of which the ethics of institutional actions are an obvious instance) have to take account of previously structured commitments and expectations within a network of relationships. In the case of a role within a formally organized institution, these commitments and expectations may also be structured by the fact that a person has limited powers and limited discretion. Thus there is likely to be a lack of clear coincidence between 'powers', actual power, and responsibility. We have often been told that there should be no power without responsibility; but a problem in modern large-scale institutions (including government) is the need for people to be prepared to take responsibility without commensurate power. In discussing the notion of responsibility I noted the distinction between responsibility as 'answerability', which can be a matter depending on constitutional conventions, and responsibility as ascribing personal power of choice to do or to forbear. In any formal institution there must be some people who, in virtue of their office, are responsible in the sense of answerable for decisions, policies and their outcome. This need not mean that they had a major share in making the decision (they may even have had their own reservations about it, or not have been able to prevent what happened). They have, however, to be prepared to take public responsibility without disclosing their private reservations or giving away confidential matter on how the decision was taken (for some things must be discussed confidentially), and particularly they must be prepared to 'carry the can' if things go wrong. This is a feature of the nature of constitutional responsibility in institutional life which can be understood, so that even if it sometimes seems hard in the individual instance, it is possible to accept it impersonally and without resentment. The relevant quality of mind is what the Stoics called *apatheia*, misunderstood in common English parlance as 'apathy' or insensitivity. Rather, it is the capacity to be

---

[41] *The Functions of the Executive*, p. 276.

detached from being influenced by how things touch one's own personal interest and self-esteem, and not to be emotionally involved through these. It is indeed part of the morality of practical reason.

Nevertheless, the lack of coincidence between responsibility and real power to get things done or altered is a genuine problem in institutional morality. Small men may fasten on this as a reason for disclaiming responsibility in the personal sense of power to do or to forbear; larger men may know the discrepancy is there, but not try to shelter behind it. Whereas smaller men may be sticklers for rules, larger men will know no organization can work without discretion.[42] They will not just accept a dissolution of responsibility into formal conventions, and be prepared to go on trying to take personal as well as conventional responsibility through accepting the loneliness of leadership. Our constitutional and institutional arrangements in a liberal democracy are designed to prevent the concentration of responsibility in a single supreme personal leader combining final power as well as formal responsibility. Critics of liberal democracy have pointed to the evasions of responsibility its conventions may make possible; those of us who distrust the *Führer-Prinzip* (we have seen what it can mean), will look on these evasions as a risk to be taken for the sake of a system in which powers and responsibilities can be spread. Yet the temptation to pass the buck is a real one; this is yet another instance of how there is a catch in everything, so that no institutional arrangements will produce Utopia. It is a temptation, particularly because of the very limited actual power of most participants in an organized institution. Yet in an 'organic' system they may all be claiming what Bagehot said were the privileges of monarchy: the right to be informed, the right to encourage, the right to warn. This may be as it should be; but in the end some people must take more responsibility (in both senses of the word) than this. Nevertheless the limits of their practical choice may be curtailed by the 'logic of the situation' in which they have to act, as well as by what others are prepared to accept. Sociological awareness of the logic of situations can help us to appreciate this; it need not, as we have seen, lead to a deterministic view that any given decision *had* to be so and not otherwise. But it can discourage 'scapegoating' and 'conspiratorial' interpretations of situations which turn out badly. This is the more important because to seek explanations of our misfortunes in the machinations of ill-disposed persons is the most primitive and natural way in which we all think until we have become sufficiently sophisticated to

---

[42] 'Discretion' can cover turning a blind eye to a certain amount of 'institutionalized deviancy' in any organization. The *reductio ad absurdum* of the lack of this is shown when an organization can be made to grind to a halt through 'work to rule'. This can be done by insisting that rules which are in the book as exceptional safeguards be treated as if they were normal practices.

think otherwise. Personal causes are easier to understand, and we can also then do something about the misfortune by taking it out on the scapegoats. It may well be that the acceptance of responsibility for something which was not in any literal sense 'his fault' by a minister as head of a department, or by others in representative positions, is a civilized relic of this demand for a scapegoat. It is also probably a necessary constitutional convention, and can be taken as such in an impersonal way without resentment.

It can probably be taken in this way the more readily where loyalty to the institution is a strong motive. For, *pace* W. H. Whyte, there *is* a problem of loyalty, which remains when we have had our laugh at Bureaucracy as Big Brother. While we may hold that no institution or organization should exact a *total* commitment (the Roman Catholic Church, with all its claims, recognizes conscience, and it is possible to leave it), clearly also few organizations would work unless some people were prepared to put more into them than could be stated in a bare contract. By 'total commitment' I am meaning abrogation of judgement and conscience in putting the demands of the organization before all other considerations in all contexts. At the end of that road can stand Eichmann, who went to his death protesting that he was being punished for obedience, and that obedience is praised as a virtue. Loyalty and deep involvement in the purposes of an organization need not mean this abrogation. 'Your representative owes you not his industry only but his judgement', as Burke remarked in another connection.[43] Burke also remarks 'his mature judgement, his enlightened conscience, he ought not to sacrifice to you, to any man, or to any set of men living'. Indeed organizations worth their salt are better served where this is recognized. We should distinguish, of course, between kinds of organizations.[44] Prisons can hardly expect to produce dedicated old lags, while a little subversion in an old boys' network or alumni association might even be desirable. Where there seems to be total dedication to the institution with no worries about other claims, it is probably when it is seen as 'not so much a programme, more a way of life',[45] and this is not necessarily the best way to further its purpose, especially in times of change. For organizations and institutions exist for purposes besides providing a way of life for those who participate in them (though this is sometimes forgotten,

---

[43] *Speech to the Electors of Bristol*, 1774.

[44] An analytic basis for the classification of different kinds of organization by their predominant means of compliance has been given by A. Etzioni, *A Comparative Analysis of Complex Organizations* (Free Press, Ill., 1961). He distinguishes those in which the major method of control is through coercion; those where it is utilitarian, through calculation of interests (especially remuneration), and those where it is 'normative' through moral involvement of participants in the organization.

[45] The title of a feature current on B.B.C. Television at the time of writing.

as by those who lamented that their Home for unmarried mothers might be closed for lack of girls needing help). We have here something of a dilemma; if an organization becomes a way of life, people get a vested interest in maintaining it as it is. But unless it holds the loyalty of its participants in maintaining its character as an institution, its serious purposes will suffer. This has been brought out well by Philip Selznick in *Leadership and Administration*; indeed he distinguishes 'organization' and 'institution' on this score. An organization can be a mobilization of energies for a special purpose. If it is to stand up and last, it must also be an institution, i.e. a community of people with the conflicts and adjustments this will involve, so that its leadership is a *political* and not just a technical task.[46] (Selznick is very good on this; he does not, however, discuss the question of limits of commitment.)

Moreover the purposes of organizations can be very different, in that they may be 'diffuse' or 'specific' as Talcott Parsons would say, and they may touch the lives of their participants at many points or at few. One way of distinguishing organizations could be in terms of the kinds of purposes they serve, and by asking how possible it is to define them operationally.

1. There are organizations whose general purpose is sufficiently specific for it to be tolerably easy to define how it could be operational, though of course this does not mean it is easy to implement it. For instance if the purpose of a firm is to survive and make a profit, the existence of bankruptcy courts and balance sheets can provide evidence of success and failure. 'Operational' here means the possibility of citing what would count as empirical evidence of success or failure; as well as showing how the purpose might be implemented through relating its general statement to a number of interlocking functional activities. In these cases the values of efficiency and inefficiency can also be judged (if not measured) in relation to empirically defined conditions of success or failure. Yet even here, underlying these clearly operational values, there will be the more general aim of maintaining the integrity of the organization as an institution, and what this entails will need continual rethinking in changing circumstances.

2. There are organizations whose general purpose is very difficult to state succinctly, and which may even be a matter of some controversy. A university is a case in point. One can say 'education and research', and there will be arguments about which has priority; 'the advancement of knowledge', and then the scales seem to be weighted in favour of research, and it can be asked whether other kinds of institutes for

---

[46] I note this way of distinguishing 'organizations' and 'institutions' and saying how they overlap. In this chapter I have been concerned with organizations which are also institutions in Selznick's sense, and have sometimes called them 'institutions'. Since, however, the word 'institution' is also used by sociologists for such things as marriage or property, I prefer in general to call specific corporate bodies 'organizations'.

advanced studies may not concentrate more effectively on this. An older generation put the purpose explicitly in a social and religious context: 'that there may not be lacking a succession of persons duly qualified for the service of God in Church and State'. It is doubtful whether in these days there can be a single clear and agreed statement of purpose, and still more doubtful whether this can be made operational by any precise tests. The attempt to do so is likely to fasten attention on the more obviously measureable output – numbers of publications, or of students, or of high Honours degrees. 'It is what they are in ten years' time that matters', Whitehead quoted someone as saying of undergraduates. By that time the university will have lost track of most of them. So indices of success and failure are likely to be misleading.

This does not mean we are completely in the dark about whether such an organization is a good instance of its kind or not. It has been said that a university may be judged by the number of intelligent enthusiasms it fosters. But these may wax and wane with the coming and going of particular personalities; a university may be strong in one thing at one time and another at another. Thus we must make a broad distinction between the kinds of organization in which there is a common purpose which can be implemented through a large number of functional contributions under division of labour with measurable indices of success, and organizations where the purpose is more elusive, and comes to life in differing emphases where the organization provides opportunities for people to do jobs which can only be done creatively if they are free to do them very much in their own way.[47] Such jobs are 'vocational' in the old sense of work done from incentives in a person's own internal springs of action, and where opportunity to do the work matters more than the exact ticket under which it is done. Yet under contemporary conditions a vocationally minded person generally has to work in and with the resources of a large organization. Scientific discoveries, for instance, are now seldom made in the shed at the bottom of the garden; they need laboratories with expensive equipment and access to considerable funds. This is likely to involve a vocationally minded researcher, especially in times of change and development, in the political processes of communication and decision making. It is at least arguable that he might have more freedom to do his own special kind of work under the conditions of a benevolent and loose kind of autocracy – tempered by what Samuel Alexander, addressing the Registrar of the University of Manchester of the day (about 1926), called 'the affectionate insubordina-

---

[47] The evidence cited in an earlier chapter of how the integrity of teachers in colleges of high quality in America was protected by the administration, when they were under accusations during the McCarthy crisis, is an example of a good mutual reinforcement of different roles in an organization.

tion which characterizes our relations with our administrative colleagues'. But no doubt this happy semblance of anarchy goes with a stable state of affairs where not many policy decisions are necessary. In times of change and growth, the demand for a more democratic system of formal and not only informal participation is natural, but as we have noted it is likely to consume a good deal of people's time and energy, especially as these processes can become absorbing through their own fascination. If in the end of the day the chief concentration is to be on the main job rather than on the mainspring of the mechanism for doing it, or even on the main chance, some countervailing measures may be necessary; for instance, readiness to allow a fairly wide discretion to those on whom certain kinds of decision may be devolved, for instance where time is an important factor. Otherwise vocational man may find himself ousted by organization man, or making a vocation out of being organization man. For some people no doubt this is as it should be; to make it general, is surely to produce a confusion of ends and means.

'A confusion of ends and means.' Organizations and their politics can become a way of life, and increasingly so where those doing the substantive work for which they have been set up are also drawn into the work of running them. No doubt in a democratic age up to a point this is as it should be. Yet there are distinctions. I have noted the need both for loyalty to institutions and for freedom of spirit over against them, and what I have said about the complexity of ethical problems and the conflicts of roles, public, private and professional, which are endemic to organizations, may seem cold comfort to those who have to live with them. Yet we need to be able to see complexity and to go on thinking without falling into Utopianism or cynicism. 'Seek simplicity and distrust it' – a maxim of Whitehead's – can be a guide so long as we see that among the simplicities to be distrusted is the ideological pursuit of a single ideal or principle without realistic appraisal of its implications in a particular setting. These may be such as to produce consequences of a kind which boomerang back on to the original ideal, frustrating it or leading to a swing from Utopianism to cynicism.[48] But the other extreme is an opportunism which neither carries moral respect nor is likely to be compatible with policy making. We come back to a view of moral judgment as neither simply rule-directed nor simply calculation of consequences, but needing to take responsible account of both. It has indeed the guiding lights of fairness and sympathy – the marks of practical reason

---

[48] See above for Selznick's diagnosis in *T.V.A. and the Grass Roots* of the effects of the pursuit of the principle of local participation. Also Merton's observations on conditions where an ideal can be frustrated by unanticipated consequences in 'The Unanticipated Consequences of Purposive Social Action', and also 'The Boomerang Response'.

in morality – but these may have to be brought to bear on a complex tangle of interests to be considered or reconciled. To meet this complexity calls not only for disinterestedness but for intelligence.

Failure to see complexity can feed tensions between those whose primary responsibility is to keep the organization or institution going and those whose primary interest is an ideal, a principle or the claims of a specific piece of work. In my preface I said that I might have dedicated this book to administrators whose hearts are with the anarchists and to anarchists who have a heart for the administrators. There are those who will want to go all out for an idea, a principle, the possibilities of a creative piece of work. There are also those concerned with ways and means, and the repercussions of the pursuit of one idea or interest on others. These will be likely to set a high value on stability, since they have the responsibility of seeing that departures from recognized procedures do not pass certain limits, and that if possible the organization survives. They will be tempted to avoid people who will be 'difficult' or who may 'rock the boat' – and there is probably a bit of an anarchist in most people of high originality. The temptation of the latter is to see the administrators as 'bureaucrats' (used as a dirty word) more interested in perpetuating the organization and their own power in it than in the real work. Both may sometimes be right; but not always. Even where they are not right, there is likely to be tension. Tension is easier to live with where we can see the reasons for it, and, above all, where each kind of person can know at bottom that he needs and depends on the other. It is no small gain if there is something in a person of the one kind which responds to concerns more often found in the other: an administrator may be a poet on the side, and an inventor or writer may have known what it is like to have a share in government.[49] Nevertheless, as St. Paul told us, there are diversities of gifts. St. Paul also spoke of a body in which there is mutual dependence of different members and functions. In a general way, this perception has come to us from our Christian tradition.[50] We need realistic and detailed understanding of ways in which these mutual dependences work, and here perhaps sociologists can help us with their interest in diagnosing multiple relationships. The point was seen by Roger Wilson, writing of Friends' Relief Work after the last war.[51] That organization was a good laboratory for the purpose, since it was set up for work which in the nature

[49] Plato warned us that we should only trust rulers who held office unwillingly. He went too far, since most things are better done by those who enjoy doing them. But he had a point: we can mistrust politicians and administrators who are only interested in politics and administration.

[50] It was something which the late Charles Williams saw; it runs through his novels, and also his books *The Descent of the Dove* and *The Figure of Beatrice*, under the themes of 'coinherence' and 'exchange'.

[51] *Authority, Leadership and Concern* (Swarthmore Lecture, 1949), p. 21.

of the case attracts a number of potentially anarchic characters – 'conscientious objectors' often not only to military service but to any kind of authority. He writes of how they found that 'ordinary' and 'extraordinary' personalities were necessary to each other and could build one another up.[52] 'For outstanding individuals are not by any means always very well balanced. Imagination often resides in those with intense inner conflicts; drive in those who lack a sense of personal inner security; inspiration in those who are careless about details; capacity for understanding people in those who do not mind much about administration; administrative ability in those who think along well-set lines. Sometimes, of course, people do emerge with exceptional qualities in the desired mixture, but ability is wasted if it cannot be used when lop-sided. The more intelligently stable the group temperament, the more readily can exceptional abilities find useful and constructive scope for their expression.'[53] Intelligent stability might be taken as epitomizing one administrative aim. To achieve it can be a difficult, creative task needing all the ability and moral toughness that Chester Barnard has said that it needs. And yet, at the same time, it is a means and not an end. Administrators need the self-abnegation of putting high ability and indeed powers of leadership into providing opportunities for other people to do something else.

Not only so within the work of an organization; this is a fact also about the wider life of society, not seen by those to whom keeping some sort of stable framework of life going just appears as one of the ways in which the 'establishment' tries to hold on to its power. Yet not only artists and others who do first-hand work of the kind which wins social recognition depend on the people who 'maintain the fabric of the world';[54] so too do those who try to contract out of society – the would-be anarchists and beats, and those who talk about 'alienation'. Their dependence is not only true in the trivial logical sense in which no one can be a rebel without something to rebel against (which is a trivial point, even when dressed up in Hegelian language about 'negation'). It is true as a practical empirical point, since we all depend on a background of routines being carried out, services maintained, basic securities provided, and so assume the existence of a host of people who are prepared to take the responsibilities of their parts in this. Spontaneity and creativity need a framework; they are not likely to flourish in social chaos. And this goes for the social rebel as well as for the original genius. One *avant-garde* pop singer, Roger Miller, has seen this.

---

[52] In commenting on this observation in my *Function, Purpose and Powers* (p. 263), I remarked that the 'ordinary' people who help build up a society in which they do not exasperate the 'extraordinary' people but help them to find constructive expression for their ideas, are not likely to be as ordinary as all that. I also discussed this question of the relations between different kinds of 'vocational' characters.

[53] *Authority, Leadership and Concern*, p. 21.

[54] Ecclesiasticus, xxxviii, 4.

'Squares make the world go round.
Sounds profane, sounds profound.
But government cain't be made do
By hipsters wearing rope-soled shoes.'[55]

This is not only a bid for tolerance, a way of saying that it takes all sorts to make a world. It means that we see how different kinds of temperament and capacity – those who produce protest, and those who produce original work, and those who produce stability – need one another, and depend on one another.

Yet, as psychologists and novelists have always known, dependence is an ambivalent relation which produces its tensions. These can best be carried when we see the reasons for them, and in our modern society some of these reasons may lie in the nature of large organizations. In these *milieux* people meet each other not only as carrying out complementary functions (as they may well do), but at the same time occupying multiple and potentially conflicting roles. This is something which cannot be wished away or organized away; it is a fact of life to be understood and lived with.

Anthony Sampson in *The Anatomy of Britain* quotes from Bagehot, 'The characteristic danger of great nations, like the Roman or the English, which have a long history of continuous creation, is that they may at last fail from not comprehending the great institutions they have created'.[56] It is a merit of Sampson's book that he sees that to understand contemporary Britain we must look at what is happening in its large organizations – the Civil Service, political parties, schools and universities, business corporations. We need a number of imaginative and well-documented sociological studies of these; it should not be left to journalists with historical and sociological sense to do most of the work. For if I am right, it is these big organizations which increasingly dominate contemporary society, and which are producing some of the most difficult and insistent moral problems we have to face. The sociologist may not just be, as Professor Sprott has suggested, 'the specialist who tries to elaborate and make precise the administrative world picture'.[57] But at least his training in studying role behaviour in networks of social relations should give him some expertise in helping us to understand a world in which administrative, executive and professional action, rather than the individual ways of the amateur, is increasingly dominant.

Organization Man need not swallow up all our life. Yet Whyte's grim diagnosis of how he may swallow up our moral initiative may well prove true if we do not see how the complex moral problems of institutionalized life, just because they are impersonal as well as personal, call for more

[55] Quoted in *Time* Magazine, March 19, 1965.
[56] *Anatomy of Britain* (London, 1962), p. 638.
[57] *Science and Social Action* (London, 1954), p. 17.

intelligence in diagnosis and more resource in moral judgment and moral courage than do those of a purely personal morality. The trouble is that though their impersonal side does call for this, it can also be invoked to allow responsibility to be evaded,[58] and the evasion can be encouraged by a popular deterministic interpretation of the findings of the social sciences. This need not be our conclusion; indeed to look further into what these can tell us, and to look behind it, may help towards a better appreciation of the person in the *persona* rather than his defacement. It will point to rules of social morality as guides rather than as determinants of judgment, of roles as played with individual style, and of social relations as relations which are still between human beings even though at many degrees of indirectness.

Moralists and sociologists may have different professional interests in these problems and the kinds of conflicts they present. To write perceptively about these they need not abrogate their special interests; but they could well be less concerned with demarcating frontiers, and more concerned with joint exploration of the no-man's-land in which we live our moral predicaments.

---

[58] Anthony Sampson also writes, 'This, surely, is the greater nightmare of a democracy—not that the government is full of sinister and all-powerful *éminences grises*, but that the will of the people dissolves itself in committees, with thousands of men murmuring about their duty to "those whom we serve"'. (*Ibid.*, p. 627.)

Some issues arising from the readings

Preliminary comments

Four main issues are discussed here. First we discuss the concept of education, since it is in the context of education that the readings need to be understood. We are concerned to ask, particularly, what sort of concept education is, and what useful understanding of it philosophy can offer. We next discuss practical reasoning (the reasoning involved in solving practical problems), and pick up a number of points for consideration, for the most part from the readings by Gauthier, Hampshire, and Emmet. The third issue we discuss arises from the reading by Entwistle and concerns the role of theory in learning how to do something (for example, to teach) and in doing it intelligently. Finally, we discuss educational theory, on such a conception as that of P. H. Hirst,[1] and comment on the limitations of educational theory for those engaged in educational practice.

The discussions of the four issues are headed as follows. The task of defining 'education',[2] Practical reasoning, Knowing in theory and knowing in practice, and, lastly, Educational theory and educational practice.

The task of defining 'education'

In this discussion, we suggest that one prevalent kind of philosophical analysis may yield an inadequate understanding of the concept of education, and that the analysis of education should be undertaken in the light of some relatively recent analyses of 'science' and, more particularly, of

---

[1] For references see page 120.
[2] We adapt this title from P. Ziff's, 'The task of defining a work of art', *Philosophical Review*, Vol. 62 (1953), pp. 58–78.

'work of art'. We develop this point to argue that 'education' is what W. B. Gallie has called 'an essentially contested concept', and we indicate some of the implications of this for educational discussion and practice. We finally suggest that R. S. Peters' account of education is not satisfactory, and make some comments on formal definitions of 'education'.

1. Conceptual analysis and defining 'education'

The request for clarification about education and educational aims is often put in the form 'What is education?' There are a number of difficulties attached to this question – some of them arising from the ambiguity of questions of the form 'What is. . .?'[3] It can be held to be a question of philosophical interest, both because philosophers might distinguish and clarify its possible meanings, and because, on one interpretation, it might be seen as a request for a definition or for an analysis of 'education'. A good many philosophers who take up such a request are likely to set about distinguishing primary, central or paradigm uses of 'education' from those variously described as secondary, peripheral, parasitic, analogous, metaphorical and so on, and to give some account of how these are related to each other, and to other concepts. This is often described as discovering the logical geography of a concept. On this conception of philosophical analysis, the philosopher's task is to map concepts. A number of questions might be raised about this.

Firstly, when we are asked to make a map of an area, its boundaries can be sharply defined (by degrees of latitude and longitude, or by gridreferences, for example). But can the area marked out by every concept be similarly (though analogously) delimited? Some concepts might have ill-defined borders – they might be inherently vague. Further, the logical area marked out by a concept is that determined by all its uses, and what these are is not given to us. We have rather to go out and look for them. But how are we to know that our collection of uses is not selective?[4] Different individuals and social groups may use concepts differently and appeals to a conformity of use that underlie such phrases as 'What we say is . . .' or 'What we would say is . . .' or 'standard use' or 'correct use' may be unjustified and simply reflect our own speech habits.

Secondly, do all concepts have uses which can be indisputably identi-

---

[3] See J. Hospers, *An Introduction to Philosophical Analysis*, 2nd edn. (Routledge & Kegan Paul, 1967), pp. 12–14; H. Staniland, *Universals* (Macmillan, 1973), p. 1, notes that questions of the form ' "What is *X*?" may be understood in many different ways; according to the context they may convey a request for almost any kind of information about *X*'. For a discussion of general relevance here see E. R. Emmet, *Learning to Philosophise* (Penguin Books, 1968), Chapter 2.

[4] cf. A. MacIntyre, *Against the Self-Images of the Age* (Duckworth, 1971), p. ix. See also Vol. I, p. 91.

fied as central, primary, and paradigm? 'Pencil' might, but does 'education'? Further, by what criteria are such uses identified? Is it by 'what we would say'? One thing is clear, the uses do not come to us labelled and categorized. Rather, philosophers bring the labels to them. And it must be asked whether, at least in some cases, the notions of 'primary' or 'central' uses do not involve, if only implicitly, a prescriptive element.[5] Philosophers may choose as a central use those which serve some further purpose they have in mind. Their choice might be connected with methodological issues or with questions of ethical justification. In the latter case the use chosen may reflect their own ethical valuations.[6]

Thirdly, the notions of mapping and of logical geography seem to imply that concepts occupy more or less fixed positions. Some, however, may not – not because they are vague, or ambiguous, or even used loosely, but rather because they are tied to essentially on-going, organic, and complex enterprises with a history behind them, and the flexibility and fluidity of use reflects and expresses the differing aims, aspirations, and orders of priority of those who take part, and have taken part in the enterprises. Mapping the logical geography of this sort of concept, if only in an interim fashion, may not bring the sort of understanding that the original question sought.[7] To understand a concept of this kind and

[5] A. G. N. Flew, in 'Indoctrination and Doctrines', in *Concepts of Indoctrination*, ed. I. A. Snook (Routledge & Kegan Paul, 1972), notes on page 87 that in determining primary and secondary uses of 'indoctrination' he may well have crossed 'the here very elusive line between description and prescription'. See also G. Maxwell and H. Feigl. 'Why ordinary language needs reforming'. *Journal of Philosophy*, Vol. 58 (1961), pp. 488–98. They write (p. 489) that they 'strongly suspect that many cases of putative ordinary-usage analysis are, in fact, disguised reformations.'

[6] To let such considerations influence an account of a concept may be both legitimate and desirable. But it is important that the influence is made explicit and that, as far as possible, the descriptive and prescriptive parts of the task be distinguished. It is worth noting here that Max Black, 'The definition of scientific method', in *Science and Civilisation*, ed. R. C. Stauffer (Madison, Wisconsin: University of Wisconsin Press, 1949), page 69, writes, 'The attempt to define scientific method or to analyse science is a search for a *persuasive* definition. I hold this to be true because I believe that the term "science" has no definite and unambiguous application.' He notes a little earlier that 'the criticism of persuasive definitions is a proceeding partly normative in character, involving considerations of an ethical as well as of a methodological and logical character.' See also W. B. Gallie, 'What makes a subject scientific?', *British Journal for the Philosophy of Science*, Vol. 8 (1957–8), pp. 118–39, particularly Section 3. For discussions of general relevance here, see S. Körner, *Fundamental Questions in Philosophy* (Allen Lane, The Penguin Press, 1969), pp. 25–32, and R. H. Weingartner, 'The meaning of "of" in "philosophy of ..."', *Journal of Value Inquiry*, Vol. 2 (1968), pp. 79–94.

[7] For a discussion that might be held to suggest that the concept of education is not amenable to analysis in the sense of logical geography, see W. H. Dray's comments in 'Philosophy and Education', *Proceedings of the International Seminar* March 23–25 1966 (Ontario Institute for Studies in Education, 1967), pp. 23–4 and R. S. Peters' reply and comments on pp. 27–29. Dray suggests that analysing the concept of education is not like analysing that of 'knowledge in general epistemology, or (to suggest what may seem a

explain and clarify its uses, may be much more like plotting its course from past to present, of trying to give some account of the reasons for its various uses, of the differing valuations reflected in changes of use, and even of the different valuations such changes may have helped to effect. It might well involve both trying to justify some of its present uses, by noting the values they reflect and asking how they can be justified, and even suggesting desirable uses for the future. Just as some activities and institutions are not likely to be understood without some grasp of their history, so, too, the concepts that reflect the changes of orientation in such activities and institutions may not be able to be understood adequately without a grasp of their history, in the light of the history of the activities and institutions.[8] To use an example of Ziff's[9] to which we return later, what sort of understanding could be had of 'work of art', without reference to the history of art and to the debates about art in which the concept had a place?

Fourthly, to interpret 'What is education?' as a demand for logical geography may be false to the most typical contexts in which such a question is asked. It might be argued that its home is not in philosophical seminars where it appears, like a body left to medical science, chilled and ready for dissection, but in discussions by interested parties about what to teach in schools, colleges, and universities. If this is true, the argument about the nature of education is taken most naturally as a normative one. To see it otherwise might be merely another example of philosophers ignoring contexts in which vocabulary is typically deployed and on which Hampshire comments in his article.[10] Ziff, in his article which has a number of implications for analyses of 'education', relates his discussion of 'work of art' to specific artistic disputes and argues that reasonable uses of 'work of art' cannot be defended without reference to normative considerations.[11] Scheffler,[12] with a reference to Ziff's paper,

(Ftn. 7 cont.)
more relevant comparison) the concepts of fact or interpretation in the philosophy of history' where 'fairly stable conceptual networks' seem to be available. See also G. Reddiford, 'Conceptual analysis and education', *Proceedings of the Philosophy of Education Society of Great Britain*, Supplementary Issue, Volume VI, No. 2 (July 1972), pp. 193–215. For a number of points that are generally relevant to our discussion here see P. L. Heath, 'The appeal to ordinary language', *Philosophical Quarterly*, Vol. 2 (1952), pp. 1–12.

[8] For the importance of a historical understanding of institutions, see W. B. Gallie, *Philosophy and the Historical Understanding* (Chatto & Windus, 1964), Chapter 6; for the importance of historical considerations to philosophy, see also Chapters 7 and 8. Both Gallie ibid., p. 190 and op. cit. (1958) and Black, op. cit. (1949) note the importance of historical considerations in analysis of science, scientific, and scientific method.

[9] P. Ziff, op. cit. See also W. B. Gallie, op. cit. (1964), pp. 170–7.

[10] See p. 37.

[11] Ziff, op. cit. particularly Section IV.

[12] I. Scheffler, *The Language of Education* (Charles C. Thomas, 1960), p. 31. He notes on page 30, that 'to offer a definition of the term "education", for example, in non-

states that 'Definitions in education thus may be said to resemble definitions in art which, though of no legal significance, also serve frequently
to express changing conceptions of the artist's task. For example, definitions of artistic innovators often extend the use of the term 'work of art'
to new sorts of objects; the counter definitions of conservatives withhold
the term from these same objects. Both sets of definitions are, furthermore, often consonant with artistic tradition, that is, they are in conformity with prior usage. The dispute can thus not be taken, in such cases, to
be a matter of the meaning of the terms alone. Rather, it is a question of
divergent artistic programs, conveyed by opposing programmatic definitions that are also descriptively accurate. An attempt to define a work of
art is not, in the words of Collingwood, 'an attempt to investigate and
expound external verities concerning the nature of an external object
called Art', but rather to give 'the solution of certain problems arising out
of the situation in which artists find themselves here and now''.'

Some support for the view that to interpret 'What is education?' as a
request for a descriptive analysis is to misinterpret it comes from some
comments of Dunlop. He writes,[13] '"This is what education is" – "now
this is what we ought to do" – the two seem oddly juxtaposed. Surely if
there is to be any point in asking the first question the answer ought to
help us to answer the second question "what ought we to do?", but what
kind of help could we get that wasn't already an indication that we ought
to do certain (perhaps very general) things?' He goes on to imply that the
philosophically important task concerning the concept of education does
not consist in descriptive analysis, and states that 'If we are interested in
the *concept* of education in a philosophically interesting way we cannot be
merely interested in how the word is used or in the distinctions people
have in mind when they use it. Clearly in these senses the concept could
be connected with all sorts of criteria in particular social groups.'[14]

Thus we might argue that 'What is education?' is a request for a pro-

(Ftn. 12 cont.)
scientific contexts is quite often to convey a program as well as, at best, to state an
equation that may be accurate with respect to prior usage', and on page 32, how decisions
governing practical orientations 'may be embodied in revision of our principles of action
or our definitions of relevant terms or both.'
[13] F. N. Dunlop, 'Education and human nature', *Proceedings of the Philosophy of
Education Society of Great Britain, Proceedings of the Annual Conference, January 1970*,
Volume IV, p. 23.
[14] Dunlop, op. cit. (1970), p. 41. Cf. M. Hollis, 'The pen and the purse', *Proceedings of
the Philosophy of Education Society of Great Britain*, Supplementary Volume, Vol. V, No.
2, July 1971, pp. 153–69. Hollis writes (pp. 168–9), 'Still less can we decide what is the
best education by analysing the concept of Education as it is standardly used. For standard
usage embodies many quaint beliefs rich in dogma, taboo, cliché, prejudice, contradiction
and error. There is more to be said for analysing the concept of Education as it ought to
be used.'

grammatic definition[15] – one that embodies a programme for an activity. To recognize that a definition of education is programmatic is to realize that it is to be defended nor merely by considerations of consistency and clarity but also by normative ones – concerning, for example, the worth of the programme, or the expected consequences for practice of adopting such a definition. One consequence of this is that the adoption of programmatic definitions 'should follow rather than precede a moral and practical evaluation of the programs they convey.'[16]

There is, in our view, at least one other important similarity between 'education' and 'work of art'. What may be said about 'work of art' is that it has, and has had, a number of different and competing uses and definitions, and that these partly reflect and partly prescribe certain valuations and orientations of members of what might be called 'artistic communities', which consist of the artists themselves, critics, aestheticians, spectators and so on.[17] Similarly, there may be a number of different and competing uses of 'education' or 'educated', which similarly reflect different and competing valuations and orientations of the educational community. Soltis notes that 'From A to Z, from Admirals to Zealots, we find almost everyone in or outside the field of education, not only ready to talk about education, but also most willing to offer *his* definition of education. In fact, it is not *a* definition of education that is lacking. Part of the problem involved in talking and thinking about education is the variety of definitions and views of education which is offered to us on all sides. We are, in fact, literally bombarded with a multitude of competing definitions which tempt us to choose among them, to mix an eclectic set of fragments from them, or even, rejecting them all, to find *the* "real" definition of education for ourselves.'[18] He goes on to say that searches for

---

[15] For this kind of definition see Scheffler, op. cit. (1960), p. 18 onwards. C. L. Stevenson's discussion of persuasive definitions is also relevant here. See C. L. Stevenson, *Ethics and Language* (New Haven, Connecticut: Yale University Press, 1944), Chapter IX. There is nothing, in our view, which precludes philosophers from offering such definitions of education, though they may be likely to embody ideal as opposed to eminently practicable programmes in that they will probably not take account of contingent restrictions which might affect their implementation. Even so they might provide a useful general orientation, though it might be one justifiable one among others. For the possibility of interpreting Peters' account of education, as programmatic see pp. 90–1 of this book.

[16] Scheffler, op. cit. (1960), p. 34. Whether there are any limits which can be laid down a priori beyond which programmatic definitions cannot be said to embody educational programmes is doubtful. Gallie's (op. cit., 1964) and Reddiford's (op. cit., 1972) discussions would seem to support this view. This does not mean that reasonable decisions cannot be made in individual cases.

[17] Cf. P. Ziff, op. cit. p. 59. Uses may be said to be competing when they embody incompatible programmes or evaluations.

[18] J. F. Soltis. *An Introduction to the Analysis of Educational Concepts* (Reading, Massachusetts: Addison-Wesley, 1968), p. 2.

the definition of education are searches for 'a statement of the right or best programme for education.'[19] Just as there might be disputes about whether this or that feature is relevant, necessary or even sufficient for a thing to be a work of art, so it might be disputed whether an educated person needs to have some knowledge of classics, or maths, or science, of the history or literature of his own country, of music, or some understanding of a religious outlook on life, or needs to be creative in some way. Disputes about these criteria will be reflected in the different and competing uses of 'educated', in debates about, for example, whether or not certain schools or members of staff in them are really concerned with education, or about whether certain curricular proposals are educationally valuable.[20]

2. Essentially contested concepts and the concept of education

These considerations about 'education' and 'work of art', give rise to a further question, and that is whether education, like work of art, can be included in the class of concepts that W. B. Gallie has called 'essentially contested'.[21] In addition to work of art and art, he cites religion, Christian life, Christian tradition, social justice, and democracy.[22] What we wish to suggest here is that 'education' and 'educated' are, like these, essentially contested concepts – that is, that arguments about whether this or that is education, or about whether this or that person is educated, are in many

[19] *Ibid.,* p 7

[20] The dispute, as we put it here, is best understood as a dispute about necessary conditions of being educated. But there might be uses of 'education' where none of the criteria individually is either necessary or sufficient. We might agree to say the criteria for the use of 'educated' are *a, b, c, d, e, f, g, h* and that no one of them is a necessary or sufficient condition of being educated, but if a person fulfils any four he will count as educated. We might even give greater weight to some than to others, and perhaps say that if a person conforms to one of the former, then he only needs two more to be educated. Thus no one criterion is necessary or sufficient, but any four together, or in some cases three together, would be sufficient. For relevant discussions, see M. Black, op. cit. (1949), and 'Definition, presupposition, and assertion', *Philosophical Review*, Vol. 61 (1952). pp. 532–50; P. Ziff, op. cit.; R. B. Edwards, *Reason and Religion* (New York: Harcourt Brace Jovanovich, 1972), Chapter 1, 'What is religion? Some problems of definition'.

[21] W. B. Gallie – 'Art as an essentially contested concept', *Philosophical Quarterly* Vol. 6 (1956), pp. 97–114; 'Essentially contested concepts', *Proceedings of the Aristotelian Society*, Vol. LVI (1955–6), pp. 167–98; 'Essentially contested concepts', Chapter 8 of *Philosophy and the Historical Understanding* (Chatto & Windus, 1964).

[22] Other essentially contested concepts might be: (*a*) Socialism – see Max Black, *The Labyrinth of Language* (Penguin Books, 1972), pp. 180–4; (*b*) the Marxist-Leninist line; (*c*) Symphonic (as used of musical compositions). See the introductions to each of the two volumes of *The Symphony*, ed. R. Simpson (Penguin Books, 1966).

cases similar enough to those concerning whether this or that is a work of art and so on, for 'education' and 'educated' to be called essentially contested concepts.[23]

Gallie says his 'main thought' with regard to such concepts is that 'We find groups of people disagreeing about the proper use of the concepts e.g. of art, of democracy, of the Christian tradition. When we examine the different uses of these terms and the characteristic arguments in which they figure we soon see that there is no one clearly definable general use of any of them that can be set up as the correct or standard use. Different uses of the term 'work of art' or 'democracy' or 'Christian doctrine' subserve different though of course not altogether unrelated functions for different schools or movements of artists and critics, for different political groups and parties, for different religious communities and sects. Now once this *variety* of functions is disclosed it might well be expected that the disputes in which the above mentioned concepts figure would at once come to an end. But in fact this does not happen. Each party continues to maintain that the special functions which the term 'work of art' or 'democracy' or 'Christian doctrine' fulfils on *its* behalf or on *its* interpretation, is the correct or proper or primary or the only important function which the term in question can plainly be said to fulfil. Moreover, each party continues to defend its case with what it claims to be convincing arguments, evidence, and other forms of justification.'[24] He says a little later that he will 'try to show that there are disputes centred on the concepts I have just mentioned, which are perfectly genuine; which though not resolvable by argument of any kind, are nevertheless sustained by perfectly respectable arguments and evidence. This is what I mean by saying there are concepts which are essentially contested, concepts the proper use of which inevitably involves endless disputes about their proper uses on the part of their uses.'[25]

Gallie lists, in all, seven conditions of a concept's being essentially

[23] This appears to be suggested by T. F. Daveney, 'Education – a moral concept', Inaugural Lecture, University of Exeter (1970), pp. 17–18. For other relevant discussions (which appeared after this book had gone to press) see A. MacIntyre, 'The essential contestability of some social concepts', *Ethics*, Vol. 84, No. 1 (October 1973), pp. 1–9 and the reply by N. S. Care, 'On fixing social concepts', ibid., pp. 10–21; A. Ryan, 'An essentially contested concept', *The Times Higher Educational Supplement*, No. 120 (1 February 1974), p. 13.

Not all concepts identified as essentially contested may be so in all of their uses. One criterion of an essentially contested concept is that it is appraisive, and 'education' or 'educated', for example, may not be so in what might be called their 'external descriptive' use (see P. H. Hirst and R. S. Peters, *The Logic of Education* (Routledge & Kegan Paul, 1970), p. 20). Gallie, op. cit. (1956), pp. 113–14, suggests that uses will inevitably be contestable (and as often as not immediately contested) in contexts of 'live criticism'.

[24] Gallie, op. cit. (1955–6), p. 168; cf. also Gallie, op. cit. (1964), p. 157.
[25] Gallie, op. cit. (1955–6), p. 169; Gallie, op. cit. (1964), p. 158.

contested.[26] Of these, the first five he describes as 'defining conditions', and the last two as 'historically justifying conditions',[27] which are necessary if an essentially contested concept is to be distinguished from one which is 'radically confused'.[28] To make this distinction is 'in effect to justify the continued use of any essentially contested concept.'[29]

Gallie's first condition is that such a concept must be '*appraisive* in the sense that it signifies or accredits some kind of valued achievement'. The second is that the achievement must be 'of an internally complex character, for all that its worth is attributed to it as a whole.' The third is that 'any explanation of its worth must include reference to the respective contributions of its various parts or features' and that 'prior to experimentation there is nothing absurd or contradictory in any number of possible rival descriptions of its total worth', where such descriptions set the parts or features in different orders of importance. The fourth is that 'the accredited achievement must be of a kind that admits of considerable modification in the light of changing circumstances', and that 'such modification cannot be prescribed or predicted in advance.' (Gallie describes 'the concept of any such achievement' as '"open" in character.)[30] The fifth is that each party recognizes that its own use of the concept 'is contested by those of other parties and that each party must have at least some appreciation of the different criteria in the light of which the other parties claim to be applying the concept in question' and that its own use has to be maintained against the uses of other parties.[31] The sixth is that the concept is derived from 'an original exemplar whose authority is acknowledged by all contestant users of the concept.' And the seventh is that it can be reasonably claimed that 'the continuous competition for acknowledgement as between the contestant users of the concept enables the original exemplar's achievement to be sustained or developed in optimum fashion.'[32]

It does not seem difficult to show that education in many of its uses conforms to at least the first five of Gallie's conditions. Firstly, it is

[26] Gallie, op. cit. (1955–6), pp. 171–80; Gallie, op. cit. (1964), pp. 161–8. Our summary uses the latter. Nos 1 to 5 occur on p. 161, and 6 and 7 on p. 168.

[27] Gallie, op. cit. (1964) p. 177.

[28] Ibid., p. 168.

[29] Cit. (1964) p. 168.

[30] Ibid., p. 161.

[31] As Gallie (ibid.) says, 'To use an essentially contested concept means to use it both aggressively and defensively.'

[32] E. Gellner, in an interesting and favourable review of Gallie, op. cit. (1964), entitled 'The concept of a story', *Ratio*, Vol. 9 (1967), pp. 49–66, offers a relatively detailed critique of Gallie's account of essentially contested concepts. Unfortunately, Gellner's review came to our notice too late for us to take account of it. But one thing he seems to suggest is that Gallie could have dispensed with his sixth and seventh conditions.

commonly used appraisively. Arguments about whether or not something is to count as educating somebody, or whether or not someone is educated, are very frequently normative arguments. This is reflected in the philosophical literature, even though there is disagreement about the analysis of 'education'.[33] Secondly, education is internally complex in that we may intend to pass on a wide and varied range of theoretical and practical competences, of attitudes and of values.[34] Thirdly, different parties may differ about the order of importance of these. Is having some conception of scientific method more important than having one of historical method? Are these more important than having some practical or even creative ability in art or in music? What priority should be given to qualities of character, such as integrity or concern for others?[35] Fourthly, education is what Gallie here describes as 'open' in character. Depending on circumstances, orientations, content and methods change. New methods and subjects are taken up; old ones drop out; some subjects are retained, but are redefined and given new directions; subjects are integrated or grouped in different combinations. These changes are not likely to be 'prescribed or predicted in advance'. Scheffler notes that 'Education, like art, literature, and other phases of social life, has changing styles and problems in response to changing conditions.'[36] What modifications there have been and are can be seen from a study of the history of education and of comparative education. Fifthly, competing and contested uses of 'education', 'educated', and 'educational', are seen in debates about what should go on in schools, colleges and universities, just as such uses of 'work of art' or of 'democracy' and of some of their derivatives are seen in debates about painting, or about political arrangements. One indication that uses are recognized as contested is that the different parties describe their uses as the proper, correct, true ones and so on, as against those of their opponents.[37] Education, thus, fulfils the fifth criterion.

[33] For philosophers' statements of 'education' as an appraisive concept see: R. S. Peters, *Ethics and Education* (Allen & Unwin, 1966), p. 25 and p. 41, for example; R. S. Peters, 'What is an educational process?', in *The Concept of Education*, ed. R. S. Peters (Routledge & Kegan Paul, 1967), p. 2, where 'education' is likened to a stamp of approval issued by *Good Housekeeping*; R. S. Peters, 'Education and the educated man', *Philosophy of Education Society of Great Britain, Proceedings of the Annual Conference, January 1970*, Vol. IV, pp. 5–20, which also contains a discussion of some objections to an analysis of 'education' which makes it a normative concept; T. F. Daveney, op. cit., pp. 5–6; and G. Langford, op. cit. (1968), p. 69.

[34] Cf. R. F. Dearden, *The Philosophy of Primary Education* (Routledge & Kegan Paul, 1968), p. 51.

[35] Cf. R. S. Peters, op. cit. (1970), p. 5; and P. H. Hirst and R. S. Peters, *The Logic of Education* (Routledge & Kegan Paul, 1970), p. 27. Disputes of this sort arise in education in any case, whether or not the concept is essentially contested.

[36] Scheffler, op. cit. (1960), p. 32.

[37] For a possible connexion between this point and ideology see P. King, 'An ideological fallacy', in P. King and B. C. Parekh, eds, *Politics and Experience* (Cambridge University Press, 1968), p. 383.

Whether education fulfils the sixth and seventh conditions is a little harder to show. In the case of the sixth, it depends on the latitude given to the notion of an exemplar. Education clearly does not possess an exemplar of the kind that Christian life does. Yet it might well be argued that it has one similar to those that Gallie assigns to art and democracy. What constitute their exemplars are held to be the tradition or traditions that lie behind them; even though, as in the case of art, there may be a number of 'different, and very often quite independent, artistic traditions',[38] and, as in the case of democracy, a number of 'historically independent but sufficiently similar' ones.[39] One educational tradition, perhaps one among others, which can provide an exemplar is embodied in the phrase 'liberal education' – a notion whose origin might be traced back to the Greeks.[40]

---

[38] Gallie, op. cit. (1964), p. 177.

[39] Ibid., p. 180. The latitude that Gallie gives to the notion of an exemplar can be seen from some of the exemplars he describes in his discussion. Firstly, there seem, in some cases, to be not only one exemplar but only one possible exemplar (and that a *comparatively* clear one), as in the case of Christian life. Secondly, there may be a *number* of possible exemplars, as in the case of art where in different discussions, different artistic traditions or different sets of artistic traditions may be used as exemplars. Thirdly, as in the case of democracy, there may be a number of independent but similar traditions which, combined, are taken to constitute the exemplar. Gallie suggests that the vagueness of such a tradition 'in no way affects its influence as an exemplar'. Gallie's comments (p. 165) make it clear that, even in the most favourable case, 'the recognition or acceptance of the exemplar's achievement must have that "open" character which we have ascribed to every essentially contested concept' and that there is 'no question of any purely mechanical repetition or reproduction' of that achievement.

[40] See P. H. Hirst, 'Liberal education and the nature of knowledge', in *Philosophical Analysis and Education*, ed., R. D. Archambault (Routledge & Kegan Paul, 1965), pp. 113–38. The first section of this paper is headed 'The Greek notion of Liberal Education'. See also R. S. Peters, 'Education as Initiation' (ibid.), particularly p. 101; R. S. Peters, *Ethics and Education* (Allen & Unwin, 1966), Chapter I, particularly Section 5; and R. S. Peters, op. cit. (1970), where on page 14 the notion of an educated man is linked to 'the Greek ideal'. Hirst, interestingly, in this context, heads a later section of his paper 'A reassertion and a reinterpretation' – that is, of the concept of liberal education. From comments on page 121 of his paper, he can be seen to be defending a use of 'liberal education' which is 'defined directly in terms of the pursuit of knowledge as liberal education *originally* was' (our italics). This is against a broader use of the concept which is additionally concerned with 'aspects of personal development, particularly emotional and moral, that may or may not be desirable.' It can be seen from Hirst's and Peters' discussions that 'liberal education' can be given a number of interpretations and might be related to 'education' in a number of ways. Hirst, in R. D. Archambault, ed., op. cit. (1965), p. 136, and in *The Cambridge Journal of Education*, No. 3 (Michaelmas, 1971), p. 112, makes it clear that on his account 'liberal education' and 'education' are not to be equated. He writes, in the latter, referring to his discussion in the former, 'I defended a stipulative definition of "liberal education" in terms of the development of knowledge and understanding. But I did guard myself by saying that in those terms liberal education is nothing like the whole of education.' Peters, op. cit. (1966), would seem to be prepared to settle for a less sharp distinction between the two. For a recent discussion of liberal education see G. H. Bantock, 'The idea of a liberal education', *Educational Review*, Vol. 21, (1968–9), pp. 3–12 and pp. 130–7. (It was suggested by a reader of a draft of this part of the book that

To establish fully a concept's conformity to the seventh condition would often seem to require a long and complex argument, particularly where the exemplar was vague.[41] Nevertheless it might be argued, at least *prima facie*, in the case of education and of other proposed essentially contested concepts, that 'the continuous competition for acknowledgement' might make optimum development more likely.[42] For even though there is no way of deciding once and for all, by general principle or otherwise, that there just is one best way of developing the exemplar, views about proposed best ways have to meet and be sustained against criticism from other contestant users of the concept.[43] To this extent, given that rational persuasion is possible in the disputes,[44] such views might be better founded than if they had not been subjected to public debate.[45] We conclude that there are grounds for believing that education is an essentially contested concept.[46]

3. Education as an essentially contested concept, and educational practice

If education is an essentially contested concept, what bearing does the fact have for educational discussion and practice? Gallie suggests that from the general recognition of a concept as essentially contested, it is to be expected that reasonable men will be less likely to underestimate, or completely ignore, the value of their opponents' positions, and will realize that rival uses of such a concept offer 'permanent potential critical value' to their own uses and interpretations of the concept.[47] This might bring about a rise in the quality of debate and remove it from the 'more or less lunatic fringe' any contestant party might have.[48] This would provide '*prima facie*, a justification of the continued competition for support and

(Ftn. 40 cont.)

'liberal education' might be a better candidate than 'education' for an essentially contested concept.)

[41] Gallie, op. cit. (1964), p. 167.

[42] Ibid., p. 168.

[43] Ibid., p. 166.

[44] Ibid., p. 182–7.

[45] Cf. ibid., p. 188. Whether this in fact happens is to a large extent an empirical matter, as is what the effect of the arguments is on actual policy. It might be worth adding here that Gallie describes his justification of the continued use of essentially contested concepts as 'conditional in the extreme'. It might, for example, frustrate the activity in question or make its pursuit too costly. Ibid., p. 167.

[46] For a discussion about different conceptions of universities, which has relevance to some of what Gallie says about essentially contested concepts, see P. Winch, 'The Universities and the State', *Universities Quarterly*, Vol. 12 (1957), pp. 14–23, see particularly pp. 17–18.

[47] Gallie, op. cit. (1964), p. 188.

[48] Ibid.

acknowledgement between the various contesting parties'.[49] But in the case of men less than reasonable, such recognition and the consequent realization that one's own use or interpretation is not 'the only one that can command honest and informed approval'[50] might bring 'a ruthless decision to cut the cackle, to damn the heretics and to exterminate the unwanted.'[51]

As regards education, the following four points can be made.

(*i*) Irrespective of whether education is an essentially contested concept or not, anyone who claims to be an educator (or even to be concerned with education, such as a policy-maker) will need to have some conception of education, if he is to understand what might be distinctive about educational institutions, what an educational problem, or an educational reason might be, what it might mean to say that something is educationally valuable, what might be distinctive about a person's role as an educator, and how decisions taken in that role are to be justified.[52] Gauthier has pointed out that a justification of some answers to practical questions depends on showing that an action is compatible with some general programme.[53] But a *complete* justification depends upon the justification of the overall programme itself, and this can only be given if the nature of the programme is clear.[54] A consequence of this is that clear statements of educational aims are required.[55] When educational aims are not clear, a good many questions about curriculum content and methods, for example, cannot be answered.[56] In such a case, a person would be in a position somewhat similar to that of a doctor who had to treat patients, and yet had no conception of what health was.[57]

But if education is an essentially contested concept, then there is likely

[49] Ibid.

[50] Ibid., p. 189. The relevant discussion in Gallie, op. cit. (1955–6), is on pp. 192–4.

[51] Ibid. A less severe consequence might be to conduct the enterprise ideologically. See Volume II of this book, pp. 55–117.

[52] For a discussion generally relevant here, see P. H. Hirst and R. S. Peters, op. cit. (1970), Chapters 2 and 7.

[53] See page 20 of this book.

[54] See page 4, and the reference to Scheffler in the footnote.

[55] We briefly discuss the relationship between educational aims and analyses of 'education' on pp. 92–4.

[56] Cf. P. H. Hirst and R. S. Peters, op. cit. (1970), p. 28. They write, 'It is essential for a teacher to get clear about his aims: for unless he does this, he will not have the criteria by reference to which he can determine successfully the content and method of his teaching'.

[57] In spite of the importance of adequate statements of aims, they are usually conspicuously absent in government reports on education, and in many other educational discussions about practice and policy. For some relevant comments, see *Perspectives on Plowden*, ed., R. S. Peters (Routledge & Kegan Paul, 1969), pp. 2–4 and pp. 21–5.

to be a number of competing views about the nature of education, and about what can count as an educational aim, and more than one of this number might be justified. In this case, it is perhaps even more important that views about educational aims are made explicit. It follows, too, that there might be a number of different justifiable views about what constitutes educational success and failure; and that since the role of an educator (like all roles) carries with it duties, responsibilities, and rights,[58] and since a person's view of his role as an educator depends upon which particular use of an essentially contested concept (namely, education) he adheres to,[59] people may have legitimately different views about their duties, responsibilities, rights, and areas of professional competence, as educators.[60]

(ii) The fact that there may be irreconcilable but justifiably different views about education and educators' roles may well be held to place stricter moral limits on the extent to which authority and power can be used to promote co-operation and concerted effort – if they ever do. For to try to achieve concerted effort in this way, may mean the imposition on others of goals which cannot be shown to be preferable to those which they themselves think desirable. Where there is much less room for rational disagreement about goals, as, for example, in hospitals,[61] it might well be more permissible to, and perhaps morally reprehensible not to, use authority and power to get such effort, even though in such institutions fairly widespread agreement on goals and concerted effort towards them might be achieved simply by rational argument, in a way that it might not necessarily be in educational institutions.

It does not follow that co-operation cannot be reasonably hoped for, even where there are apparently irreconcilable disputes of the sort that essentially contested concepts give rise to. There may well be areas of agreement existing prior to any discussion about co-operation, and discussion might bring voluntary compromises[62] on the part of the contestant

---

[58] See R. S. Downie, *Roles and Values* (Methuen, 1971), Chapter 6.

[59] Cf. Gallie, op. cit. (1955–6), pp. 194–5 and op. cit. (1964), pp. 190–1.

[60] Cf. D. Emmet, 'Ethics and the Social Worker', in *Social Work and Social Values; Readings in Social Work*, Vol. III, ed. E., Younghusband (Allen & Unwin, 1967), pp. 15–16, who writes, 'In a profession such as medicine, the professional code is designed so that the doctor can properly carry out a generally accepted and recognised purpose. His professional ethics are, therefore, concerned with means. But in the case of some professions, notably social work and education, the end itself is controversial and difficult to state, and any way of stating it is likely to have some ethical notion built into it, either overtly or in a concealed way.' See also Aristotle, *Nicomachean Ethics*, 1112*b* following. It would be a mistake to say that medicine gives rise to *no* controversial moral issues.

[61] We refer here to hospitals concerned with physical health.

[62] These compromises are likely to be complex and in so far as they are rationally worked out require a fair amount of moral sensitivity. There may not necessarily be any determinate answer to whether this or that is undeniably the best compromise

parties. Co-operation might be willingly and rationally undertaken, even in areas of apparently intractable disagreement, where there are grounds for thinking that the results of co-operation, achieved at the cost of some compromise in the values of individuals, are to be preferred to the results of individuals privately pursuing their own goals, with merely a prudential regard for those of others. Even so, all that might come about is some central area of agreement, and beyond this individuals might, within an area of moral indeterminacy, be left to pursue their own goals.

It can be argued, therefore, that it is not justified to lay down one coherent set of ordered, fixed, and all-embracing goals for a school to which (granted that they were feasible) all who work in the school or come into it are required to subscribe. Rather, the goals might be said not merely to alter, as a matter of fact, depending on the educational and other values of those who work in the school (and on those of other people too), but justifiably to do so. It follows, too, that schools within an educational system ought not necessarily all to share a common set of aims but rather that there should be a diversity of aims reflecting current contestant justifiable views of education.[63]

(*iii*) If education is an essentially contested concept, there may be different and contestant views about the education of teachers, and part of such an education ought to be to draw to the attention of trainees that education is an essentially contested concept, and that, as a consequence, not only will they have 'opponents' (to use Gallie's word) but also that having them is 'an essential feature of the activity' they are about to engage in.[64]

(*iv*) The fourth point we make concerns the distinction between education and other concepts. It is important to note that it no more follows from education being an essentially contested concept that complete freedom of stipulation is permitted, or that there is nothing distinctive about education (where this is taken to mean that no useful and defensible distinctions can be drawn between education and other activities), any more than it follows from Christian life being such a

(Ftn. 62 cont.)
possible. Discussion should cease, in any case, at a point where its continuance begins to endanger the activity which constitutes its subject, and other things of value.

[63] The issues raised in the article by Dumont and Wax are relevant here. See pages 158–73. If our argument is cogent, what appear to be current restrictions on choice of school, at least for parents who are not relatively rich, become harder to justify. It is important to note that we are not advocating an extreme educational laissez-faire, nor any extreme moral or educational scepticism, nor asserting that everyone's normative judgements about education or anything else are equally justifiable. We are saying that within certain limits education is an indeterminate enterprise, and we are asking what this implies. This is one way in which the analogy between education and medicine breaks down. Physical health is not an essentially contested concept.

[64] Gallie, op. cit. (1964), p. 187.

concept that anything might count as living a Christian life. The very identification of education as an essentially contested concept depends on it being distinguishable from other concepts. What is central to the distinction being drawn is the exemplar appealed to, in debates about whether something is or is not education. But the exemplar is a guide only, and might well permit uses of education in which education is distinguished from other concepts in a number of different ways. It might, of course, be possible to give an account of education which encompasses most or all contested uses but it is likely to be abstract and general, and will have to be revised as new uses arise and old ones lapse.[65] It is unlikely to be specific enough to offer much useful guidance to practice.

It might turn out on investigation, therefore, that at the level of specific contested uses of 'education' (and probably at the level of general accounts even, depending on exactly how they attempt to encompass the specific uses), the distinction between education and socialization, for example, or between educational and social reasons, might be defensibly drawn in a number of ways. It *might* even be that a case could be made out for a use of 'education' which made very little and perhaps nothing of such distinctions.[66]

To end our discussion of the concept of education, we raise two further issues. One concerns the relationship of our account of education to Peters' account of it,[67] and the second the relationship of accounts of education to statements of educational aims.

---

[65] Cf. Ziff, op. cit., p. 78, where it is stated that 'As new and different kinds of work are created, as the character of society changes and the role of art in society varies, as it has so often done throughout history, it may and most likely will be necessary to revise our definition of a work of art'.

[66] For discussions of the two distinctions, see P. White, 'Socialization and education' in R.F. Dearden, P.H. Hirst and R.S. Peters, eds, *Education and the Development of Reason* (Routledge & Kegan Paul, 1972), pp. 113–31; P. Renshaw, 'Socialisation: the negation of education?', *Journal of Moral Education*, Vol. 2 (1973), pp. 211–20; and K. Thompson, 'A critique of the distinction between "social" and "educational" issues as a basis for judgements concerning secondary school reorganisation', *British Journal of Educational Studies*, Vol. 18 (1970), pp. 18–31. Consider the different ways in which the distinctions between works of art and other objects might be drawn (*a*) by those who call the ready-made objects exhibited by Duchamp works of art (among them are a typewriter cover, a hat-rack, a coat-rack, and a urinal turned on its back, entitled 'Fountain') and (*b*) by those who do not. See also the quotation, a propos of 'Fountain', on p. 56 of the Catalogue of the 1966 Duchamp Exhibition at the Tate Gallery, Arts Council 1966 – 'The only works of art America has given are her plumbing and bridges.' See also C. Barrett, 'Are "bad works of art" works of art?', in A. Cashdan and E. Grugeon, eds, *Language in Education: A Source Book* (Open University, Routledge & Kegan Paul, 1972), pp. 233–8. See particularly p. 236.

[67] See the following discussions by R. S. Peters – *Authority, Responsibility and Education* (Allen & Unwin, 1959), Chapters 7, 8, and 9; *Education as Initiation* (London University Press, 1964); 'Education as initiation', in R. D. Archambault, ed., op. cit. (1965) (another version of the previous item); op. cit. (1966), Part I; 'What is an educational process?',

4. Education as an essentially contested concept and R. S. Peters' account of education

Peters' account of education might at first be thought to be incompatible with ours in that his seems to imply that there is only one appraisive concept of education.[68] If it is so, it might be to the advantage of ours. For there are grounds for thinking that his account is unsatisfactory. Some objections to it seem difficult to meet.[69] Dunlop[70] has suggested that Peters may not have guarded himself 'against the suggestion that there might be three, or four, or five etc.' concepts of education and Reddiford's discussion would seem to support this. He writes, 'In the first place it is clear that there are many "correct" uses of a particular concept within a given conceptual system. There are no good grounds for insisting that there is, or are just one or two; there is more than one concept of "education". In the second place, the idea of "correct use" or "correct application" is of very limited value in the analysis of conceptual systems, nor is "correctness" at all basic to such analyses.'[71] This would seem to be compatible with 'education' being an essentially contested concept.

(Ftn. 67 cont.)
in R. S. Peters, ed., op. cit. (1967); 'Aims of education – a conceptual inquiry' – with commentary by J. Woods and W. H. Dray and reply by R. S. Peters in Philosophy and Education, Proceedings International Seminar, March 23–25, 1966 (Ontario Institute for Studies in Education, 1967), pp. 1–32; 'Education and the educated man', op. cit. (1970), pp. 5–20; P. H. Hirst and R. S. Peters, op. cit. (1970), Chapter 2.

For discussions of Peters' account of education see – R. D. Archambault, 'Manner in education', *Proceedings of the Philosophy of Education Society of the U.S.A., 24th Annual Meeting*, 1968, p. 22–33; J. F. Soltis, op. cit. (1968), Chapter 1; J. F. Soltis, 'On defining education: an apology', *Proceedings of the Philosophy of Education Society of the U.S.A.*, 25th Annual Meeting, 1969, pp. 172–6; A. Thompson, 'Definition and policy; R. S. Peters on "education",' A. E. Martin, 'Perspectives on Peters', R. S. Peters, 'Reply to Arnold Thompson and E. A. Martin', all in *Education for Teaching*, No. 81 (Spring 1970), pp. 12–29; F. Dunlop, op. cit. (1970), pp. 21–44; K. Robinson, 'Education as initiation', *Educational Philosophy and Theory*, Vol. 2, No. 2 (1970), pp. 33–46; G. Reddiford, op. cit. (1972), pp. 193–215; K. Robinson, 'The task-achievement analysis of education', *Educational Philosophy and Theory*, Vol. 4, No. 2 (1972), pp. 17–24; F. Murphy, 'The paradox of freedom in R. S. Peters' analysis of education as initiation', *British Journal of Educational Studies*, Vol. XXI, No. 1 (1973), pp. 5–33; J. Earwaker, 'R. S. Peters and the concept of education', *Proceedings of the Philosophy of Education Society of Great Britain*, Vol. VII, No. 2 (July 1973), pp. 239–59. A number of interesting issues are raised in this paper, which was published too late for us to take into account.

[68] There seem roughly to be three uses of 'education' to be distinguished in Peters' work:-an appraisive use linked with the notion of worthwhile; an external descriptive use dependent upon the previous use; and an undifferentiated use.

[69] See for example Peters' comments on the Spartan education example in 'Education and the educated man', op. cit. (1970), p. 7. See also Dunlop, op. cit. (1970), p. 32 and Reddiford, op. cit. (1972), p. 210.

[70] Dunlop, op. cit. (1970), p. 21.

[71] Reddiford, op. cit. (1972), p. 208.

Further, Reddiford's comments on conceptual changes, on there being a number of concepts of education, and on the relation of both of these to social purposes[72] has strong points of similarity to things Ziff says about 'work of art'. Ziff notes that what will be considered a reasonable use of this phrase will depend both 'on the characteristic social consequences and implications of something's being considered a work of art, but also the purposes to be accomplished by means of these consequences – i.e. the various functions of a work of art in society.'[73] Neither of these is likely to remain unchanged over time. This similarity, together with the fact that Ziff's account of work of art is compatible with it being an essentially contested concept,[74] provides a further reason for thinking that education might be one.

It might be argued that, even as it stands, Peters' account is not incompatible with education being an essentially contested concept. Gallie suggests that in the case of democracy there might be 'a single general use made up, essentially, of a number of mutually contesting and contested uses of it.'[75] In the case of education, Peters' account might be held to identify one such general use which, in its turn, is made up of a number of contesting and contested uses, which themselves may embody, to some degree or other, reasonably specific educational programmes. The contestedness may arise from groups differing both as to what is valuable or worth-while, and as to the internal order of importance of whatever is so identified.[76] Peters' account of a general use will now mark out the area within which constitutive contesting concepts are to fall, if they are to be concepts of education, as opposed to concepts of something else. This compatibility, however, does not make Peters' account less vulnerable to the sorts of consideration that Reddiford's article gives rise to. It is still possible to argue that linking education either entirely or even in part to what is worth-while is simply to mark out one possible use, general or otherwise.

But it might also be argued that because Peters' writings on education

---

[72] Ibid., particularly Section VI.

[73] Ziff, op. cit., p. 73.

[74] Gallie, op. cit. (1964), pp. 170–8.

[75] Ibid., p. 180.

[76] Cf. R. S. Peters, 'Education and the educated man', op. cit. (1970), p. 5, where it is stated that '"valuable" would have to be interpreted in terms of the valuations of the person, or group of people, using the word'; P. H. Hirst and R. S. Peters, op. cit. (1970), p. 27, where it is stated that 'Content would be given to the general form of "an educated man" provided by the analysis in terms of desirability and knowledge conditions. Arguments, of course, would have to be produced for emphasising some desirable qualities rather than others'; and R. S. Peters, op. cit. (Ontario, 1967), p. 8, where Peters states that since 'multiple criteria' are involved in being educated, 'emphasis will be given at different periods to different aspects of what it means to be educated. Such emphases emerge as "aims of education"'.

offer an account of education, a substantive account of what things are worth-while,[77] and of some order of priority among them, he thus can be said to be defending one essentially contested use of 'education' and of 'educated' against others. What he defends (and Hirst too), if only on a very general level, seems to be a conception of education in which theoretical activities are given greater weight than practical ones.

This emphasis on theoretical activities and, in consequence, on what is often described as the academic side of schooling, has given rise from time to time[78] to the charge that Peters' account of education is a conservative one. If it is conservative (and 'conservative' is not a notably unambiguous word), one reason might be that the kind of analysis that Peters uses on 'education' tends to preclude adequate reference to concrete social and historical contexts in which debates about educational programmes occur. As a consequence, the existing use(s) of one social group at one particular time tends to be identified as *the* use, or as the proper or correct use. It might not be coincidental that Peters, who is a university teacher, offers an account of education related to one traditional and, it might be said, conservative (as opposed to radical) view of a university–that of a university whose central purpose is the pursuit of truth. Its specifically educational purpose is to introduce students to this activity at a relatively advanced level. If educational institutions are seen as hierarchically related, and this university conception of education is seen as paradigmatic, then it will be held to set orientations, with some contingent restrictions, for other institutions, in so far as they are held to be educational. What the lack of historical and social considerations in the analysis might do, is to sanction one or other existing orientation, and so give rise to the sort of conceptual and moral parochialism to which MacIntyre, for one, has drawn attention, when he suggests that philosophy which fails to give sufficient attention 'to the historical and social sources' of concepts (as he holds some contemporary academic philosophy has done) may 'appear to guarantee one way of looking at the world by seeming to demonstrate its necessity; and this is the key role of inadequate philosophy in underpinning ideology.'[79]

But even if it is admitted that Peters' view is conservative or, as Powell

---

[77] R. S. Peters, op. cit. (1966), Chapter V. Part of the difficulty in gaining a clear understanding of Peters' account of education is that Chapter I of *Ethics and Education* appears to offer a piece of descriptive analysis (of education) and Chapter V seems to turn this into a programmatic account.

[78] See J. P. Powell, 'On justifying a broad curriculum', *Educational Philosophy and Theory*, Vol. 2, No. 1 (March 1970), p. 57.

[79] A. MacIntyre, op. cit. (1971), p. ix. See also Gallie, op. cit. (1955–6), pp. 197–8. Peters offers some etymological and historical considerations in support of his analysis. See, for example, R. S. Peters, op. cit. (1970), p. 11 onwards. But compared with what is required, they might be said to be meagre.

suggests,[80] that it 'amounts to a vindication of the *status quo* as far as the curriculum is concerned,' or even that it is progressive (to use what here seems to be the relevant antonym) and vindicates current changes nothing is thereby proved about its worth. This depends on the force of the arguments that can be brought in support of and against it. Further, even if it is true, as Gallie suggests of essentially contested concepts,[81] that we may need to call upon psychological, sociological, and historical factors to explain a person's 'present preferences and adherences . . . to admit this is not to deny the existence, or at least the possibility, of logically appraisable factors in an individual's use, or change of use, of a particular contested concept.'

5. The concept of education and aims of education

Our discussion of education might provoke the comment that we have not been concerned with the concept of education itself but with the nature of statements of educational aims, in that contested uses of the concept are likely to reflect substantive differences about educational programmes, whereas any analysis of 'education' should be content-free.[82] Such a comment might be true without being an adverse criticism of our discussion, and we offer one or two considerations in support of this.

Firstly, we have already suggested that questions about what education is are not, in their typical contexts, philosophers' questions, where this implies that all that is required is a piece of descriptive analysis.[83] In discussions about the nature of education, the concept will frequently be defined and used programmatically, and the adequacy of the definitions and uses will be defended not merely by what people say, but also by substantive normative arguments about what should go on in schools, colleges, and universities. Such substantive debates provide much of the data by which the adequacy of formal definitions of 'education' are to be tested, just as substantive debates about whether this or that is a work of art provide much of the data against which any formal definition of 'work of art' is to be tested. The adequacy of formal definitions is tested by their ability to cope with the substantive uses rather than the formal definitions laying down, almost a priori, the limits within which substantive uses of 'education' are to be considered correct and permissible, and so within which substantive debates are to be considered debates about

[80] Powell, op. cit. (1970), p. 57.

[81] Gallie, op. cit., 1964, pp. 186–7. See also p. 185.

[82] See for example, R. S. Peters, *Ethics and Education* (Allen & Unwin, 1966), p. 27 and R. S. Peters, op. cit. (Ontario, 1967), p. 25.

[83] See pp. 76–8.

education.[84] If it is argued that one of the aims of education is purely utilitarian (for example, to fit people for certain sorts of job), it need not and may not be a decisive objection to say that such an aim is not an aim of education because it is logically impossible for an aim to be both purely utilitarian and educational.[85] The force of the objection depends particularly upon whether it can be shown that such a use of 'education' cannot be referred back to the common exemplar. If it cannot, it is no longer a question of the utilitarian use being an essentially contested use of 'education', but of it being a different concept altogether, even though it shares the same name[86]. If it can be referred back, then the formal definition, which does not encompass it, is deficient.

Secondly, to offer a non-substantive account of education is to offer an account whose bearing on practice will be hard to see. This in our view is a defect in an account of education, just as it might be in accounts of scientific method or of social justice. Black argues, in the case of scientific method, that 'a useful definition will be a controversial one, determined by a choice made, more or less wisely, in the hope of codifying and influencing scientific procedures.'[87] And though scientific method and science do not seem to be essentially contested concepts, the point about practice is relevant to education.[88] Barry makes a somewhat similar point

---

[84] For the sort of a priorism in question, see B. Williams' review ('Philosophy and imagination' of *Education and the Development of Reason*, ed. R. F. Dearden, P. H. Hirst, and R. S. Peters (Routledge & Kegan Paul, 1972), in *The Times Educational Supplement*, 28 March 1972, p. 19. Williams says of Black's contribution, 'Reasonableness', that 'the writer already knows what concept he is dealing with – he is not in fact recovering it from these data.' Something similar may underlie W. H. Dray's question as to whether Peters might be really fabricating 'a concept of education out of his vision of what people ought to become.' See 'Philosophy and education', *Proceedings of the International Seminar, March 23–25, 1966* (Ontario Institute of Education, 1967), p. 24. Peters' reply is on page 28.

[85] Cf. R. S. Peters, op. cit. (1966), pp. 24–30.

[86] For the role of the exemplar in distinguishing these two cases see Gallie, op. cit. (1955–6), pp. 174–80 and Gallie, op. cit. (1964), pp. 163–8. For points of general relevance here see G. Reddiford, op. cit. (1972), particularly Section VI. It might be argued that because of the variety of uses of 'education', contested or otherwise, and because of a consequent lack of clarity, the word should no longer be used in discussions about policy for schools, etc., but that discussions should be conducted simply in terms of what ought and ought not to be done. Cf. Gallie, op. cit. (1964), p. 167. Dunlop's remarks (Dunlop, op. cit. (1970), p. 42) might be held to suggest such a view. A similar case might be made out for 'indoctrination'. Brian Barry, 'Social justice', *Oxford Review*, No. 5, (Trinity, 1967), p. 29, notes a related view about 'justice'. See also the comments on the word 'need' in B. P. Komisar, 'Should we meet the needs of the students?', in H. W. Burns and C. J. Brauner, eds, *Philosophy of Education: Essay and Commentaries* (New York: Ronald Press, 1962), p. 36.

[87] Black, op. cit. (1949), p. 94. See also pp. 70–1 and pp. 82–3. He notes on page 82 that it is difficult to decide what a proper level of abstraction would be. For a similar dilemma see Gallie, op. cit. (1956), p. 98.

[88] Gallie, op. cit. (1964), p. 190. Social justice on the other hand does seem to be (ibid., pp. 181–2).

in his discussion of social justice. He says, 'The uselessness of most verbal formulae, as guides to the application of "justice" in actual situations, is so manifest that I shall not labour the point. "To each his own" – a popular classical tag – obviously gets us back to square one pretty quickly, and a popular recent formula, that justice requires "relevant differences" to be taken into account hardly manages to get off square one at all.' He goes on to say that he thinks that there is 'one formula which breaks out of the circle and thus carries the promise of at least providing workable prescriptions in concrete situations.'[89] It is an account of this sort which he sets out to defend.

What these two points amount to is, firstly that substantive uses of 'education' have a logical priority over formal, non-substantive definitions, in the sense that the former provide the data which alone make attempts at adequate formal definitions possible; and secondly, that formal, non-substantive accounts of education are likely to be irrelevant to practice, and this is a defect of them. We argue from this that, for philosophers and for others who discuss the nature of education, talk about education must start at the level of aims, that is of substantive programmes, and not at the level of formal definitions.[90]

Against the charge that we ourselves have not provided an account of education that has practical bearing we make the following brief comment. Practical consequences should ensue from the recognition of education as an essentially contested concept, and we have indicated some of them earlier in the discussion. And though the identification of education as an essentially contested concept is more an issue in what might be called 'the methodology of definition' than a matter of criticizing or advocating uses of 'education' which embody normative views about practice and policy, questions about the way that such terms as 'education' might be defined have important implications for the way that the enterprises denoted by them are to be understood.

Practical reasoning

This discussion of practical reasoning is in three parts. In the first, we discuss the relationship between theoretical and practical judgements; in the second, we discuss disagreement about solutions to practical problems; and in the third, we discuss the bearing of the limitations of our knowledge on solutions to practical problems.

1. Practical reasoning and ethical naturalism

It can be seen from the readings of Gauthier and Hampshire that the

---

[89] B. Barry, 'Social justice', *The Oxford Review*, No. 5 (Trinity, 1967), p. 29.
[90] Though see G. Langford, *Philosphy and Education* (Macmillan, 1968), pp. 70–1.

point of practical reasoning is to come to some justifiable conclusion about what the best thing is to do. Hence it involves evaluation. It also involves theoretical reasoning, since anyone faced with a practical problem needs to ascertain, as far as possible, the relevant facts of the situation in which he has to act and, in particular, to discover the consequences of adopting each of the alternatives open to him.[91] He will need to evaluate the alternatives in the light of what he takes the facts to be, to identify features of the alternatives which constitute reasons for or against their adoption. And since each of the alternatives is likely to have reasons both for and against it, he will have to determine the comparative strength of these.[92]

Hampshire has argued that theoretical problems, and practical problems of a moral sort, are of two irreducibly different kinds. A consequence of this view is that to settle all the empirical issues about alternative courses of action is not to settle ipso facto the practical or evaluative issue about which alternative to adopt. It is, on this view, one thing to settle the empirical and other theoretical issues about, for example, streaming, comprehensive schools, and discovery methods, and another to justify practical moral judgements about them.

Underlying this distinction between theoretical and practical (moral) issues is what is usually described as an anti-naturalist thesis that value judgements (and in this context, specifically, a sub-class of them, namely practical moral judgements) are not deducible from premisess which do not contain at least one value judgement – that is to say, from premisess which consist entirely of theoretical statements.[93] This thesis in its un-

---

[91] Cf. S. Körner, 'On the concept of the practicable', *Proceedings of the Aristotelian Society*, Vol. LXVII (1966–67), p. 3, who writes, 'Empirical beliefs and methods of reasoning are part of practical thinking.' It should be noted that our discussion of practical reasoning is as it relates to moral rather than to what Hampshire calls 'technical' problems.

[92] Cf. J. Wheatley, 'Reasons for acting', *Dialogue: Canadian Philosophical Review*, Vol. VII (1969), p. 557, who writes, 'Life being as complicated as it is, there are usually for any contemplated action, reasons for not doing it (or doing something incompatible with it) as well as reasons for doing it.' Our discussion of practical reasoning can usefully be read in conjunction with K. Baier, 'The Moral Point of View', Random House, New York, Abridged Edition, 1967, Chapters 1 and 2.

[93] There is another version of the anti-naturalist thesis – namely that value terms are not *definable* by non-value ones. See for example R. F. Dearden, *The Philosophy of Primary Education* (Routledge & Kegan Paul, 1968), pp. 154–5, and P. W. Taylor, *Normative Discourse* (New Jersey: Prentice Hall, 1961), Chapter 9. The two versions are stated by Taylor, op. cit., p. 246, to be logically connected. A. N. Prior, *Logic and the Basis of Ethics* (Oxford University Press, 1949), p. 95, takes the definitional version to be a special case of the entailment version. A person may be said to be a naturalist, in this context, when he holds that such definitions and entailments are possible. For introductory discussions of naturalism see A. C. Ewing, *Ethics* (English Universities Press, 1953), Chapter VI; J. Hospers, *Human Conduct* (New York: Harcourt, Brace & World, 1961), pp. 542–56; J. Hospers, *An Introduction to Philosophical Analysis*, 2nd edn. (Routledge & Kegan Paul, 1967), pp. 568–72; R. F. Atkinson, *Conduct: An Introduction to Moral Philosophy* (Macmillan, 1969), pp. 57–64. For more advanced discussions, see

restricted[94] form has had a fairly wide use, not least in educational philosophy, and we wish here to raise briefly two issues about it: (*i*) how is its truth to be established? (*ii*) if it is true, what does it imply?

(*i*) R. Wollheim notes that the thesis can be defended in two ways – by a posteriori considerations, and by a priori ones.[95] The a posteriori way is to show, case by case, that for every attempt to produce an argument which purports to show that a value judgement is deducible from non-value premisess, it is possible with consistency to assent to the premisess and deny the conclusion. The weakness of this method is that it does not show that such entailments are in principle impossible. It might merely be the case that the right premisess have not been found.[96] And it is important to notice that if the thesis is defended by G. E. Moore's 'open question'[97] argument or one of its variants, then the defence is by means of a posteriori, and not a priori considerations.

The a priori way of defending the anti-naturalist thesis is to produce a general account of the nature of value judgements, and to show that this logically precludes them from being the validly drawn conclusions of arguments whose premisess contain no such judgements.[98] Such an attempt is made by R. M. Hare.[99] But whether Hare's attempt is successful is not clear. R. S. Downie and E. Telfer argue that it is not.[100] J. R. Searle brings a number of counter examples against the unrestricted thesis which he describes as a 'dogma',[101] and in a related discussion produces considera-

---

(*Ftn. 93 cont.*)
G. Warnock, *Contemporary Moral Philosophy* (Macmillan, 1967), Chapter 6; W. D. Hudson, ed., *The Is/Ought Question* (Macmillan, 1969); W. D. Hudson, *Modern Moral Philosophy* (Macmillan, 1970); R. L. Franklin, 'Recent work on ethical naturalism', *American Philosophical Quarterly*, Monograph Series No. 7, *Studies in Ethics*, N. Rescher, ed. (Oxford: Blackwell, 1973), pp. 55–95.

[94] By 'unrestricted' here we mean that the thesis applies to all value judgements, moral and non-moral.

[95] R. Wollheim, 'Philosophie analytique et pensée politique', *Revue Française de Science Politique*, No. 2 (1961), pp. 299–301.

[96] Ibid., p. 300.

[97] G. E. Moore, *Principia Ethica* (Cambridge University Press, 1903), Chapter I, Section 13. See also J. Hospers, op. cit. (1961), pp. 534–5; R. S. Downie and E. Telfer, *Respect for Persons* (Allen & Unwin, 1969), p. 136; G. C. Kerner, *The Revolution in Ethical Theory* (Oxford University Press, 1966), pp. 16–21.

[98] R. Wollheim, op. cit. (1961), p. 301.

[99] See, for example, R. M. Hare, *The Language of Morals* (Oxford University Press, 1952).

[100] R. S. Downie and E. Telfer, op. cit. (1969), pp. 136–7. See also pp. 137–8, for an argument against what appears to be Hampshire's view of the non-redundancy of practical judgements.

[101] J. R. Searle, *Speech Acts* (Cambridge University Press, 1969), p. 135.

tions to suggest that a characterization of value judgement such as Hare gives in *The Language of Morals* is incorrect anyway.[102]

What all this seems to suggest is that the unrestricted thesis is less than securely established. Wollheim would seem to agree with this. He suggests that neither a priori nor a posteriori attempts to defend it have been entirely convincing.[103]

The thesis might however be defended in a restricted form, as applying only to moral judgements. Searle's counter examples, if they were accepted, would appear to hold against the restricted thesis, only in so far as its truth depends on the truth of the unrestricted one.[104] But since the truth of the former is usually made to depend upon that of the latter, it seems that if the restricted thesis is to be shown to be true, its truth needs independently establishing. It is doubtful whether this has been done and, in consequence, whether the restricted ethical thesis is securely established. Atkinson, for example, who is inclined to think that 'ethical naturalism is *in principle* unacceptable' says that he does not know how its unacceptability could be 'conclusively established'.[105] It must be said that attempts to demonstrate that empirical or metaphysical statements, about what society approves of or about what God commands, for example, entail or define moral judgements seem to fail;[106] and even a more general and plausible candidate seems to run into difficulties[107] and, in any case, does not facilitate greatly the justification of value judgements, which is often taken to be one of the motives behind naturalism. As a consequence the validity of any proposed naturalistic entailments or definitions, in education and elsewhere, between, say, empirical (theoretical) statements of psychology, sociology, or common sense, and practical moral judgements certainly cannot be simply assumed, but rather will need to be demonstrated, if it can.[108]

[102] J. R. Searle, op. cit. (1969), Chapter 6, in particular Sections 1, 2 and 4, and Chapter 8. There are discussions of Searle in W. D. Hudson, ed., op. cit. (1969), and W. D. Hudson, op. cit. (1970).

[103] R. Wollheim, op. cit. (1961), p. 301.

[104] Cf. J. Searle, op. cit. (1969), pp. 187–8. Searle uses the terms 'general' and 'special' for our 'unrestricted' and 'restricted' respectively.

[105] R. F. Atkinson, op. cit. (1969), p. 63. He also says that it is 'a good deal more certain that all naturalistic views produced so far are defective'.

[106] J. Hospers, op. cit. (1967), pp. 568–70.

[107] R. S. Downie and E. Telfer, op. cit. (1969), pp. 138–43.

[108] The anti-naturalist thesis, in one or other of its versions, has been widely used by philosophers of education, though with more confidence (it might be said with hindsight) than is perhaps immediately warranted. See, for example, E. Best, op. cit. (1964), p. 163, P. H. Hirst, op. cit. (1965), p. 8, C. D. Hardie, 'Religion and education', *Educational Theory*, Vol. 18 (1968), pp. 213–14, R. F. Dearden, op. cit. (1968), p. 20, J. White, op. cit. (1971), p. 103. These writers all discuss what might be taken to be intended entailments (or

(*ii*) But even if the anti-naturalist thesis is true, perhaps only in a restricted version, what follows from it?

The first thing to say is that a lot has been taken to follow from it. Edel[109] records his 'amazement at the proportions to which a limited logical proposition[110] has been blown up, and the weight of theory it has been made to bear.' The thesis seems to be one of those underlying the ethical theories of Ayer, Stevenson, Ross, and Hare, for example, which, different as they are, all seem to find it difficult to meet the charge that they leave less room than is required for rationality in moral discourse. This difficulty may arise from the fact that, as Warnock notes, 'the temptation has not always been resisted to dramatise the anti-naturalist thesis, as it were, by turning it round' – that is, to argue (fallaciously) from the thesis that 'no one is ever logically obliged to accept any given feature as a criterion of merit', that 'absolutely anything *might* be regarded as a criterion of merit.' [111].

The second thing to say is that even if a proposed naturalistic entailment (or definition) is shown to fail, whether by an appeal to the thesis or by an appeal to Moore's argument or a variant of it, it follows neither that the evaluative conclusion is false nor that the premises (or the definiens) as they were taken to be, fail to constitute adequate grounds for the truth of the conclusion.[112] For, as Hampshire's and Melden's comments quoted below suggest, it might be the case that a number of statements, none of which is a value judgement, fully justify a statement about what ought to be done, without entailing it. To show, therefore, that a practical (moral) judgement is not entailed, say, by a number of empirical statements, may be to show neither that the judgement is false nor that it is ill-founded. Hampshire makes this point when he argues that not all rational arguments need be deductive, and that it is fallacious to infer 'from the fact that moral or practical judgements cannot be logically derived from statements of fact that they cannot be based on, or established exclusively by reference to, beliefs about matters of fact.' [113] A. I. Melden[114] holds a

---

(*Ftn. 108 cont.*)
definitions) between factual and value statements and cite the thesis as the reason for the failure of the entailments. But the failure in each case would appear to be more readily established than the truth of the thesis and, if this is so, it would be better to argue from the failure of the entailments to the truth of the thesis than from the truth of the thesis to the failure of the entailments.

[109] A. Edel, *Ethical Judgement: the Use of Science in Ethics* (Glencoe: Free Press, 1955), p. 75.

[110] i.e. the proposition expressed by the anti-naturalist thesis.

[111] G. Warnock, op. cit. (1967), p. 66.

[112] A. Edel, op. cit. (1955), p. 76, who writes 'no ethical view is crushed by hurling the logical maxim as a thunderbolt'.

[113] See p. .

[114] A. I. Melden, 'Reasons for action and matters of fact', *Proceedings and Addresses of the American Philosophical Association*, *Vol. XXXV* (1961–2), p. 58. See also K. Baier,

view similar to Hampshire's. He writes, 'Surely, then, it is false that an *ought* cannot be derived from an *is* – an evaluation from any statement of fact. Here one need only take seriously the notion of a reason for acting. For a reason for acting is a consideration that provides some warrant for the conclusion that an action should be performed. If good and sufficient, it is a consideration from which it *follows* that the action should be performed. But something is a reason for acting precisely because and just to the extent that it refers us to a relevant matter of fact. Accordingly, matters of fact can be good and sufficient justifying considerations. That is to say, matters of fact as *such* can and do fully establish matters of evaluation. It follows that if there are reasons for action, moral or otherwise, an *ought* most certainly is derivable from an *is*. The question is not whether, but how, and from what facts, matters of morality do follow.' Like Hampshire, he does not believe that he is thereby committed to ethical naturalism.[115]

In the light of this, the anti-naturalist thesis, even if it were known for certain to be true in its unrestricted form, would appear to be a weapon of limited philosophical power, and to grant the truth of the thesis in its restricted form only is not thereby to grant that moral judgements cannot be rationally grounded. Nevertheless, questions about what particular considerations are relevant to what sort of evaluative judgements, moral or otherwise, and about justifiable modes of argument in evaluative matters, are still outstanding. Their investigation might reasonably be held to be a philosophical task,[116] and one which is likely to involve philosophers in evaluative issues in that to justify criteria of relevance and modes of argument is to defend an account of what is rational in the area of discourse under discussion. And this is 'to undertake a normative commitment'.[117]

(Ftn. 114 cont.)
The Moral Point of View (New York: Random House, 1967), Chapter I. Compare the general tenor of Hampshire's and Melden's views with that of J. White's, op. cit. (1971), p. 103, who writes 'But how can empirical research alone determine what should be taught? No empirical fact can alone justify a conclusion that something is right or ought to be done (in this case, that the objectives of curriculum x are educationally all right). For how do you pass from an empirical statement, about something which is the case (and contains no value-term) to a statement which *does* contain a "right" or an "ought"? There is just no argument here: it simply cannot be done.' For a relevant discussion see Nelson Pike, 'Rules of inference in moral reasoning', *Mind*, Vol. LXX (1961), pp. 391–9; and A. Sloman, 'Rules of inference or suppressed premisses?', *Mind*, Vol. LXIII (1964), pp. 84–96.

[115] A. I. Melden, op. cit. (1961–2), p. 60.
[116] Ibid. See also Hampshire's article.
[117] A. G. N. Flew, *Hume's Philosophy of Belief* (Routledge & Kegan Paul, 1961), pp. 89–92 and also p. 82. Flew is discussing the standards of inductive argument but the point is applicable to moral argument too. Cf. C. K. Grant, 'Belief and action', Inaugural Lecture, University of Durham (1960), p. 3, who writes 'In philosophy we must consider,

2. Practical reasoning and moral disputes

One reason for attempts to reduce moral (and other value judgements) to other sorts of judgement is that unless this can be done, the apparently widespread and intractable disagreements about what are justifiable solutions to practical (moral) problems seem unlikely to be settled. Unless, it seems to be argued, moral judgements can be seen to be reducible to a class or classes of judgement (for example, to empirical ones), the truth or falsity of which can be determined by recognized procedures (at least in principle, whatever the difficulties in practice), there is no way of deciding between incompatible moral judgements, and moral problems become insoluble. Our previous discussion suggests that whatever the truth about the impossibility of naturalistic reductions, no such reduction of moral judgements seems to have been successfully made. What we wish to raise here are a number of points about moral disagreement, in the light both of these remarks and those of Hampshire and Melden.

The first thing to say is that the mere existence of disagreements about moral issues no more entails that they are insoluble in principle than do disagreements about empirical issues.[118] It may be that a particular moral judgement can be and has been conclusively established and that one party to the dispute, perhaps because of intellectual or psychological factors, is unable or unwilling to understand or to be moved by considerations that show the judgement to be justified.[119] This sort of dispute, of course, may not be settled in practice, in that, as a matter of empirical fact, nothing can be done to make the individuals see the relevance of the considerations.[120] Such a situation is important for anyone who has to

---

(Ftn. 117 cont.)

not only the ways in which we do in fact reason, but also the ways in which we are *justified* in reasoning. This is part of what is meant by saying that philosophy is a normative enquiry, and which marks it off from another subject that even today is often confused with it, namely psychology.' For the relevance of this point to social science see, A. C. MacIntyre, *Against the Self Images of the Age* (Duckworth, 1971), Chapter 21, called 'Rationality and the explanation of action'. For further relevant discussion see Volume II, pp. 39–55 and pp. 147–51.

[118] A moral issue may be said to be insoluble in principle when it cannot be shown that just one of a number of incompatible answers to it is justified. See the examples on pp. 101–2.

[119] Cf. G. Warnock, op. cit. (1967), p. 72, who writes, 'That moral argument is not more effective than we find it to be is probably attributable to the cross that all arguments have to bear: an argument offers reasons to people, and people are not always reasonable.'

[120] There is an ambiguity about 'settle' worth noting. An issue may said to be settled simply when the parties agree. In this sense, nothing is entailed about the adequacy of the conclusion they have agreed upon. Parties may agree upon a solution that is mistaken. This shows the limitations of appeals to consensus. In a second sense of 'settle', an issue may be said to be settled when grounds are produced which show that one answer is the correct one and another not. Even, so, the parties may not agree and the issue not be settled in the first sense. In a third sense, settle may take in both of the first two senses

decide what to do, where the implementation of the decision depends to any extent on the individuals' consent. For it might be better to adopt a course of action that can be justified and made acceptable to them rather than one which, though better in the abstract, cannot.

Secondly, moral problems might be insoluble in practice (though not in principle) because their solution depends upon prior answers to certain empirical problems, about which there might be legitimate differences of opinion, given the state of knowledge at the time. Any empirical discipline will provide examples, wherever disagreements about solutions fall within the area of professional competence. There might be legitimate differences of opinion among social scientists, for example, about the general import of a number of studies carried out on various forms of school organization. With time, resources, and research the ambiguity of the import might diminish, and with it some of the disagreement, but the decision about what to do may need to be taken forthwith.

Thirdly, individuals may use different criteria of evaluation, or use the same ones but give them different weight, and there may be no way of showing that one set of criteria or one weighting is to be preferred. In this case, some moral issues may be insoluble in principle. Parties might disagree, and there be no way of showing that one of them is wrong or mistaken. The existence of such competing sets of criteria and weightings would appear to be entailed by, though not to entail, the existence of essentially contested concepts, and debates about general programmes for education concerning, for example, the relative importance of imparting theoretical skills as opposed to practical ones or to qualities of character might be in principle insoluble.[121]

The issues about criteria of evaluation are some of the most fundamental and controversial of moral philosophy[122] and all we can do here is to note them and give some tentative support to the possibility of in principle insoluble moral disagreements, by giving possible examples.[123]

(a) One example which we have used before, is that of the reading scheme

---

(Ftn. 120 cont.)
together. There is a fourth sense of 'settle', in which an issue is sometimes said to be settled simply when one party gets his way (that is, his answer *counts*), even though the other party disagrees with it.

[121] See T. F. Daveney, op. cit. (1970), p. 17. For a discussion relevant to points that Daveney makes here see M. Hollis, 'The pen and the purse', *Proceedings of the Philosophy of Education Society of Great Britain*, Supplementary Issue, Volume V, No. 2 (July 1971), pp. 153–69.

[122] For a detailed survey of contemporary moral philosophy see W. D. Hudson, op. cit. (1970). R. W. Beardsmore, *Moral Reasoning* (Routledge & Kegan Paul, 1969) contains clear discussions of moral disagreement and criticisms of the work of R. M. Hare and Mrs P. Foot. These three philosophers hold different views about the nature of moral reasoning and of moral disagreement. See also G. Warnock, op. cit. (1967), and G. Warnock, *The Object of Morality* (Methuen, 1971).

[123] See also Vol. I, Section 2, pp. 186–8.

Imagine that it can be established that it is in children's interests to learn to read as quickly as possible and at the same time to spell as well as possible. Now when scheme A is used children generally learn to read more quickly but misspell more than when scheme B is used. Is scheme A to be preferred to B?

(b) Another example is suggested by a current debate. Imagine that a proposed reorganization could be shown to affect adversely the attainment of one category of children and to affect favourably that of another. Should the reorganization be undertaken?

(c) Imagine that it could be shown that a method of discipline, say corporal punishment, was the most effective deterrent in cases of behaviour known to be wrong (for example, bullying) but that it had perhaps in the long term some adverse psychological effects on its recipients. Should it be used?

(d) Imagine that one consequence of allowing parents to choose which school to send their children to was increased inequality of educational opportunity. Should such a choice be permitted? If so, to what extent? This issue, which is about the relative importance of the principles of equality and liberty, arises not only in debates about the public schools but also about some current schemes of reorganization of the state system.

The four examples (and the one about the relative importance of theoretical and practical skills) all involve determining the strength of competing considerations. Wheatley suggests that there is no general procedure for doing this.[124] Warnock talks of a 'metaphorical weighing' which 'though of course not impossible is not susceptible of great exactness.'[125] Griffiths makes similar points and suggests that 'perhaps in many cases in moral matters *the* right answer is a chimaera. Perhaps in many cases we must be satisfied with *a* right answer.'[126] Even so, given the criteria of evaluation[127] and, in spite of the lack of general procedures for assessing their comparative weight, it might be able to be shown, for example, in (b) that if one group was very badly affected and the other only minimally, then the reorganization should not be undertaken. A similar case might be made out for the other examples. But where there is not this obvious disparity between considerations, it is by no means clear that there is just one justifiable answer to the problem. There might, of

[124] J. Wheatley, op. cit. (1969), p. 562. See also R. W. Beardsmore, op. cit. (1969), Chapter 9.

[125] G. Warnock, op. cit. (1967), p. 69.

[126] A. P. Griffiths, 'Justifying moral principles', *Proceedings of the Aristotelian Society*, Vol. LVIII (1957–8), p. 124. Griffiths also notes that such a view does not justify what he calls 'indifferentism'. He says that 'it is only when all the serious reasoning which can be done, has been done, that any degree of eclecticism is in place'.

[127] Our examples tend, if anything, to underestimate the possibility of insoluble moral disagreement – at least on such an account of moral reasoning as Hare's (as opposed to say Warnock's). The examples are also oversimple and this, too, might tend to minimize the possibility of insoluble moral disagreement.

course, be no dispute. People might share the same criteria and methods of application. The point is that there does not have to be agreement even[128] when people are open to rational considerations.

If these points about criteria and their application are true,[129] it would be misleading, even on such an account as Melden's and Hampshire's of the relationship between 'is' and 'ought', to argue that empirical data could be used in any simple way to settle practical (moral) issues; that practical (moral) disagreements could in principle be settled by producing a requisite amount of empirical data; that practical moral judgements could be directly read off or calculated from such data; that from the work, say, of Piaget or of Bernstein (even if the claims contained in it were securely established) there could be straight-forwardly derived one indisputable set of prescriptions for educational policy and practice. For questions about relevance and weighting arise, to which the data themselves do not supply the answers.[130]

3. Practical reasoning and limited knowledge

A claim that arises from Emmet's discussion of 'bounded rationality' is that practical judgements are made and have to be made where the relevant empirical data about situations and consequences of proposed courses of action are always less than complete.[131] This may be said to be

---

[128]Insoluble issues about criteria make insoluble moral disagreements only possible and do not entail their actual existence.

[129]If the points about criteria are true, then the prospects for naturalism appear poor. For given even a little scope in the range of possible criteria of moral evaluation, the entailment or definition offered will have to be put in such general terms that it will offer little help in justifying practical judgements. Where the definition or entailment embodies a less general criterion or criteria, and so is apparently more useful in justifying practical judgements, it will need to be justified against other definitions and entailments embodying competing criteria. Our discussion about criteria suggests that it is not clear how this can be done. Justifying the definition turns out to be the same in practice as justifying a particular moral viewpoint. See W. F. Frankena, *Ethics* (New Jersey: Prentice Hall, 1963), pp. 83–4.

[130]For some comments about public justification where the application of criteria is complex, see S. Körner, op. cit. (1966–67), pp. 9–10 and S. Körner, *Fundamental Questions in Philosophy* (Penguin Books, 1971), pp. 121–2.

[131]Cf. H. J. Paton, 'Can reason be practical?', in H. J. Paton, *In Defence of Reason* (Hutchinson, 1951). He writes on page 122, 'The world as known to the agent is known to be full of undiscovered possibilities and so to be imperfectly known; but the agent must act on what he knows (including knowledge that his knowledge is limited).' It might be plausibly argued, as a consequence of the discussion in the present section, that this last piece of knowledge is or at least ought to be the most important for any agent who has to act on limited knowledge. Paton says a little later (p. 123) that 'We have to act here and now, and even what we call inaction is a kind of action. Hence we have always to act on imperfect, and sometimes on very imperfect knowledge. It is not always intelligent

true of almost all practical problems in education. It will be true of a teacher who has a practical teaching or disciplinary problem, of a head of department trying to decide whether to change the old maths for the new, of an education committee trying to decide what sort of comprehensive scheme to adopt, of secretaries of state trying to make decisions about the 11 plus, educational priority areas or nursery schools. The situations in which such judgements are made are rarely, if ever, fully understood. Empirical beliefs about outcomes are unlikely to be well founded and in some cases may be no more than guesses.[132]

It would be over-sceptical to claim that in every such case practical judgements have to be made in absolute ignorance. Some knowledge and beliefs, ranging from the reasonably sure to the very tentative, may come from our experience in schools and elsewhere. The value of these need not be denied.[133] Other knowledge and beliefs may come from the more specialized investigations of psychology or sociology.[134] But given the variety of institutional and personal factors in education, the extent to which we can confidently generalize, even from these disciplines and our experience taken together, is not likely to be large.[135]

The question we now raise is 'What bearing do the limitations of our knowledge have on the solution of practical problems?'

The first thing to say is that in so far as it is justifiable to act on limited knowledge, then the distinction between (*a*) the ideal or the objectively

(Ftn. 131 cont.)
to refrain from outward action till we have gathered all possible relevant knowledge, if this means the opportunity for relevant action will have gone for ever. It is unintelligent to let our will be paralysed and left at the mercy of circumstances while we seek for knowledge. It is equally unintelligent to let our will be blind when there is relevant knowledge to be had for the asking.' See also the following remark of A. G. N. Flew in his *God and Philosophy* (Hutchinson, 1966). He writes on page 184 that 'The realistic and the courageous moral to draw from the fact that we have constantly to act without that basis for certainty which we should like to have is: not that we must delude ourselves into believing that our condition is other, and better, than it is; but that, having once recognised that the facts are what they are, we ought to learn to live with them with our eyes wide open.' This is the import of our discussion in this section.

[132] See Vol. I, Section 2, pp. 192–5.

[133] Cf. K. R. Popper, *The Poverty of Historicism*, paperback edn. (Routledge & Kegan Paul, 1961) pp. 85–6.

[134] It is important to notice that different studies on the same topic may present incompatible conclusions. To establish the import of competing studies may be a sophisticated task. See Vol. II pp. 157–64. What we imply here about the lack of empirical knowledge in education requires support from the disciplines in question. The amount of empirical information available may vary from area to area. Some teaching methods may have been comparatively well investigated compared with others, or with certain methods of school organization. It would be rash in our view to say that the amount or reliability of empirical information in education is anything like that in medicine or agriculture.

[135] See Vol. I, Section 2, pp. 196–7.

right solution to a practical problem and (*b*) what, given the circumstances, it was reasonable to hold was the best thing to do, must be insisted upon.[136] To justify a solution where knowledge is limited, it will be enough to show that it was the one supported most strongly by the information the agent could reasonably be expected to have had at the time.[137] It follows that incomplete knowledge of outcomes or of other relevant empirical factors does not *entail* uncertainty about what to do, though it does entail uncertainty about ideal or objectively right solutions.[138] For in some cases the available empirical data, even though incomplete, might, nevertheless, clearly support the adoption of just one of the alternatives under consideration.[139] Moreover, anyone who adopts a solution on the basis of incomplete knowledge is not open to censure even if what is done turns out to be disastrous, provided that he can show that the decision was taken with reasonable care, on the information available.[140] In a similar way, a decision, made at random or carelessly, may turn out to be almost ideal, and yet not be one for which credit can be claimed or given.

Secondly, the limitations of our knowledge not only make it impossible to identify in advance (if at all) objectively right solutions to practical problems but also affect the extent of the changes which, offered as solutions, can be justified in the way described in (*b*) above. For though almost all proposed changes in education will outrun our predictive power, there are limits to the extent that they can do so, and, at the same time, be

[136] This point can be made in terms of the distinction between the 'subjectively rational' and the 'objectively rational'. The former is what in the circumstances an agent has grounds for thinking is the best thing to do, the latter is what in *fact* is the best thing to do. Thus, J. Rawls, op. cit. (1972), p. 422, writes that 'a rational person may regret his pursuing a subjectively rational plan, but not because he thinks his choice is in any way open to criticism. For he does what seems best at the time, and if his beliefs later prove to be mistaken with untoward results, it is through no fault of his own. There is no cause for self reproach. There was no way of knowing which was the best or even a better plan.' For a similar distinction see J. Hospers, *Human Conduct* (New York, Harcourt, Brace & World, 1961), pp. 216–20.

[137] It is important to notice that one such solution might, on occasion, take the form of letting things go on as they are (i.e., of doing nothing). For it may be reasonable to conclude that none of the things that can be done will ameliorate the situation.

[138] Cf. M. Scriven, *Value Claims in the Social Sciences*, Publication No. 123 (Social Science Education Consortium, 1966), pp. 27–8. The points made in the paragraph hold true also for a naturalistic account of practical judgements. Even if issues of evaluation were bypassed by a naturalistic account, those about uncertainty are not.

[139] It need not of course always have such a straightforward import. See Gauthier's example (*iv*). It might on occasion be so indeterminate that, even, given agreed criteria of evaluation, it offers very little guidance for choosing between alternatives.

[140] This may well happen. As J. Rawls, op. cit. (1972), p. 422, points out, 'Nothing can protect us from the ambiguities and limitations of our knowledge, or guarantee that we find the best alternative open to us.'

justified. There are at least three reasons why this is so. (*i*) The less reliable that predictions about the outcomes of a change are, the weaker the grounds are likely to be for believing either that it can achieve its goals, or that, even given the feasibility of the goals, it will be better overall than some other change whose outcomes are equally unknown or uncertain, or than no change at all, or than a change (perhaps of lesser scope) whose outcomes can, to some extent, be more reliably predicted.[141] (*ii*) Almost any change will have some adverse consequences. The less they can be predicted, the more difficult it will be to anticipate or minimize the problems they give rise to. (*iii*) In so far as practice can be improved only by learning from past practice, there are reasons against undertaking changes that preclude this. The greater the extent of a change and the more limited our knowledge, the more difficult learning from past practice becomes. For it then becomes harder, and perhaps impossible, to discover what was brought about by what, and so to acquire data that might be used to improve future practice.[142]

It follows that the extent of justifiable change cannot be determined without reference to the limitations of our knowledge, and that there are moral, prudential, and intellectual reasons against undertaking changes which ignore them.

Thirdly, in so far as practical problems have to be met in conditions of limited knowledge, it is unreasonable to expect them to be solved once and for all. They may be met only partially. And even the best of solutions may give rise to further practical problems which in turn may be met only partially, and in turn give rise to further practical problems.[143] As Emmet says, 'The "solution" of one problem may bring others in its train; and

---

[141] On the general point here of R. F. Atkinson, *Sexual Morality* (Hutchinson, 1965), p. 56, who writes, 'Reformatory proposals can only be rationally founded upon, and hence are limited by, our capacity to make social predictions, to say, with reason, what will happen if such and such is done. But all we can make with confidence are rather short term predictions in narrow fields.' For the issue of feasibility see pp. 190–204 and Nagel's comments in Vol II, pp. 20–2. It is important to note that in conditions of bounded rationality any current state of affairs is itself imperfectly known and understood. When, therefore, a proposed change is being evaluated, it is not a matter of comparing something known (the current state of affairs) with something only imperfectly known (the change and its outcomes) but of comparing two things each of which is imperfectly known. Nevertheless, our knowledge of the future can at best be no better than that of the present and is likely to be somewhat worse.

[142] See K. R. Popper, op. cit. (1961), Chapter III, pp. 88–9. The whole of this chapter of Popper is relevant here and is usefully read with C. E. Lindblom 'The science of "mudding through"', reprinted from *Public Administration Review*, Vol. 19 (1959), in *The Making of Decisions*, ed. W. J. Gore and J. W. Dyson (Glencoe: Free Press, 1964), pp. 155–69 and pp. 422–4.

[143] Cf. C. E. Lindblom, op. cit. (1959), on page 166 of the 1964 reprint, who writes that 'policy is not made once and for all; it is made and remade endlessly.'

wisdom may lie in being able to decide which problem to live with at any given time.'[144]

Fourthly, in so far as we are concerned to improve practice, solutions need to be monitored. Attempts need to be made to identify outcomes, intended and unintended, of changes, and causes and effects.[145] This may be done informally on a day-to-day basis and lesson by lesson, or by full-scale research projects lasting a number of years. It may take energy, time, and money, and resources that might have been used on something else. The extent to which it should be done is a practical problem which has to be met by people at all levels of the educational system, from assistant teachers to secretaries of state. Answers to it will depend on, among other things, how satisfactory current practice is held to be, or on what is an acceptable degree of ignorance about outcomes or of risk. There may be a number of justifiable views about these matters.

What this discussion implies is that practical problems in education are rationally met by a 'piecemeal' approach and not by 'Utopian' leaps in the dark, to use Popper's terms.[146] The justifiable scope of any proposed change will vary from problem to problem, depending on the amount of relevant empirical information available. There is no general rule by which the scope can be decided. Each case has to be judged on its merits, and agreement may not be easily achieved where empirical data have apparently contradictory imports, or where there are disputes about the adequacy of current practices, or about justifiable degrees of risk.

Knowing in theory and knowing in practice

We continue here a discussion of an issue raised by Entwistle, namely the relationship between thinking about what to do and how to do it, and actually doing it.[147] We begin by distinguishing knowing in theory

---

[144] See page 52 of this book.

[145] Cf. D. Emmet's comments on pp. 51–62.

[146] K. R. Popper, op. cit. (1961), Chapter 3. The piecemeal approach might be called 'conservative', dyslogistically, by those who hold it implies an over-cautious and irrational adherence to current practices. Three things can be said briefly in reply. (*i*) If there are grounds for holding that the piecemeal approach is the only rational one, where knowledge is limited, then 'conservative' is inappropriate. (*ii*) Since 'conservative' here carries a charge of irrationality, it needs to be *demonstrated* that, in spite of the arguments produced in its support, the piecemeal approach is irrational, and that there is some better method. (*iii*) The piecemeal approach cannot be practised without change. This is a banal logical truth. The approach itself, however, implies nothing about the desirability of current practice or of change. What can be said is that if improved practice is required with least likely cost, then such an approach is the way to set about getting it. Some people may be strongly attached to whatever happens to be current practice and indifferent to its improvement. But this attitude is not entailed by the piecemeal approach.

[147] See pp. 38–50.

and knowing in practice. We then discuss Ryle's account of practical knowledge, some elements of practical knowledge which cannot be expressed in propositions, and finally the role of theory and theorising in imparting, acquiring, and exercising such knowledge.

1. Introduction

By discussing the relationship between theoretical problems, reasoning, and judgements on the one hand, and practical problems, reasoning and judgements on the other, we have indicated one way of drawing a distinction between theory and practice, and of interpreting the claim that there is a gap between them. We now discuss a second way.

It is always possible, as MacIntyre[148] points out, to 'be able to see what to do, but never have the requisite skill to do it.' In such a case we might say that a person knew how to do something in theory but not in practice.[149] We might deny that he had practical knowledge, on the grounds that this is usually attributed only to people who know how to do something in practice – whether or not they know how to do it in theory. This way of making a distinction between theory and practice is reflected in a remark of O'Connor's – 'When in ordinary speech we contrast theory with practice we refer to a set or system of rules or a collection of precepts which guide or control actions of various kinds.'[150] It is possible to know the theory (in this sense) of an activity and not be able to carry out the activity in question (for example, driving a car) and, further, to be able to carry out an activity for which very few, if any, precepts are available. A person, therefore, not only might know in theory and not know in practice how to do things, but also might know in practice and not know in theory (where this last phrase means 'not know the theory'). Knowing in theory, then, is knowing the precepts or being able to give

[148] A. MacIntyre, 'Purpose and intelligent action', *Proceedings of the Aristotelian Society* Supplementary, Vol. XXXIV (1960), p. 82.

[149] Cf. D. W. Hamlyn, *The Theory of Knowledge* (Macmillan, 1971), p. 104 – 'It remains true that a man cannot be said to know how to do something unless he can do it, except in the sense that he knows in theory how to do it although he cannot do it in practice' and G. E. M. Anscombe, *Intention* (New York: Cornell University Press, 1963), p. 88– 'A man has practical knowledge who knows how to do things, but that is an insufficient description, for he *might* be said to know how to do things if he could give a lecture on it, though he was helpless when confronted with the task of doing them.' Miss Anscombe also notes (page 89) that 'although the term "practical knowledge" is most often used in connexion with specialised skills, there is no reason to think that this notion has application only in such contexts.' Practical knowledge, specialized or otherwise, is required for the solutions of practical problems which are solved by doing something. It can be seen to be not the same as the knowledge that so and so is the best thing to do to meet a practical problem.

[150] D. J. O'Connor, *An Introduction to the Philosophy of Education* (Routledge & Kegan Paul, 1957), p. 75.

a verbal account of what requires to be done, and knowing in practice is being able to carry out the activity they prescribe. The sense of 'theorizing' related to 'knowing in theory' is one which includes considering or calling to mind the precepts, or even discovering or establishing them by one form or other of practical reasoning.

2. Ryle's account of practical knowledge

There is a claim that arises from the work of Ryle, particularly, that knowing in practice how to do something, and therefore practical knowledge are independent of theory and theorizing, as just described.[151] Ryle holds that theorizing is neither a necessary nor sufficient condition of intelligent performance, whether in practical or theoretical activities. He sets out to show 'that there are many activities which directly display qualities of mind, yet are neither themselves intellectual operations nor yet the effects of intellectual operations. Intelligent practice is not a step-child of theory. On the contrary theorizing is one practice amongst others and is itself intelligently or stupidly conducted.'[152] He begins by drawing attention to the distinction between 'knowing how' and 'knowing that'.

---

[151]G. Ryle, 'Knowing how and knowing that', *Proceedings of the Aristotelian Society*, Vol. XLVI (1945–6), p. 1–16; G. Ryle, *The Concept of Mind* (Hutchinson, 1949), Chapter 2.

[152]G. Ryle, op. cit. (1949), p. 26. See also p. 30, and Ryle, op. cit. (1945–6), p. 9. Cf. M. Oakeshott, 'Political education', in M. Oakeshott, *Rationalism in Politics and other Essays* (Methuen, 1967) paperback edn. He writes, page 119, that 'it might be supposed that an ignorant man, some edible materials, and a cookery book compose together the necessities of a self moved (or concrete) activity called cooking. But nothing is further from the truth. The cookery book is not an independently generated beginning from which cooking can spring; it is nothing more than an abstract of somebody's knowledge of how to cook: it is the stepchild, not the parent of the activity. The book, in its turn, may help to set a man on to dressing a dinner, but if it were his sole guide he could never, in fact, begin: the book speaks only to those who already know the kind of thing to expect from it and consequently how to interpret it.'

It is important to notice that Entwistle distinguishes theoretical and practical learning in terms of the distinction between theoretical and practical tasks but that practical knowledge is·not always restricted to knowing how to (and being able to) carry out practical tasks. Oakeshott, for example, distinguishes not theoretical and practical knowledge but technical and practical knowledge. Technical knowledge consists of knowledge of the rules that govern a task or activity. A cook has technical knowledge if he can recite the recipe for a dish. He has practical knowledge (on Oakeshott's distinction) if he can in fact produce the dish. The distinction Oakeshott makes is roughly that between knowing how in theory and knowing how in practice. On this account, practical knowledge can be manifested both in practical activities (e.g. cooking) and in theoretical ones (e.g., science and history). See M. Oakeshott, 'Rationalism in politics', in M. Oakeshott, op. cit. (1967), pp. 7–13. Ryle's distinction between knowing that and knowing how has close similarities to Oakeshott's distinction, and applies both to theoretical and practical activities. See G. Ryle, op. cit. (1945–6), p. 1. Briefly,

Knowing that is knowing that so and so is the case[153] and includes propositional knowledge expressed in prescriptions;[154] knowing how is knowing how to do things[155] and knowing how to perform certain tasks;[156] knowing how is further equated with performing critically and this is equated with performing intelligently and the notion of intelligent performance is explicated as follows[157] – 'an action exhibits intelligence, if, and only if, the agent is thinking what he is doing while he is doing it, and thinking what he is doing in such a manner that he would not do the action so well if he were not thinking what he is doing.' This implies that any agent, if he is acting intelligently, is 'ready to detect and correct lapses' and 'applies criteria in performing critically, that is, in trying to get things right.'[158] Ryle holds that there has been a view that intelligent behaviour of the sort described is only intelligent in so far as any agent first goes through the 'internal process of avowing to himself certain propositions about what is to be done ('maxims', 'imperatives', or 'regulatative propositions' as they are sometimes called)' and executes his performance in accordance with them. On this account, 'to do something thinking what one is doing is ... always to do two things; namely, to consider certain appropriate propositions or prescriptions, and to put into practice what these propositions or prescriptions enjoin. It is to do a bit of theory and then to do a bit of practice.'[159] He holds that such a view of intelligent performance is 'false in fact and refutable in logic'[160] and that to describe a person's performance as intelligent is not to attribute to him 'the double operation of considering and executing.'[161]

As Entwistle implies, this creates a difficulty. For if practical knowledge is independent of theorizing what could the role of theorizing be? To attempt an answer to this question, it will be necessary to look at Ryle's views in more detail.[162]

(Ftn. 152 cont.)
'practical knowledge' in a narrow sense is used of someone only in so far as he knows in practice how to carry out some practical task or activity, and in a wider sense of someone who knows in practice how to carry out a task or activity, theoretical or practical.

[153] G. Ryle, op. cit. (1945–6), p. 4.
[154] G. Ryle, op. cit. (1949), p. 29.
[155] G. Ryle, op. cit. (1945–6), p. 4.
[156] G. Ryle, op. cit. (1949), p. 29.
[157] Ibid.
[158] Ibid., pp. 28–9; see also pp. 46–51.
[159] Ibid., p. 29.
[160] G. Ryle, op. cit. (1945–6), p. 9.
[161] G. Ryle, op. cit. (1949), pp. 29–30.
[162] The most detailed discussion and criticism of Ryle's views is by D. G. Brown, 'Knowing how and knowing that, what', in *Ryle*, ed. O.P. Wood and G. Pitcher (Macmillan, 1971), pp. 213–48. Other relevant discussions are: I. Gallie, 'Intelligence and intelligent conduct', *Proceedings of the Aristotelian Society*, Vol. XLVIII (1947–8), pp. 187–204; J. Holloway, *Language and Intelligence* (Macmillan, 1951), Chapters 4, 5

Ryle's main argument against the traditional view is a regress one. Selecting and applying the appropriate maxims to guide a performance is an activity which can itself be done intelligently or stupidly. If the performance is to be intelligent then the selection of the maxims must be intelligent. But we now need to explain what intelligent theorizing is, and this will have to be explained by a further prior act of theorizing, which itself will have to be intelligent and which in its turn will need to be explained by a further prior act of intelligent theorizing – and so on.[163] A second argument is that theory in the sense of rules, maxims, precepts and prescriptions, etc., is logically second to practice – that is, we can only derive precepts that might bring about intelligent performances from intelligent performances that have already taken place.[164] In addition, people do act intelligently and carry out intelligent performances, without prior acts of theorizing,[165] and there are some activities for which the theory is unformulated.[166]

What then is intelligent performance? Ryle's general view is that it consists in the ability and readiness to cope as well as possible with whatever contingencies arise during the course of the performance – thus, say, in boxing, not only to keep to the rules but to minimize adverse contin-

(Ftn. 162 cont.)
and 6; A. D. Woozley, 'Knowing and not knowing', *Proceedings of the Aristotelian Society*, Vol. LIII (1952–3), pp. 151–72; J. Hartland-Swann, *An Analysis of Knowing* (Allen & Unwin, 1958), Chapter 4; A. MacIntyre, op. cit. (1960); J. R. Martin, 'On the reduction of "knowing that" to "knowing how"', in *Language and Concepts in Education*, ed. B. O. Smith and R. H. Ennis (Chicago: Rand McNally, 1961), pp. 59–71: I. Scheffler, *Conditions of Knowledge* (Glenview, Illinois: Scott Foresman, 1965), Chapter 5; M. Black, 'Rules and routines', in R. S. Peters, ed., op. cit. (1967), pp. 92–104; W. B. Gallie, 'The idea of practice', *Proceedings of the Aristotelian Society*, Vol. LXVIII (1967–8), pp. 63–86; D. W. Hamlyn, op. cit. (1971); G. Langford, *Human Action* (Macmillan, 1972), pp. 36–42. For an adequate account of practical knowledge all this and a lot more would need to be discussed. We are particularly concerned here with practical skills which, W. B. Gallie (op. cit. (1967–8), p. 78) suggests, Ryle has shown need not 'be steered by prior acts of appreciating theory-based prescriptions.'

Other material relevant to the discussion here and to that of practical reasoning can be found in: R. B. Raup, G. E. Axtelle, K. D. Benne and B. O. Smith. *The Improvement of Practical Intelligence* (Harper Bros, 1949); T. Kotarbinski, 'De la notion de méthode', *Revue de Metaphysique et de Morale*, Vol. 62 (1957), pp. 187–99; T. Kotarbinski, 'Practical error', *Danish Year Book in Philosophy*, No. 1 (Copenhagen, 1964), pp. 65–71; T. Kotarbinski, *Praxiology* (Pergamon Press, 1965); T. Kotarbinski, 'The methodology of practical skills: concepts and issues', *Metaphilosophy*, Vol. 2 (1971), pp. 158–70; H. Hiz, 'Kotarbinski's Praxeology', *Philosophy and Phenomenological Research*, Vol. 15 (1954), pp. 238–43.

[163] G. Ryle, op. cit. (1949), pp. 30–2. See also G. Ryle, op. cit. (1945–6), pp. 5–8, and P. Winch, *The Idea of a Social Science* (Routledge & Kegan Paul, 1958), pp. 51–7, on the application of precepts to practice.

[164] See the passage quoted from Oakeshott in a footnote on page 00; G. Ryle, op. cit. (1949), p. 30.

[165] A. C. MacIntyre, op. cit., p. 85.

[166] G. Ryle, op. cit. (1949), p. 30.

gencies, to seize on and use those that can be used advantageously, to detect and correct lapses in one's own performance. That such performances are carried on without prior deliberation can be seen from Ryle's examples of a person arguing,[167] or of the tennis player[168] who far from 'both making muscular movements and also . . . doing lots of short, sharp bits of reflecting,'[169] is mostly '*un*reflective or *un*pensive.'[170] His 'thinking almost consists in his whole and at least slightly schooled attention being given to, *inter alia*, the flight of the ball over the net, the position of his opponent, the strength of the wind, and so on.'[171] Thinking of the reflective sort might even, it is suggested, militate against success.[172]

It can be seen that a necessary condition of intelligent practice is that any agent should be able to recognize features of the situation in which he is performing that either constitute processes relevant to the success and failure of the performance, or are signs of such processes – that is, the agent should be able to read the situation in the light of the task in which he is engaged. Indeed, the concept of purposive action itself presupposes beliefs of this and other sorts.[173] A batsman, for example, needs to be able to recognize a ball that is likely to drop short either, say, from its flight, or perhaps from a movement of the bowler's arm or wrist at the time of delivery. A driver of a car should be able to recognize when there is an adverse camber on a bend, or a tennis player when a ball is likely to land almost dead. Teachers will need to be able to read the social situations in which they have to teach.[174] What needs to be recognized will depend on the task in hand. In philosophy it might be recognizing ambiguities, in teaching recognizing when the class is bored or tired, and so on. How such skills are learnt and how they might be improved, and what limits are placed on their development by the intel-

---

[167] G. Ryle, op. cit. (1949), pp. 47–8.

[168] G. Ryle, 'Thinking and reflecting', in *The Human Agent*, Royal Institute of Philosophy Lectures, Volume I, 1966–7 (Macmillan, 1968), pp. 210–12.

[169] G. Ryle, op. cit. (1968), p. 216.

[170] Ibid., p. 211.

[171] Ibid.

[172] Ibid., p. 215.

[173] See G. Langford, *Human Action* (Macmillan, 1972), pp. 90–4. See also S. Hampshire and H. L. A. Hart, 'Decision, intention and certainty', *Mind*, Vol. LXVII (1958), p. 8; and C. Olsen, 'Knowledge of one's own intentional actions', *Philosophical Quarterly*, Vol. 19 (1969), pp. 332–4. G. Langford, op. cit. (1972), pp. 41–2 and p. 91, argues that though intelligent performance need not be preceded by theorizing in the sense of calling to mind the maxims (i.e. the theory) of an activity, it does require theorizing in a wider sense which includes the acquisition of empirical beliefs about the situation in which the performance is taking place. It is unlikely that Ryle would deny this. See, for example, G. Ryle, op. cit. (1949), p. 49 and the example of the tennis player just cited from G. Ryle, op. cit. (1968), p. 211.

[174] The articles by P. Bohannan, and by R. Dumont and M. Wax, in Volume I Section 2 draw attention to how difficult this can be. See also pp. 184–6.

lectual and psychological make-up of individuals, cannot be settled without empirical investigation.

3. Unspecifiable elements of practical knowledge

The ability to read a situation is in our view a skill which, like all skills, has its unspecifiable element, as a discussion of Polanyi's suggests.[175] He draws a distinction between what he calls the 'particulars' of a 'physiognomy' and the relationship of these particulars to each other. Because he wishes to suggest similarities between recognizing human faces and recognizing some other things, he uses 'physiognomy' in a wide sense to cover, for example, the appearances of mental and physical diseases and 'the characteristics of wines and blends of tea which only experts can recognize.' A physiognomy consists of certain individual items (particulars) related to each other in certain ways, and constitutes a comprehensive entity or 'a whole'. In the light of this, Polanyi discusses 'the recognition of a disease by its physiognomy' as follows: '(1) We cannot identify, let alone describe, a great number of the particulars which we are in fact noticing when we diagnose a case of the disease. (2) Though we can identify a case of the disease by its typical appearance, we cannot describe it adequately, and there are four closely related reasons for this. (a) We are ignorant (according to 1) of the unspecifiable particulars which would enter into the description. (b) The relation between the particulars – even if they could all be identified – could be described only in vague terms which the expert alone would understand. (c) Our identification of a disease in any one instance comprehends unspecifiably as its particulars the whole range of cases which, in spite of their individual differences, we have identified in the past, and (d) it relies on this comprehension for the future identification of an unlimited number of further cases which might differ from those known before in an infinite variety of unexpected ways.'[176]

In so far as this is true and can be taken as analogous to reading social situations, particularly those in education, then the possibility of putting into words all that we know and might wish to pass on is small.[177] For in

---

[175] M. Polanyi, 'Knowing and being', *Mind*, Vol. LXX (1961), pp. 458–70. See also M. Polanyi, *Personal Knowledge* (Routledge & Kegan Paul, 1958).

[176] M. Polanyi, op. cit. (1961), pp. 466–7.

[177] There are differences between medicine and diagnosis, on the one hand, and education and reading social situations in education, on the other. There is a fairly large body of semi-codified and so explicit knowledge of symptoms in medicine, and the correlation between the occurrence of the symptoms and the occurrence of the disease, is better established in many cases than the correlation between what might be taken to be signs of social processes and the occurrence of these processes. In many cases in education, all we may have are the symptoms, as it were, and never the disease. Knowledge of what

such cases, 'our knowledge may include far more than we can tell.'[178] Indeed Polanyi describes the topographic knowledge a surgeon has of the areas in which he operates as 'ineffable'[179] and suggests that knowledge of this sort is such that articulation of it is 'virtually impossible'.[180] Where knowledge has been made explicit as, say, when medical students learn a list of a disease's symptoms together with all their variations, 'only clinical practice can teach him to integrate the clues observed on an individual patient to form a correct diagnosis of his illness, rather than an erroneous diagnosis which is often more plausible.'[181] Thus the only way to learn to read and make sense of an X-ray plate, he suggests, is in the end by watching experts do it and by listening to them.[182]

Even so it would be wrong to deny that the precepts, maxims, etc. that govern intelligent performances (or in O'Connor's word their 'theory') could ever be formulated.[183] In some cases the task is likely to be a difficult one,[184] whether at the level of precepts, maxims, and procedural formulae, or the level of what Oakeshott calls 'the underlying *rationale*'.[185] But where the precepts are formulated, they will leave a lot

---

(Ftn. 177 cont.)
to do in the light of these symptoms would seem to be better founded in medicine on the whole than in education. Further, ignorance about what to do is often more immediately apparent in medicine than in education, in that the criteria of failure are more clearcut – that is, the patient either fails to improve or dies. See also pp. 184–6.

By what extent, if any, the study of the social sciences can increase our ability to read and understand social situations, and to what extent they can offer concepts and knowledge which additional to, or instead of, those of common sense might improve our teaching, is given some account of better teaching, an empirical matter. One view is that of D. J. O'Connor (op. cit. (1957), pp. 95–6), who writes the 'A good teacher knows enough of the workings of human nature from common experience to enable him to teach effectively.' If this is true, then the reason for the inclusion of the social sciences in training courses for teachers might be for purposes other than for classroom skills. H. Entwistle, 'The relationship between theory and practice', in *An Introduction to the Study of Education*, ed. J. W. Tibble (Routledge & Kegan Paul, 1971), pp. 95–113, provides reasons for thinking that common sense is not always enough. See for example pp. 101 and 106. For a relevant discussion about common sense and its relation to specialized knowledge see L. R. Perry, 'Common sense thought, knowledge, and judgement, and their importance for education', *British Journal of Educational Studies*, Vol. 13 (1965), pp. 125–38. For the place of theoretical disciplines in the education of teachers see Volume II.

[178] Polanyi, op. cit. (1961), p. 467.
[179] Polanyi, op. cit. (1958), pp. 88–9.
[180] M. Polanyi, op. cit. (1958), p. 87.
[181] M. Polanyi, op. cit. (1961), p. 460.
[182] M. Polanyi, op. cit. (1958), p. 101.
[183] D. W. Hamlyn, op. cit. (1971), p. 104. See D. J. O'Connor quoted on p. 108.
[184] M. Polanyi, op. cit. (1958), p. 52. See also M. Oakeshott, op. cit. (1962), p. 7.
[185] M. Oakeshott, 'Learning and teaching', in *The Concept of Education*, ed. R. S. Peters (Routledge & Kegan Paul, 1967), p. 166. See also M. Polanyi, op. cit. (1958), pp. 49–50. This is the level at which laws of mechanics, for example, may explain how certain movements made by a cyclist enable him to keep his balance, or how a certain

unsaid.[186] Comments of Gallie suggest that, even in cases where the precepts can be made out very fully, 'factors of personal judgement' are still 'required by inexhaustible minor variations in the special circumstances.'[187] Consequently, merely following the precepts uncritically will in general not bring success. They need to be interpreted in the context in question, to be modified, to be applied. The precepts themselves do not state how they are to be applied, and, even if others do, this set of precepts which prescribes how the first set are to be applied will itself need to be applied. Winch points this out, saying that 'The activity "goes beyond" the precepts.'[188]

Thus even where we know in theory how to do something and have, to use Oakeshott's term, technical knowledge which is 'susceptible of formulation in rules, principles, directions, maxims – comprehensively in propositions',[189] something additional is required to turn this into practical knowledge. Oakeshott calls this additional element 'judgement', which is 'the tacit and implicit component of knowledge, the ingredient which is not merely unspecified but is unspecifiable in propositions.'[190] We may not of course have technical knowledge, in Oakeshott's sense. We may be able to carry out some performances intelligently and successfully but the rules, precepts, and maxims which we follow might be completely unformulated. For as Gallie[191] notes there are tasks for which no procedural 'formulae are forthcoming, and for which . . . the so-called theory is at best a later rationalization of successful practice'; and there are some too where one important and perhaps major determinant of success may be 'characterological' as opposed to 'intellectual preparation and endowment'.[192] He suggests that characterological factors are particularly important in practices that 'revolve around conflicts or

(Ftn. 185 cont.)
way of hitting a golf ball causes it to fade. On this level in particular, we may be in complete ignorance of why what we do brings success. Thus, we know how to relieve some sorts of pain by giving people aspirin but not what the bio-chemical explanation of this is. So too, we may know that certain sorts of method, at least in some contexts, promote quicker learning, and yet have no idea of what sort of socio-psychological account of this could be given.

[186] See pp. 44–5.
[187] W. B. Gallie, op. cit. (1967–8), p. 72.
[188] P. Winch, op. cit. (1958), p. 55. Cf. H. Entwistle, op. cit. (1971), p. 98 and G. Langford, op. cit. (1972), p. 39.
[189] M. Oakeshott, op. cit. (1967), p. 10.
[190] M. Oakeshott, in R. S. Peters, ed., op. cit. (1967), p. 167; see also his discussion there of 'information'. P. H. Nowell-Smith, 'Purpose and intelligent action', Proceedings of the Aristotelian Society, Supplementary, Vol. XXXIV (1960), p. 105, notes that 'we can speak of intelligence and stupidity only where we can speak of exercising judgement, of good or bad choices, right or wrong solutions, and all of these entail the concept of intentional action.' This again suggests a conceptual link between judgement and practical knowledge.
[191] W. B. Gallie, op. cit. (1967–8), p. 70.
[192] Ibid., p. 71

tensions between two or more human wills' and that success in these cases (though not only in these) 'is a matter of will as much of skill; of seizing opportunities and moving on in faith as much as applying theoretical knowledge and displaying irreducible "knowledge how".'[193]

Practical knowledge then, in which we include the intelligent and critical exercise of skills, and the ability to perform intelligently in an activity, requires knowledge of a kind which cannot be put into propositions.[194] Further, in so far as practical knowledge depends upon characterological factors and so on the acquisition of various dispositions, there is a further element of it which is not expressible in propositions nor acquired by learning them.

4. Practical knowledge and the role of theory

Now in so far as practical knowledge cannot be put into propositions, it cannot be passed on by them. Oakeshott states that 'it exists only in practice, and the way to acquire it is by apprenticeship to a master . . . it can be acquired only by continuous contact with one who is perpetually practising it.'[195] But Peters, in his discussion of Oakeshott, suggests that this view is too parsimonious.[196] Practical knowledge together with its constituent of judgement might be self-taught, or might be acquired by on-the-spot criticism from someone adopting the role of a coach, who need not be particularly proficient in the skill. What a coach needs to have mastered rather is the 'art of commenting on and encouraging the performances of others'.[197] He needs, according to Ryle,[198] 'ability to abstract, ability to express and ability to impress' – irrespective of his proficiency in the skill in question.

[193] Ibid., p. 72. Intelligent and successful performances, therefore, whether of a theoretical or practical kind, may well depend very much on non-cognitive factors. See in this context M. Oakeshott, in R. S. Peters, ed., op. cit. (1967), p. 174; J. Passmore, 'On teaching to be critical', in ibid.; P. Hirst and R. S. Peters, op. cit. (1970), pp. 39 and 50–1; R. S. Peters, 'Reason and passion', in *The Proper Study* Royal Institute of Philosophy Lectures, Vol. 4, 1969–70 (Macmillan, 1971) pp. 132–53.

[194] Cf. G. Ryle, op. cit. (1945–6), p. 14 – 'But knowledge-how cannot be built up by accumulation of pieces of knowledge-that.'

[195] Oakeshott, op. cit. (1967), p. 11. Polanyi writes, op. cit. (1958), p. 53, 'An art which cannot be specified in detail cannot be transmitted by prescription, since no prescription for it exists. It can be passed on only by example from master to apprentice.' Oakeshott's and Polanyi's points apply to both theoretical and practical activities. Oakeshott's account of judgement applies to both, as does Ryle's of 'knowing how'.

[196] R. S. Peters, 'Michael Oakeshott's philosophy of education', in *Politics and Experience*, ed. P. King and B. C. Parekh (Cambridge University Press, 1968). See, in particular, pp. 48–58.

[197] R. S. Peters, in P. King and B. C. Parekh, eds., op. cit. (1968), p. 56.

[198] G. Ryle, op. cit. (1945–6), p. 13.

How exactly judgement and so practical knowledge are imparted and acquired is difficult to say.[199] Peters suggests that the area within which the concept falls is uncharted and one which it would be fruitful for philosophers, psychologists and sociologists to explore.[200] But however it is acquired or imparted, it has certainly been acquired only when a pupil has passed beyond what he could have copied from his teacher. As Winch says, 'Learning how to do something is not just copying what someone else does; it may start that way, but a teacher's estimate of his pupil's prowess will lie in the latter's ability to do things which he could precisely *not* simply have copied.'[201] Thus practical knowledge goes beyond both the propositional knowledge and the model a student may have used in his attempt to acquire it.[202]

In the light of all this, what might be said about the role of theory and theorizing in imparting, acquiring, and exercising practical knowledge?

Theorizing itself is an activity, which, like others, can be done well or badly, intelligently and stupidly, and so on.[203] Intelligent theorizing depends, for example, on distinguishing relevant from irrelevant factors, and taking only the former into account. The value of theorizing will depend on how well and intelligently it is done.

Even on Ryle's account of intelligent performance, there is a place for deliberation, reflecting what to do, planning, and calling maxims to mind, and other things he includes under theorizing. He himself says, 'Certainly we often do not only reflect before we act but reflect in order to act properly.'[204] This is the gist of Entwistle's argument on pp. 40–3. MacIntyre points out that 'it is a true empirical generalization that deliberation on what to do commonly promotes success in or acting relative to our purposes.'[205] One way in which deliberation may play a part is discussed by Entwistle.[206] It consists in deciding in the light of the context which skill or techniques to bring into play.

---

[199] For a relevant brief discussion see W. Hare, 'The teaching of judgement', *British Journal of Educational Studies*, Vol. XIX (1971), pp. 243–9.

[200] R. S. Peters, in P. King and B. C. Parekh, eds., op. cit. (1968), p. 58.

[201] P. Winch, op. cit. (1958), p. 58; Cf. G. Ryle, 'Thinking and self-teaching', *Proceedings of the Philosophy of Education Society of Great Britain*, Supplementary Volume, Vol. V, No. 2 (July 1971), pp. 217–18.

[202] The model may, nevertheless, determine for the pupil what the point of the activity is and what are appropriate procedures and appropriate ways of coping with contingencies, and so what will count as good and bad judgement.

[203] Cf. G. Ryle, op. cit. (1949), pp. 30–2.

[204] G. Ryle, op. cit. (1949), p. 29.

[205] A. C. MacIntyre, op. cit. (1960), p. 86. MacIntyre's own thesis is stronger than this – he holds that at least some cases of intelligent behaviour must be preceded by deliberation (p. 86); and that deliberation is neither a necessary nor sufficient condition of intelligent behaviour (pp. 85 and 86) although 'the concept of intelligent behaviour cannot be elucidated except with reference to the concept of deliberation' (p. 85).

[206] See page 42.

In spite of its limitations, theorizing and theory might well be useful in promoting intelligent and successful performances, and so in imparting practical knowledge. Ryle suggests that the maxims which constitute the theory have a pedagogic role. Their place is 'in lessons to those who are still learning how to act. They belong to manuals for novices.'[207] They are 'for the half-trained'.[208] What such maxims might do is to mark out the area outside which success is either unlikely or impossible. Theorizing cannot ensure success both because it may omit relevant factors which could be made explicit, and because of the tacit and unspecifiable elements in practical knowledge which can only be acquired by practice. Theorizing prior to a performance may make it more difficult to commit some sorts of mistake[209] and may be most helpful when it is carried on 'in close association with practice'.[210] The extent to which these generalizations are true cannot, however, be established in advance of empirical work.

The *way* the theorizing is done and the way theory is imparted may have important consequences. Dewey argues that certain sorts of criticism might produce not thoughtful and independent teachers but those who have merely some of 'the knacks and tools of the trade'. He says, 'It ought to go without saying (unfortunately, it does not in all cases) that criticism should be directed to making the professional student thoughtful about his work in the light of principles, rather than to induce in him a recognition that certain special methods are good, and certain other special methods bad. At all events, no greater travesty of real intellectual criticism can be given than to set a student to teaching a brief number of lessons, have him under inspection in practically all the time of every lesson, and then criticize him almost, if not quite, at the very end of each lesson, upon the particular way in which that particular lesson has been taught, pointing out elements of failure and of success. Such methods of criticism may be adapted to giving a training-teacher command of some of the knacks and tools of the trade, but are not calculated to develop a thoughtful and independent teacher'[211] – nor,

[207] G. Ryle, op. cit. (1945–6), p. 12.

[208] Ibid., p. 14.

[209] See Entwistle, pp. 46–7.

[210] See Entwistle, p. 45.

[211] J. Dewey, 'The relation of theory to practice in education', in The Third Yearbook of the National Society for the Scientific Study of Education, Part 1, ed., C. A. McMurry, Chicago Illinois: Chicago University Press, 1904, p. 28. Dewey makes an important related point a little earlier (p. 15) to the effect that 'immediate skill may be got at the cost of power to go on growing' – that is 'immediate skill may be pursued at the cost of not making students 'thoughtful and alert'. Dewey counts among the costs of such methods (p. 16) 'the lack of intellectual independence among teachers, their tendency to intellectual subserviency. The "model lesson" of the teachers' institute and of the educational journal is a monument, on the one hand, of the eagerness of those in

as Entwistle suggests, a teacher 'who has the resource to adapt himself to novel circumstances'.[212]

Finally, issues arise about the justification and validity of the maxims and advice given and used in acquiring and exercising practical knowledge, and teachers and learners need to be aware of them. In a good many cases, the maxims and advice are unlikely either to consist entirely of, or to be understood as, value-free technical judgements about how to attain certain ends. They are likely to contain, explicitly or implicitly, or to be understood as containing, value judgements about ends and procedures. Embodied in rules-of-thumb about teaching or discipline, for example, are likely to be value judgements about desirable educational ends, about good discipline, and about appropriate ways of achieving these.[213] Further, the efficacy of the procedures contained in the maxims and advice will depend on inductive inferences from past experience.[214] We have already suggested that there are comparatively few reliable generalizations which educators can use.[215] One consequence is that we are likely to be ignorant of the limits within which the maxims and advice hold, and we may continue with them even though changed circumstances have rendered them ineffectual.[216] This may be particularly the case in the absence of any sort of underlying rationale. O'Connor[217] seems to suggest that theoretical explanations which constitute such rationales may in fact enable us to amend educational practice in the expectation of improved results. To what extent this can be done depends, at least in part, on the relevance and reliability of such explanations. It is not obvious, for example, that some sorts of learning theory are at all relevant to classroom practice.[218] Sometimes theoretical explanations or what are intended to be such are taken over in an attempt to provide firm backing for some practices by giving them an underlying rationale, even though the uncertain status of the explanations may in fact preclude this.[219]

(Ftn. 211 cont.)

authority to secure immediate practical results at any cost; and, upon the other, of the willingness of our teaching corps to accept without inquiry or criticism any method or device which seems to promise good results. Teachers, actual and intending, flock to those persons who give them clear-cut and definite instructions as to just how to teach this or that.'

[212] See Entwistle p. 43.

[213] Cf. G. Langford, *Philosophy and Education* (Macmillan, 1968), pp. 131–2.

[214] G. Ryle, op. cit. (1945–6), pp. 10–11.

[215] See pp. 103–7

[216] Cf. E. Nagel, *The Structure of Science* (Routledge & Kegan Paul, 1961), p. 5.

[217] D. J. O'Connor, op. cit. (1957), p. 109.

[218] Cf. R. S. Peters, *Authority, Responsibility and Education* (Allen & Unwin, 1959), Chapter 10.

[219] See E. V. Sullivan, *Piaget and the School Curriculum – a Critical Appraisal*, Bulletin 2 (Ontario Institute for Studies in Education, 1967). Nevertheless it would be over-sceptical to doubt the existence of a skill because of the absence of any underlying rationale.

Educational theory and educational practice

We make one or two brief comments here, in the light of our previous discussion, about a conception of educational theory, such as that of Hirst.[220]

Hirst holds that there could be something called 'the theory of education'.[221] Such a theory is not akin to a scientific theory but is rather 'constructed to determine and guide the activity',[222] in this case education. Those engaged in constructing such a theory will be concerned to establish 'a body of rational principles for educational practice'.[223] These will constitute the theory and will be justified, certainly in part, by reference to the various theoretical disciplines that are relevant to education – psychology, sociology, history, philosophy, and so on.[224] What Hirst seems to mean by the term 'principles' here is 'practical generalizations', which are statements which prescribe (or proscribe) certain types of action. They will include practical judgements about educational ends, means, and procedures, and so will include statements of aims, and the sort of procedural formulae and maxims mentioned earlier.[225]

Our previous discussion suggests that there might be a number of different but justifiable views about the nature of education, its organization, and its methods. If this is so, then to the extent that the phrase 'the theory of education' implies there could be just one justifiable collection of rational principles for educational practice, it is misleading. There might rather be a number of justifiable educational theories, each reflecting justifiable differences in evaluations about aims, organization, and methods. To establish such principles is not, in any case, to provide educators with ready-made answers to specific practical problems they might face. The principles will need to be applied. They will, almost

(Ftn. 219 cont.)

M. Polanyi, op. cit. (1958), pp. 50–2, draws attention to two instructive cases where this was done.

[220]See P. H. Hirst, 'Educational theory', in *The Study of Education*, ed. J. W. Tibble (Routledge & Kegan Paul, 1966), pp. 29–58; see also D. J. O'Connor, op. cit. (1957), Chapters 4 and 5; M. Struthers, 'Educational theory: a critical discussion of the O'Connor-Hirst debate', *Scottish Educational Studies*, Vol. 3, No. 2 (1971); 'The nature of educational theory', Symposium by D. J. O'Connor and P. H. Hirst, in *Proceedings of the Philosophy of Education Society of Great Britain*, Vol. VI, No. 1 (January 1972), pp. 97–118. See also J. Gribble, *Introduction to Philosophy of Education* (Boston: Allyn and Bacon, 1969), Chapter 7.

[221]See P. H. Hirst, in J. W. Tibble, ed., op. cit. (1966), p. 40.

[222]Ibid.

[223]Ibid., p. 41.

[224]Ibid., pp. 50–1.

[225]P. H. Hirst, in J. W. Tibble, ed., op. cit. (1966), p. 52–4; cf. M. Struthers, op. cit. (1971), pp. 77–8.

certainly, be defeasible since there will be circumstances in which they do not hold.

Hirst's view of educational theory is not so much a description of what is now possible, but rather an outline of a long-term and perhaps unending programme. For it is by no means clear that the knowledge on which the possibility of reliable practical generalizations depends is available or will be in the near future. Hirst, it can be argued, would acknowledge this. He says that 'the answers we give to most major educational questions, above all about what we ought to do in schools, necessarily involve us in committing ourselves on important philosophical issues.'[226] We suggest in Volume II that there may be very little in philosophy that could count as securely established. He says a little later that there is a 'significant body of work in such areas as Philosophy, Psychology, Sociology which has practical significance for work in schools' but that it is 'small'.[227] All this (as well as our previous discussion) suggests that practical educational generalizations of whatever kind are likely to be at best tentative and unreliable.

What educational theory is likely to be able to offer those engaged in educational practice is not firm guidance but only suggestions and hints about what might be best done, and when and how. There is little, if any, possibility of it offering practical generalizations which, if followed, will solve practitioners' practical problems and ensure successful practice. Where theory is available, it will have to be applied, and this will inescapably require initiative from the practitioner. If this is the case, then Entwistle's words are particularly relevant. He writes, 'The job of a theory is to evoke judgement rather than rote obedience. The application of theory to practice is the bringing to bear of critical intelligence upon practical tasks rather than the implementation of good advice.'[228]

[226] 'Conversation with Paul Hirst', *Cambridge Journal of Education*, No. 3 (Michaelmas, 1971), p. 110.

[227] Ibid., p. 115.

[228] H. Entwistle, 'The relationship between theory and practice', in *An Introduction to the Study of Education*, J. W. Tibble, ed. (Routledge & Kegan Paul, 1971), pp. 101–2. One important task for educational theory is, in our view, to make explicit to practitioners its own limitations. See also M. Naish and A. Hartnett, 'What theory cannot do for teachers', *Education for Teaching*, No. 96, Spring, 1975, pp. 12–19.

2
The work of classroom teachers

Introduction to the readings

In Section 1 an attempt has been made to indicate some elementary ways in which 'theory' and 'practice' might be distinguished. In the course of the discussion it was suggested: (*i*) that teachers and others in education work in an area where difficult value issues arise; (*ii*) that they have to solve their practical problems and exercise their skills in situations of 'bounded rationality', that is, on the basis of incomplete understanding and knowledge of the contexts in which they work, and in particular of the outcomes of actual or proposed courses of action; (*iii*) that the help that educational theory can provide is limited. The discussion in Section 1 was for the most part philosophical and concerned with conceptual and logical matters. It was also general. Little was said about the specific practical problems that might face teachers, the specific skills they might require, or the specific contexts in which they might work. In this section three readings have been chosen to provide evidence in each of these areas.[1]

S. Hilsum and B. S. Cane, 'The teacher's day'

This study[2] presents evidence about the 'total job' performed by a group of 129 teachers working in 66 different primary schools in Surrey, and it

[1] It should be noted that the discussion of the teaching profession in this section, and teachers' work, is highly selective. The intention is only to provide evidence for points made in Section 1. For a more formal review of the literature see Anthony Hartnett, 'The teaching profession', Section 7 in *The Sociology of Education: an Introductory Guide to the Literature*, Anthony Hartnett, ed., Library Publication No. 3 (School of Education, University of Liverpool, 1975). (Copies available from the Library of the School of Education.)

[2] National Foundation for Educational Research in England and Wales, 1971. See also another version published in Sidney Hilsum, *The Teacher at Work* (Slough: NFER, 1972). See also the study by Roy Nash, *Classrooms Observed* (Routledge & Kegan Paul, 1973),

shows that teachers' work involves a great deal more than is conventionally understood by 'teaching'. Three sections are included from the study: most of Chapter 2, 'How the teaching days were observed and described'; part of the 'Summary and conclusions'; and part of Chapter 17, 'Disruptions in the teaching day: contingencies and interruptions'. The study provides examples of the practical activities which primary-school teachers had to undertake as part of their working day, and shows some of the factors with which they had to deal. It explores the context in which teachers had to make judgements about what to do. Further data on different groups of junior-school teachers, and teachers in other organizational settings (comprehensive, grammar, middle, etc.) would be valuable.[3]

Paul J. Bohannan, 'Field anthropologists and classroom teachers'[4]

Bohannan outlines a number of comparisons between American teachers and field anthropologists, and suggests that teachers may have to deal with groups and individuals whose values they may not share.[5] He examines some of the consequences of this for teachers.

Robert V. Dumont Jr and Murray L. Wax, 'Cherokee school society and the intercultural classroom'[6]

This article is based on an empirical study undertaken in schools for the children of Cherokee Indians in the USA. The teachers in such schools attempt to educate the Cherokee children, and to integrate them within

---

(Ftn. 2 cont.)
and also N. Gross, J. B. Giacquinta, and M. Bernstein, *Implementing Organizational Innovations* (New York: Harper & Row, 1971). This work will be cited as 'The Gross study'.
   [3] See the American study *Life in Classrooms*, by P. W. Jackson (New York: Holt, Rinehart & Winston, 1968), especially Chapter 1, 'The daily grind' and Roy Nash, *Classrooms Observed*, op. cit.
   [4] *Social Education*, Vol. 32. No. 2 (February 1968), pp. 161–6.
   [5] For some British evidence see Charles Hannam, Pat Smyth and Norman Stephenson, *Young Teachers and Reluctant Learners* (Penguin Books, 1971); Nell Keddie, ed., *Tinker, Tailor: the Myth of Cultural Deprivation* (Penguin Books, 1973). See also this book, pp. 179–90. For some further literature on anthropology and education see: Peter S. Sindell, 'Anthropological approaches to the study of education', *Review of Educational Research*, Vol. 39, No. 5 (1969), pp. 593–605; George D. Spindler, ed., *Education and Culture – Anthropological Approaches* (New York: Holt, Rinehart & Winston, 1963); Murray L. Wax et al., eds., *Anthropological Perspectives on Education* (New York: Basic Books, 1971), see especially the bibliography (pp. 310–84) in the Murray L. Wax collection of readings. On philosophy and anthropology see Abraham Edel, 'The contribution of philosophical anthropology to educational development', pp. 69–91 in *Philosophy and Educational Development*, G. Barnett, ed. (Boston: Houghton Mifflin, 1966). See also H. Otto Dahlke, *Values in Culture and Classroom* (New York: Harper & Row 1958).
   [6] *Human Organization*, Vol. 28. No. 3 (Fall, 1969), pp. 217–26.

'American society'. Dumont and Wax characterize the process of Indian education as unidirectional, and imposed on a target population. It is unidirectional because the educators teach the children but do not learn from them, and the transformations which have occurred within Indian society are neglected. They examine the consequences of this view for the teachers and students involved. As we argue when we discuss 'educational categories', it would be useful to have additional data from the UK about the 'images' teachers have of the culture of the groups they teach; the evidence upon which such 'images' are based; and how the 'images' alter over time for different teachers.[7]

Dumont and Wax make the point that to enter the world of the Cherokee is 'as demanding as the mastering of an utterly foreign tongue'. The authors give a number of examples of the distinctive cultural background of the Cherokee. They point out that in the classroom the children wish to preserve their identity as Cherokees, and that knowledge and skills which the teacher has to offer will be evaluated in terms of how they contribute to life *as Cherokees*. The students set up the terms on which they will learn, and the conflict between students and teachers may be complex, subtle, and implicit in classroom interaction.[8] It may result in 'a wall of silence impenetrable by the outsider'. Such a form of conflict may be as important in schools as conflict which is explicit and obvious.

[7] See N. Keddie, 'Classroom knowledge', in *Knowledge and Control*, ed. M. F. D. Young (Collier-Macmillan, 1971), pp. 133–60; D. Hargreaves, *Social Relations in a Secondary School* (Routledge & Kegan Paul, 1967). On 'educational categories' see this book, pages 179–83.

[8] The readings by Bohannan, and Dumont and Wax raise interesting questions about the relationships between notions of worth-while activities; cross-cultural disputes about 'rationality', 'knowledge', etc.; and the concept of education. On this see this book, pages 73–92. The whole issue is discussed in greater detail in A. Hartnett and M. Naish, eds, *Education, Conflict and Values* (in preparation). See also John Eggleston, 'Decision making on the school curriculum; a conflict model', *Sociology*, Vol. 7, No. 3 (September 1973), pp. 377–94.

Readings

5 The teacher's day S. HILSUM and B. S. CANE

(S. Hilsun and B. S. Cane, *The Teacher's Day*,
National Foundation for Educational Research,
1971: (a) from Chapter 2, (b) from Summary and
Conclusions, and (c) from Chapter 17)

(a) How the teaching days were observed and described*

Several investigators, mostly in the USA,[1] have studied what was called
'teaching load', but the data on which their findings were based were
the subjective estimates made by the teachers themselves about their
work. In attempts to introduce greater objectivity into the analysis of
teacher behaviour, increasing use has been made of methods of systematic,
direct observation, and various tools or instruments have been developed
for this purpose,[2] but most of these instruments were designed specifically
for studying the teaching or learning *process* rather than the work a
teacher was called upon to undertake.[3] Also, these researchers were
confined to the classroom situation, whereas our project was to be concerned with the total job performed by the teacher – in the classroom,
in the school building, and, indeed, outside the school.

The teacher's work as such was investigated by Hagstrom (1960),

* For full references to works cited see pp 301–03 of the bibliography to *The Teacher's Day*.
[1] California Teachers' Association (1947); Adolphson and Umstattd (1949); Douglas
(1950); US State Department of Education (1955); Rudd (1965); NEA Research Division's
five-year cyclical surveys (1962, 1967).
[2] The use of mechanical aids in observing is discussed by Howsam (1960); Herbert and
Swayze (1964) developed the idea of 'wireless observation'; reviews of both observing and
recording instruments have been written by Withall (1960), Medley and Mitzel (1963a,
1963b), Boyd and Devault (1966), and Biddle (1967).
[3] Researchers who used direct observation methods in studying aspects of the teaching
learning processes (and in some cases they designed their own instruments to do this)
include: Anderson (1945, 1946a, 1946b); Withall (1949); Huges (1959); Ryans (1960);
Smith (1962, 1967); Leacock (1963); Bellack (1963, 1965, 1966); Poole (1964); Flanders
(1965); Gardner and Cass (1965); Waimon (1966); Herbert (1967) and Brown *et al.* (1968).

Stukat and Engstrom (1967), Hornbrook (1968) and Bates (1970), all using direct observation methods, but Hagstrom's inquiry involved teachers in only one school, while the other researchers studied only the classroom work of the teacher.

As far as the present authors are aware, there have been only two large-scale surveys which used direct observation and which were also concerned with the total teaching task, and both were conducted in the USA[4]; in each of these, however, the survey was incidental to a larger programme investigating the problem of utilizing 'teacher-assistants', and the survey was intended to identify and quantify the teacher's non-professional work rather than construct a comprehensive, descriptive account of the teaching day.

Nearer home, the researchers involved in the Scottish Primary School Survey[5] also used direct observation of teachers, and, as with the two studies just mentioned, their objective was to describe only the non-professional aspects of the teacher's job. There was no attempt to arrive at a description of the overall task undertaken by teachers.

It appeared, then, that the project we wished to embark upon was a novel one, and we would have to develop our own methods of observing and recording.

THE FEASIBILITY STUDY

It was clear that before we could begin to investigate ways of observing and recording teachers' activities we had to enlist the assistance of the teachers themselves: we had to know whether they would co-operate in the project and we also required their knowledge and advice about various facets of their work. The feasibility study thus had as its objectives: to seek the co-operation of teachers, and then, in consultation with them, to test ways of observing, identifying and recording teacher activities. These four aspects of the feasibility study[6] are summarized below.

1. Teacher co-operation
The feasibility study took place in and around the area of Slough during the period 1967–68, and was conducted in close consultation with the heads' and teachers' associations. We laid special stress on establishing personal contacts between the researchers and the teachers, and, as we shall show, this matter of liaison became an essential feature of our methodology.[7]

We had made no decisions at that time about the type of school or teacher to be studied; indeed, we were anxious to observe as many

[4] Bay City Experiment (1956, 1958); Yale-Fairfield (1959).
[5] Duthie (1970).
[6] Hilsum, Bell and Cane (1969).
[7] See Appendix I for a fuller discussion of liaison procedures.

different teaching situations as possible. Four working parties of teachers (Infant, Junior, Modern, Grammar) prepared the way for trial observations: during the Spring and Summer of 1968, 41 teachers were observed, 10 in secondary grammar/technical schools, 6 in a secondary modern school, 13 in junior schools, 11 in infant schools and one in a nursery school.

2. Observation methods
Several methods of observation were tried out: these included the use of 'mechanical' observers (television camera with a video-tape recorder; sound tape recorder; combined audio-video-tape recorder) and human observers (an outside observer recording in shorthand, narrative form; an outside observer keeping systematic, objective records; the teacher himself recording from memory). We concluded that, for our purpose, the outside observer recording systematically was the most suitable observing method, provided the teacher wore a radio-microphone which transmitted to the observer: this 'mechanical aid' was required so that the observer could hear the teacher even when the latter was speaking quietly to a pupil. The reasons for selecting this particular observation method are discussed in the report of the feasibility study.

As the teacher's work extended beyond school hours and included evenings, weekends and vacations, it was decided to ask the teachers to complete 'diaries' for these periods. We tried out various forms of diary until we arrived at a version which was structured to provide the researchers with the information they required but which teachers could complete fairly easily (see Appendix II). The reliability of these subjective records is discussed in the feasibility report and in Chapter 7 of this book.[8]

Thus, during school hours a system of continuous recording by observers was adopted, and outside these hours, teachers kept their own records, summarized under categories that corresponded broadly to those used in school-time.

3. Categorizing the teacher's activities
There was extensive discussion of the classification system used to describe teachers' work. Obviously, this system played a major part in the research, and it was developed with considerable care. At first, the

---

[8] There is one question that may here arise in the reader's mind and which we should answer immediately: why did we reject the use of subjective records made by teachers about work done *during* school hours, but accept them when made about work performed *outside* these times? The fact is, that the two estimates are made about quite different circumstances: the classroom and school situation entails a series of complex interaction patterns in which the teacher is himself intimately involved, but outside school hours the teacher's work occurs in a relatively simple context; his memory of the events of the classroom situation will therefore be liable to much greater distortion than will his recall of out-of-school work.

teachers in Slough drafted and tested out their own categories (see Appendix III). The research team developed these, checked and re-checked them during their observations in all types of school, from nursery to sixth form. There was a constant reference back and forth from office discussion to classroom trials: the video-tapes of 30 lessons were played and replayed in further tests of the category system.

In all this work, constant efforts were made to ensure that the categories included all possible teacher activities, and did not involve any judge-ments on the observer's part as to which activities were 'educational' or 'non-educational'. Also, none of the categories were to be in any way evaluative of the teacher's success or failure. Our aim was merely to report what the teacher was seen to be doing; the later interpretation of grouping of the observed categories of activity should be seen as an exer-cise separate from the actual recording process.

Gradually, a list of activities appropriate to the junior teacher's work was arrived at, and it was this list that researchers used in their recording throughout the study in Surrey. It had been found, as was to be expected, that there was an enormous number of activities undertaken by teachers, but there were sufficient common elements among these multifarious tasks to warrant reducing them to 55 categories. (The category system also included a few supplementary coded observations: for example, one sign was used to show that the observed activities had occurred simultaneously; other signs indicated whether the activities recorded were related to attendance registration, dinner registration or 'milk-time'; another sign denoted that the teacher's lesson had been interrupted from outside the classroom. The complete list of categories and the kind of teacher activity described under each category are shown in Appendix IV.

A more detailed discussion of the rationale used in developing the category system is presented in Appendix III; here we only wish to emphasize most strongly that the system was developed *empirically*. Its effectiveness depends on the extent to which every conceivable activity was covered, and the precision with which each category was defined and understood by each observer.

4.   Recording methods
Various types of recording sheet and recording procedure were tested during the feasibility study, and Appendix II gives the details of the method finally adopted for the main study in Surrey. The following pro-vides an outline of the procedure.

Each observer arrived at the school before school began on the sampled day, and stayed with the sampled teacher for the whole day until the school timetable finished, i.e. during breaks and lunchtime as well as during teaching sessions. Every activity – other than private matters – was observed and recorded on the specially devised schedule (see Appen-dix II). When an activity began, the observer made a down-stroke on a horizontal time-scale, followed by the number that symbolized the activity; when that activity finished and the next began, another down-stroke was made, followed by the number allocated to that next activity; thus the record continued throughout school hours – down-stroke, number, down-stroke, number, and so on.

Experience showed that this was the only practical way of proceeding: the teacher's work was so diverse, and so often broken up into tiny intervals of a fraction of a minute, that an accurate record in terms of larger sections of time would have been impossible if a time interval as long as five minutes, or even one minute, had been adopted. The summation of many large errors would have given a misleading picture of the whole day. In any case, the very frequent change of activity in junior school work would have been missed from the record.

We had originally thought in terms of recording in the way described during randomly sampled parts of the day only, rather than continuously throughout the whole of school hours, but we agreed with our committee of advisers that a great deal of the qualitative side of the teacher's work might then be lost: activities occurring at one part of the day were frequently directly related to those happening at other times of the same day; and to understand or explain the incidence of a day's specific activities one needed knowledge about the total activities occurring on that day.

What emerged from our records, therefore, was a descriptive sequence of each day's activities from '9 to 4', plus a summary of evening, weekend and holiday work. The description was in terms of the time devoted to each category of activity, and, for school hours, the frequency of that category and the order in which activities occurred.

In order to enrich the eventual description and to assist our later analysis, the observer also recorded items thought to be relevant to the context of the day's work. Apart from biographical information about the teacher, these items included notes about the weather (e.g. raining, windy, very cold), the school (e.g. pupil roll, type of building), the class (e.g. size, year-group), and any points about individual pupils that the teacher believed the observer ought to know (e.g. the presence of new pupils, of immigrant pupils who spoke no English, of maladjusted pupils). Whether the teacher was standing or sitting or moving outside the classroom was also noted, as were periods when he was 'on duty' and periods when he was 'free'.

5. Observers

The feasibility study provided us with the opportunity to consider all matters relating to the qualifications, qualities and training required in an observer. Details are given in the feasibility report: we need only state here that for the project described in the present book we decided to use three observers, all of whom had been teachers. As they were to observe in schools independently, it was vital that they be trained thoroughly in the identification and recording of categories, and observer agreement tests were carried out prior to and during the course of the project. These tests (described in Appendix VI) showed that the observers achieved a remarkable degree of unanimity.

THE MAIN STUDY

The feasibility study in the Slough area had shown us how to approach the main study: the observation method, the categorizing system and the recording procedures had been established and have been outlined in the previous section. The approach to teachers, however, needs further exposition, for this is vital to the issue of 'abnormality in the observed situation'. In the rest of this chapter, therefore, we discuss the procedures used in the main study to achieve 'normality', and follow this with an explanation of the way we have collated the data recorded in the study; to begin with, the sampling is discussed, for this provides the framework within which the main study operated.

1. The sample of schools, teachers and days
Records of work done in school hours were obtained on 197 schooldays during the year 1969. (A school year contains about 200 schooldays.) These recorded days were distributed over the spring, summer and autumn terms of that year, and apart from the first and last weeks of each term (which were excluded, as being exceptional) all parts of each term were represented in the sample days. We received 185 'diary' records of work done in out-of-school hours on schooldays; the distribution of these during the year corresponded to the in-school records. The records of weekend work related to 75 weekends, also distributed throughout the three terms of the year, and, finally, the holiday work was recorded on 150 days and included the half-term breaks, plus the three main holidays of the year (Christmas, Easter and Summer).

A total of 129 teachers, working in 66 different schools, were involved in the records. During the spring term, two teachers in 18 different schools were observed; and each teacher was observed on two days. This pattern of observation was repeated for the summer term, i.e. two teachers in a further 18 schools were each observed on two days; but in the autumn term, it was decided to expand the teacher sample, and two teachers in a further batch of 30 schools were observed, this time on one day each instead of two.[9] Fuller details of the sampling design of days, schools and teachers, and the reasons for the change in the design for the third terms are provided in Appendix VI.

The large number of days sampled guaranteed that most kinds of

---

[9] This design should have resulted in a sample of 132 teachers; the reduction to the sample of 129 who were actually observed was due to the absence through illness of three of the teachers.

situation were covered in a representative way, i.e. school situations, different teachers, and variations in days of the week and month. Some heads in the sampled schools queried whether the particular teachers and days selected for observation in their school were really typical: the answer is that individual days or teachers would be unrepresentative, but for large numbers of days or teachers, chosen at random, the overall picture must be representative, provided we spelt out the degree of variation and the nature of the variation – as we have tried to do.

2. 'Normality' of the observed days

Readers may accept the statistical sampling, but still have doubts about the reliability of the recording situation: how can the teacher act normally when being continuously observed throughout the day? This was one of the key issues we tackled in our feasibility study. We accepted that there must be some degree of abnormality in the day of a teacher who was being observed; our task was to minimize this to a point at which it was relatively unimportant.

As a result of our experience in Slough schools, we concluded that it was the teacher rather than the pupils about whom we should be concerned. Pupil 'abnormality' soon disappeared once the novelty of the observer's presence had faded; most teachers, however, would only feel relaxed and 'normal' if they sensed that the observer's presence constituted no threat of any kind, either to their own position or to their relationship with their pupils. Our aim, therefore, was to reassure the teacher so that he became unperturbed by, and even indifferent to, the observer's presence – we wanted to achieve a situation where, in fact, the teacher simply forgot that he was being observed.

The procedure we adopted in Surrey was as follows: the project was explained first to the representatives of the several county associations of heads and teachers, and an advisory committee was formed. Eleven separate meetings were then held in different parts of the county, and all primary heads in the county were invited to attend any of these; at these meetings we outlined the project and answered any questions put to us. With the permission of the heads concerned, we then visited all the 66 sampled schools, and in each school we introduced ourselves to the two teachers who had been sampled. We explained that all records obtained would remain anonymous and that our observations contained no element of judgement about the teachers' methods or attitudes. We tried to make them thoroughly familiar with the procedures and aims of the research; we encouraged them to ask any questions or make any comments about what was involved. At that point the teachers were asked if we could arrange an 'acceptance visit' for each of them.[10]

---

[10] We have summarized the 'approach' procedure here. The reader is referred to Appendix I for further details and discussion.

On an 'acceptance day', the observer attended at the school for a whole day and gave the teacher and his pupils a chance to familiarize themselves with the whole observing and recording procedure, including the use of the radio-microphone. Samples of the teacher's work were recorded and shown to the teacher if he wished to see them. (These were intended only as 'practice' samples; none were used in our analysis.) At breaks and lunch-time the teacher was again encouraged to ask any questions, and the out-of-school diary schedules were explained to him. The acceptance day also provided the observer with an opportunity to acquaint himself with the classroom and school situation and, through their conversations during the day, the teacher and observer could develop a relaxed relationship. (It was understood, of course, that on the 'real' observation days, the observer would become a spectator, divorced from the situation. There would be no observer-teacher or observer-pupil interaction, apart from the normal civilities of a 'Good morning', etc.).

During the preliminary conversations, some teachers declared themselves already contented about the position and said they did not require an acceptance visit; others, during the course of the acceptance day, said they were satisfied and it was not necessary for the observer to stay for the full day. However, we always tried to keep to our arranged procedure, partly to make sure we were seen by the other pupils and staff, for they also had to accept us around the school and in the staffroom. We regarded one acceptance day as a minimum acclimatization period; we always offered to return for another if the teacher had any doubts about his or the pupils' 'normality', but no teacher who had experienced the acceptance visit said he needed a second.

At the end of the acceptance day, the teacher was asked if he would participate in the project.[11] The careful introduction for the teacher had ensured that each participant had the maximum opportunity to assuage his doubts, to get his queries answered, and to gain confidence both in the observer as a person and in the procedure of recording. We felt that this part of the project was much appreciated by the teachers, to the extent that, of 141 teachers approached, 132 agreed to participate.[12] This degree of response, in our opinion, was an indication that the teachers had accepted in a positive way the notion of having an observer in the classroom, i.e. their anxieties or feelings of insecurity had been dispelled; this had been the objective of the whole preparatory exercise,

---

[11] This is an important point. The teachers were randomly selected and *then* asked to volunteer; thus the research procedure ensured that no suggestion could be made to the effect that the sample of teachers consisted of 'special' teachers.

[12] Some of the refusals were concerned with the teacher's ill-health, the remainder with hostility to the project. All refusals occurred during early discussions, well before the matter of an acceptance visit could be raised.

for it was the teachers' anxieties, we believed, that might have made the observed classroom situations 'abnormal'.

We were satisfied, then, that the element of 'abnormality' in the observed situation had been reduced to a minimum; that when the actual observation day arrived, the classroom situation would be almost completely unaffected by the presence of the observer. However, we wished to test our belief. Accordingly, at the end of the actual observation day, the teacher was asked if, and to what extent, he believed he himself or the pupils had been affected by the observer's presence. In Appendix V, this issue is discussed in further detail, but we can say here that the conclusion of our feasibility study, viz. that if our procedure was followed, then the classroom situation would be altered very little, was substantially confirmed.[13]

One point about the observation procedure remains to be mentioned, and it is most important with regard to the credence the reader will give to our findings. In order to remove any suggestion of 'preparation' on the part of the teachers, we did not give any advance notice to either heads or teachers of the actual days on which we would visit schools for the sampled observation visits. The observer just arrived at the school about 8.45 a.m. without warning, and recorded the day as he found it. The teachers who agreed to take part knew that this would be the method of proceeding, although they also understood from our discussions with them that there was to be no 'judgement' of their work and no advantage would be gained for them or for the project if they modified their day to impress the observer.

3. Collating the data: periods of time recorded

For the purpose of our analysis, the teaching day was divided into three sections of time:

(a) *C-time* This is the major part of the school day and refers to the teaching sessions, when the teacher is timetabled to be with a class. Typically, there would be four sections of C-time: from the start of the day to the beginning of morning break, from the end of morning break to the start of the lunch period; from the end of the lunch period to the start of the afternoon break; from the end of afternoon break to the end of the timetabled day.

(b) *S-time* This includes the morning and afternoon breaks, and the lunch period. During S-time, teachers might be expected to be fairly free to drink their cup of tea, eat their lunch, and to relax. Our study indicates to what extent this expectation was fulfilled.

(c) *O-time* This covers all the unobserved time outside school hours, i.e. before the school timetable commences in the morning, and after the

---

[13] Oddly enough, although in the previous literature this matter of abnormality resulting from an observer's presence is discussed at some length, the only attempt to gauge some measure of the observer's effect was made during the study by Stukat (1967).

timetable has finished in the afternoon. O-time will therefore include any professional work undertaken in the evenings of the schooldays observed. We have extended the meaning of O-time to cover non-schooldays, i.e. weekends and holidays.

4. Collating the data: the grouping of the categories

The fifty-odd categories of activity, referred to previously and detailed in Appendix IV, provided the basic data for the researchers to study, and several of these individual categories are of considerable interest in their own right. It was felt, however, that it would be easier for readers to understand the general findings if the categories were grouped, where possible, into the kind of descriptive system most educationists are familiar with.

There are, of course, certain dangers in this procedure: first, it is well known that the various parties interested in educational matters differ remarkably in the connotations they attach to educational terms, and any label attached to a group of teacher activities will probably convey different ideas to different people; secondly, even if all readers agreed on the definitions of the terms used, it is quite feasible that they might differ in the way they allocated specific categories to main groups or sub-divisions. It must be understood, therefore, that the labels under which categories are subsumed, as given in Table 2.1 are very general terms – in fact, they are defined by the activities as listed in Appendix IV.

The main divisions of teacher activity are briefly described below, under their arbitrarily chosen titles.

I. '*Teaching*' This covers the most obvious aspects of teaching: the moments when the teacher explains a point in the lesson, asks and answers questions about the lesson, tells a story to the class, listens to and joins in discussion of a lesson topic, shows a group how to read a map, demonstrates to an individual pupil how to multiply, watches and calls out evaluative comments to pupils as they perform gymnastic skills, instructs pupils in mixing colour paints, and so on. These and similar activities, all of which involve interaction with pupils and which the teacher may do sitting, standing or moving about, come under the sub-division called lesson instruction. But under teaching we have also included activities concerned fairly closely with lessons but where there is no interaction with pupils, for example the planning of lessons, marking, professional reading. These we have subsumed under the general label of lesson preparation. Other components of teaching are school games fixtures, educational visits, attendance at a professional course.

II. '*Organization*' In this main division we have placed observation categories that relate to organization for, and during, teaching. This includes grouping children and giving them their lesson assignments; arranging the collection or distribution of books and equipment; dealing with contingencies and incidents that arise in the middle of a lesson;

dealing with messages in and out of the classroom; planning a coach trip, a sports fixture list, a list of classroom jobs for monitors. Also included under this main heading were various forms of staff consultation (with colleagues, or with non-teaching staff) since these contacts generally relate to organization.

III. '*Control and supervision*'   The most obvious aspect of this section was discipline – the reprimanding of a child or group. It also covered the supervision of pupils moving about a building, supervising when another teacher was in charge (e.g. at assembly), patrolling the building or playground when on duty, invigilation of examinations, looking after children moving to and from an annexe.

IV. '*Clerical/mechanical tasks*'   Many jobs done by teachers are simple routine tasks that are required as support to the welfare or instructional work of the teacher. For instance, there are various kinds of recording done by teachers – copying lists or marks, marking the register, making out class lists. All teachers have to make, collect, store and distribute equipment (e.g. books, paper, pens), and some have additional items to consider (e.g. PT apparatus, film projector, tape recorder, musical instruments, craft tools). Most teachers spend time in simply clearing out a cupboard, tidying the room, moving chairs or desks. Activities of this general nature we have called clerical/mechanical.

V. '*Pastoral*'   There are many moments during a school day when teachers are concerned with the personal welfare of an individual child: it may be that the pupil has lost his spectacles or dinner money, or is not feeling well; the teacher may talk to a boy or girl about his or her hobbies, a family outing or a brother's success at the secondary school; in a few cases, the child may have some serious personal problem that needs attention. Any of these events may result in a teacher talking with parents, and this time would also be called pastoral. Added to these personal contacts, there are the broader activities such as Sports Day or Open Day, clubs and societies, which can often create an important opportunity for pastoral work.

VI. '*Private*'   Sometimes, during the day, a teacher will move around the building alone or wait in his classroom for pupils to arrive; and no 'work-activity' will appear to be involved. At other times, especially in the staff room, teachers will be relaxing, taking part in social conversation that has no content of work; perhaps they will read the newspaper, do a crossword or just sit and smoke a cigarette. They will go to the cloakroom. Some staff will do professional work (for payment) that has nothing to do with their school appointment, e.g. mark evening-class books. All these occasions, and similar ones, were classified as private.

VII. '*Unrecorded*'   The observers could not observe all the teachers all the time: for example, a few teachers left the school building at lunchtime to go home or shopping. In a small number of cases, the observer was unable to classify an activity under one of the agreed categories, even after subsequent discussion with research colleagues. It was thought best to classify such instances as unrecorded.

A tabular summary of the main divisions and sub-divisions is given in Table 2.1, together with examples of the activities covered. The full list of individual categories is described in Appendix IV.

TABLE 2.1: *The grouping of teacher activities*

	A Lesson instruction	e.g. instructing class, group or individual in lesson topic.
I. TEACHING	B Lesson preparations, etc.	e.g. marking; planning, professional reading.
	C Teaching but detail not recorded	e.g. educational visit.
	A Organizing in classroom or school	e.g. allocating pupils to assignments; arranging distribution of equipment.
II. ORGANIZATION	B Staff consultation	e.g. talking to head/ colleagues/advisers about professional matters.
III. CONTROL AND SUPERVISION	A Discipline	e.g. reprimanding pupils.
	B Supervision	e.g. escorting pupils along corridors; playground patrol; dinner supervision.
IV. CLERICAL/ MECHANICAL TASKS		e.g. clearing up spilt milk; marking registers; duplicating maps; collecting monies.
	A Individual pupil	e.g. joking with pupils; speaking to pupil about personal matter; talking to parent; dealing with unwell pupil.
V. PASTORAL	B Special occasions	e.g. concert, sports afternoon, school jumble sale.
	C Extra-curricular activity	e.g. football club, chess club.
	A Personal	e.g. chatting with

		colleagues about personal matters.
VI. PRIVATE	B Moving/waiting alone	e.g. walking along corridor, with no pupils present; waiting in classroom for pupils to arrive.
	C Professional work not connected with school job	e.g. at lunch-time, marking books of evening class students.
VII. UNRECORDED		e.g. observer could not see/hear teacher.

(b) Summary and conclusions

In order to provide a background to the proposed description of the teachers' work, information about the sampled schools, their staffs and their pupils was collected, and the most striking feature of this survey was the considerable variation reported in school circumstances and situation within one county area. The obviously different characteristics of school roll and location masked an infinite variety of working conditions arising from different standards of accommodation, differences in the ability range of pupils taught, differences in staffing provision (including part-time and specialist help), differences in class size and – possibly most important – differences in the teachers themselves (Chapter 3).

School hours
A teacher's daily round (on schooldays) is conducted within the framework of a school's timetable. In most of the sampled schools there were four teaching sessions during the day, with three break periods dividing these sessions from each other: the first and third breaks were short (about 10 or 15 minutes) and were intended to split up the morning and afternoon sessions respectively; the middle break was the lunch period and lasted on average 1 hour and 20 minutes. (The teaching sessions we have called 'C-time', and the breaks 'S-time'.) The average time allocated to the C-time part of the day was about four and three quarter hours, and that to S-time about one and three quarter hours; the average length of school hours was just over six and a half hours.

Schools varied considerably in several aspects of their school hours: notably, in the time they finished, the length of the lunch period, the total time allocated to C-time and to S-time, and the total length of school hours. Longer school hours appeared to be a feature of schools in the North Division of the county, but the other variations were distributed in a more complex manner across the schools.

These differences among the schools have extremely important implications regarding (*a*) the relative capacities of individual schools and teachers to undertake either curricular or extra-curricular activities, or both, and (*b*) the conditions of work for teachers in different schools (Chapter 4).

The teacher's work
During the teaching sessions of schooldays, only about 43 per cent of the time was, on average, allocated to lesson instruction as such; another 15 per cent was assigned to organizing pupils in the work. About a tenth of the time was spent on general supervision and another tenth on clerical or mechanical tasks. There were large day-to-day variations in these times, but it was noted that some activities which occupied only a small amount of the teacher's time, like pastoral work with individual pupils, might nevertheless be extremely important for both teacher and pupils.

Several of the observed activities occurred frequently during the sessions and thereby broke up the continuity of the teacher's work; in particular, many lessons involved a sequence of teacher activity in which short periods of instructing pupils alternated with still shorter intervals of organizing them (Chapter 5).

During breaks and the lunch period on schooldays only a quarter of the time was spent relaxing, eating or chatting privately: a further quarter of the time was taken up with talking to colleagues about professional matters; supervision, mechanical tasks, lesson preparation and club work occupied most of the remaining parts of S-time (Chapter 6).

In out-of-school hours the mean time spent each schoolday on all teaching activities was two hours and ten minutes, but this varied a great deal from day to day. The jobs that on average contributed most to each evening's professional work were marking, lesson planning and mechanical jobs, which together accounted for over half of the out-of-school work, with another fifth of this work being allocated to professional reading and staff discussion. Certain activities, like clubs and attendance at meetings, happened less often, but when they occurred they usually lasted much longer than other activities (Chapter 7).

When combining the time spent on professional work during the three parts of a school day, i.e. during the teaching sessions (C-time), in the breaks and lunch period (S-time), and in out-of-school hours, it was found that a teacher's average working day was eight and a quarter hours, or $41\frac{1}{4}$ hours per week. Teachers who worked in schools with short school hours appeared to do more out-of-school work than colleagues in schools with longer school hours.

A finding of great significance was that 42 per cent of the teacher's work was undertaken in his own time (S-time and O-time), most of it away from the classroom, and it was therefore suggested that future discussion of, and research into, the teacher's role in education should bear this fact in mind. Obviously, this finding is also very pertinent to the training of student teachers.

Analysis of the activities that made up the junior teacher's complete working day demonstrated that only 26 per cent of the day was spent actually instructing pupils; about 40 per cent was occupied in the essential related work – organizing pupils (10 per cent), consultation (12 per cent), marking (10 per cent), lesson planning and professional reading (8 per cent). Nearly 25 per cent of the day was spent on clerical and mechanical chores and supervision; almost as much time as was spent instructing (Chapter 8).

The amount of time spent on professional activities at weekends varied a great deal from one weekend to another, but the average amount of work done each weekend was three and a quarter hours. Thus, when weekend work was added to schoolday work, the teacher's working week during term-time amounted to an average of $44\frac{1}{2}$ hours.

Marking and lesson planning often accounted for over half the weekend work, and clerical or mechanical tasks took up another eighth; the rest of the work usually consisted of professional reading or jobs connected with school administration (Chapter 9).

With regard to holiday work, it was found that the teacher was engaged on activities connected with his job on about three-fifths of the days allocated as school holidays during the school year, and on these 'working days' the amount of work done ranged from a few minutes to over four hours. Over the whole sample of recorded holidays the average time allocated to teaching work each day was 74 minutes.

The teaching tasks which occupied the teacher most at holiday times were those concerned with the preparation of schemes of work; background reading of a professional nature, evaluating pupils' progress, and the various mechanical jobs associated with lesson planning and school administration (Chapter 10).

It was thought desirable to make a re-calculation of the teacher's working week, such that his 'long holidays' were taken into account; allowing the teacher only 28 days of 'legitimate' holiday (inclusive of statutory holidays), and regarding the remaining 337 days as days when he 'ought' to have been at work, the total amount of work actually observed and recorded during the year 1969 was equivalent to a working week of 38.2 hours throughout the 48-week year.

Variations in 'teaching days'

A study was made of the possible effect certain characteristics of the teachers, schools and classes in the sample might have exerted on the pattern of the teacher's work. The teacher characteristics studied (teaching experience, sex, dependants and school responsibility) appeared to have little influence on what many consider the chief activity of the classroom, namely lesson instruction. The chief differences found were: less experienced teachers appeared to be less organized in the classroom and had more disciplinary incidents; men teachers organized and reprimanded pupils less frequently than women; teachers who discharged school responsibilities but received no additional payment did more teaching work in out-of-school hours than deputy heads or teachers holding 'Burnham' posts. Similarities that were unexpected included: lesson preparation in evenings was undertaken as much by experienced as by inexperienced teachers; the more experienced teachers did as much extra-curricular (club) work as newer recruits; this club work was undertaken as much by teachers who had family commitments as by those without any (Chapter II).

The school characteristics examined were the school's size, the school neighbourhood, and the school's administrative area; the class variables considered were class size, year group and ability range. The principal finding was an unexpected one: the class-size and the ability range of a class appeared to have little effect on the pattern of classroom teaching adopted by the teacher, i.e. similar amounts of class teaching and individual teaching seemed to be undertaken regardless of the size of the class or the ability range of pupils. The only positive significant point to stress is the conclusion that teachers of large classes had to do most of their marking in their own time, while teachers of small classes were able to mark their pupils' work in lesson-time, with the pupils interacting. Two findings that were expected and were realized were: lessons with younger pupils were more fragmented than those with older pupils, and teachers in small schools supervised pupils during breaks and lunch periods for longer than other teachers did.

The divisional area in which a teacher worked almost certainly had an effect on much of the teacher's work, but the influence was not easy to identify: effects of local administration were probably mediated through such items as policy regarding school hours, the amount of ancillary help and part-time teaching assistance made available to a school, programmes of in-service courses, and so on, i.e. items that only indirectly affected the specific activities undertaken by teachers in and out of school (Chapter 12).

Special aspects of the teaching day
In an attempt to examine the problems of non-professional work, an analysis was made of those activities which were performed by the teachers but which, in the researchers' view, might have been carried out by a 'helper'. The chief activities concerned were those labelled mechanical, clerical and supervisory tasks; in our sample the average time spent on these jobs by the teacher was 1 hour and 41 minutes each schoolday. It was believed that our findings offered clear evidence of the need for 'helpers', but because there were many problems of organization involved which might affect the full utilization of a helper-service, it was suggested

that a carefully evaluated exercise should be conducted in which helpers were introduced into a limited number of schools, and the results of this exercise should guide policy-makers in any discussions on the future of a schools helper-service (Chapter 13).

One aspect of supervisory work that was studied in some detail was what teachers called duties, i.e. periods at playtime and/or lunch time when teachers were required to be on call on the school premises. Schools varied considerably in the way they organized duties, and individual teachers adopted different approaches in the way they carried them out. On average a teacher was on duty once every three or four days: a day involving playtime duty arose about once a week, as did a day when lunch-time duty was undertaken. These frequencies appeared to decrease as the size of the school increased, and to vary according to administrative area and teachers' school responsibility. About half the teachers seemed to have opted-out of supervising pupils at lunch periods (Chapter 14).

A study was made of free periods – those times during the day's teaching sessions when the teacher was not timetabled to be with a specific class or group. A teacher was timetabled to receive, on average, one free period in every two days, the mean length of a free period being between 25 and 30 minutes. In practice, one out of every five of these allocated periods was either cancelled or reduced.

The features that marked most free periods were: they contained very little personal activity on the part of the teacher; he was engaged in a variety of work tasks (chiefly those connected with mechanical chores, marking, consultation and lesson planning) rather than a single activity; many of these work activities entailed interaction with pupils and were conducted away from the staffroom (Chapter 15).

An analysis of the extra-curricular club activities organized by the teachers in their own time (S time and O-time) showed that on average a club session was recorded once every three or four days: a lunchtime club was organized once in six days, and an after-school club once in eight days. The average time of a club session was about half an hour, with after-school clubs lasting generally longer than lunchtime clubs. About a third of the teachers in the sample were recorded as running a club, and it was suggested that the relatively short lunch hour in some schools might be a factor deterring teachers in such schools from greater involvement in club activities. The clubs recorded catered for a very wide range of interests.

Very little club work was reported at weekends (Chapter 16).

(c) Disruptions in the teaching day: contingencies and interruptions

From the previous chapters, the reader will have gathered that the teacher's work in the classroom rarely proceeded steadily in a regular fashion. The interaction between pupil and teacher during the normal teaching situation was such that intermittency rather than continuity of activity was a prominent feature of each day.

Although the teacher-pupil interaction contributed largely to the fragmentation of the teacher's work, continuity was affected also by various disrupting factors that upset the teacher's planned programme. These interruptions – sometimes short, sometimes long, sometimes stemming from inside the classroom, sometimes from outside – occurred on most days, so that each teaching day contained an element of unpredictability. Occasionally the teacher could anticipate an abnormal day if he knew in advance of some adjustment to the normal school programme, e.g. all pupils were going to have a medical examination, or a touring drama company were to give a performance to the school; but often a situation would arise that could not have been predicted.

It was fairly obvious to the researchers that these abnormalities or disruptions were really part of the normal teaching day, and should be explicitly recognized as such.[14] We identified two types of disrupting or abnormal situation: (a) the expected event, known in advance, but happening relatively infrequently, e.g. a concert afternoon, a sports afternoon, a student arriving to take some lessons or observe; and (b) the emergency or contingency situation, unpredicted but needing to be attended to on the spot. The former kind of occasion is reviewed in Chapter 18; the latter type of disrupting incident which happens almost every day, is studied below, followed by an analysis of the interruptions caused when an adult or pupil enters the classroom with a message of some kind.

CONTINGENCIES

We recorded contingencies in one of two ways: there was the very specific situation involving a pupil's health or physical well-being, and there was the more general event affecting several pupils or the whole class.[15] We show in Table 17.1 how long and how often the teacher was called upon each day during class-time to deal with each kind of contingency. These data refer specifically to the contingency as observed – the events leading up to the contingency and any after-effects not seen as closely related to the contingency were excluded from the category and recorded under another appropriate category.

[14] In order to preserve the reality of a disruption, we regarded it quantitatively and qualitatively, as a single happening, although in fact it usually was made up of many small specific activities. There were also practical difficulties related to observing and recording these situations in detail. These methodological points are discussed in Appendix III.

[15] Although both kinds of emergency situation entailed the teacher in a variety of activities, for the purpose of later analysis we classified the health emergency as pastoral work and the general emergency situation as organization.

TABLE 17.1: *Contingency situations – duration and frequency during teaching sessions*

| | TIME (IN MINS,) | | FREQUENCY | |
	Mean	SD	Mean	SD
Health contingencies	1.3	2.4	6	6
General contingencies	2.8	3.6	5	5

The average time spent each day on contingencies was very small, but we would stress that although many of these situations were minor incidents, often lasting only a few moments, their effect on the teacher and pupils was often very considerable indeed. For this reason, we believe the quantitative summary presented in Table 17.1 needs to be supplemented by qualitative description.

Minor incidents

We list a variety of incidents that were observed at some time during the year's observations. It is by no means an exhaustive list, but it will convey to the reader the kind of situation in which the teacher had to stop what he was doing and deal with the matter as he saw fit.

(*a*) *Incidents lasting less than one minute*

Pupil asks to go to toilet – teacher permits.

Pupil asks to go to toilet – teacher queries request, tells pupil to wait till playtime.

Pupil complains of earache – teacher sends pupil to secretary.

Teacher pauses, wonders (out loud) why pupil so long in toilet – sends another pupil to find out.

Teacher about to start lesson pupil returns from playtime with cut knee – teacher attends to cut.

Teacher interrupted by pupil whose tooth has come out teacher checks and puts tooth in envelope for pupil (!).

Pupil starts hiccoughing and cannot stop – teacher tells pupil to go out and get drink of water.

Lesson just begun – pupil goes to front and asks for medicine – teacher takes bottle from drawer and gives pupil spoonful (!).

(*b*) *Incidents lasting between one and five minutes*

Pupil stung by wasp in classroom – teacher inspects, and sends pupil to secretary.

Pupil tells teacher she is unwell and wants to go to cloakroom – teacher permits, sends another pupil to check if first pupil all right. Second pupil returns – unwell pupil having nosebleed – teacher tells her to take unwell pupil to secretary. Later, second pupil returns – cannot find secretary – told to stay with unwell girl. Both pupils return – report bleeding stopped. Several times later teacher checks with unwell girl to see if feeling better. (This example of one incident intruding spasmodically into lesson time was not uncommon.)

Pupil enters after playtime – complains of being hit on head during playground fight – teacher inquires into fighting incident, sends implicated pupils to head.

Secretary enters and tells teacher that parent has complained about paint being thrown on daughter's jumper – teacher stops lesson and investigates how incident happened.

Craft lesson – pupil reports classroom sink blocked with paste – teacher investigates – finds outside drain blocked – pupil sent outside and works at drainpipe while teacher tries to clear drain from inside – head comes in and also helps. (This incident occurred in 'bursts', with the teacher trying simultaneously to check the work of the rest of the class, organize them packing up materials and clear up the sink mess.) . . .

TV lesson – picture becomes faulty and teacher tries to adjust – sends for another teacher – they twiddle knobs and try to re-capture picture. (Television breakdowns were fairly commonplace – sometimes the teacher(s) managed to remedy the fault, sometimes the lesson was abandoned, and sometimes the lesson continued with the teacher standing by the set with a hand fixed on a knob or holding up some wires!). . .

Major incidents

The previous notes recorded examples of situations that occurred fairly commonly; a teacher might expect one or several such contingencies to happen on any teaching day. There were other occasions which appeared to affect the teacher's work more noticeably, and some of these are described below. These descriptions were written by the observer a short while after the incident occurred and were the expanded versions of notes recorded on the spot. We acknowledge that they are subjectively written accounts, in that the observer was attempting to capture the 'flavour' of the event, but as we are here trying to convey the qualitative realities of the classroom situation, we feel these descriptions are worth reproducing.

Mrs D. ('mature' teacher, recently qualified)

Mrs D, a probationary teacher in her second term of teaching, was taking a class of seven-year-olds while her own was being taught by another teacher. She was reading a story that some pupils had requested, and she had told those pupils who did not want to listen to read their own books.

The observer heard the teacher occasionally refer to 'John', asking him to hurry and choose his book from the class library, and while the teacher was reading, John could be seen sliding along the back wall of the class, picking at books, poking at other children and generally making a great nuisance of himself. The observer wondered why Mrs D did not take any action, but as it was obvious that the teacher knew exactly what was happening, the observer assumed that she was deliberately trying to ignore John's activities. She told the other pupils to take no notice of John.

As Mrs D continued to read, John could now be seen going up to other pupils, pulling at them and punching them. Mrs D quietly reprimanded John each time he disturbed other pupils, and each time John stayed quiet and inactive for a moment. Little by little, however, one could sense a build-up of tension and the observer realized that the teacher had been trying to 'play down' John's activities. In a few moments, however, she could no longer continue the pretence of ignoring the boy's misbehaviour. John had moved over to Terry and begun punching him continually. Terry, a rather docile lad, tried to ignore him, but when John put his hand round Terry's neck and began tightening his grip, Terry and the other children round him called out to Mrs D. She was already up and moving towards the area of trouble, but John ignored her approach and continued his hold round Terry's throat. When the teacher tried to pull him away, he resisted strongly, and as soon as she had pulled him off, she went to fetch the headmaster, asking the observer as she passed him to watch the class. The moment she left, John began to threaten other pupils, and when the observer stood in his way so that he could not reach them, his face turned pale, his eyes glared vacantly and his body became quite rigid. The head teacher returned with Mrs D in a matter of seconds, and he escorted John out of the room.

Mrs D tried to continue reading to the class but was obviously very disturbed. Later she told the observer that John was a special case who, in the staff's view, should really be in a school for maladjusted children but advisers had thought it best to keep him in a normal class. She had, therefore, known about John's peculiarities and for that reason had attempted to play down his misbehaviour in the hope of his settling down. She said she had heard a great deal about John in general staff conversation and had found him a bit of a problem before; but she had never known him as bad as that day.

As John's behaviour that day caused no great surprise to his own teacher and the rest of the staff, it was clear that the observer's presence had not inspired the contingency. The recorded time for the emergency was four and a half minutes.

Mr J. (class of 34 pupils, 7–9 years old)

Earlier in the morning the observer had heard the headmistress talking to Mr. J about a mother who had come to the school that morning and reported that her son had had some hair trouble. The observer had heard the head say a few words about contacting the clinic.

At 11.34 the head entered and interrupted the teacher's work, and began organizing the pupils for 'head inspection' in the cloakroom. As the pupils filed out in line, those staying in the class had to continue working, but as pupils returned they giggled and joked and pulled faces, so that within a few minutes, the class, while not noisy, were completely distracted from work. Mr J tried to keep the work going, but the nature of the situation, with the head also entering to speak to him and confer with him every few minutes, was such that concentrated effort was out of the question. Finally, as the last pupils returned, Mr J appeared most anxious to be inspected himself and the head stayed in the room while the teacher made sure that the fleas in his hair was one perk in the teacher's job that he most certainly did not want to receive. A final word with the nurse on how to continue hair protection concluded the incident, but the class remained excited, gossipy and bubbly for the next half-hour.

Even then, the incident's impact was not over, for during most of the lunch hour it naturally formed the centre of staff discussion, past experiences of such situations and present anxieties being aired freely.

The actual contingency from arrival of the nurse till the end of the inspection lasted twelve minutes, but the visible effects of the contingency on the class routine and on the teacher's task lasted much longer. (There was, of course, no way of measuring the teacher's concern for the physical welfare of the class or for himself, but that evening one NFER observer, if himself observed on his return home, might have been seen discarding the calm, objective approach of his training and, with only a hurried, muffled greetings to his family, rushing into his bathroom and washing his hair vigorously and uninterruptedly for the ensuing half-hour.)...

INTERRUPTIONS

The previous section of this chapter studied various class-room incidents which tend to disrupt the teacher's work. Another source of disruptions is the person entering the classroom during teaching time, to deliver a message or report. Such interruptions are often only momentary, like a pupil coming for the dinner register, or some pupils bringing in the milk crate, but they can very easily break the flow of a lesson, mar a teacher's train of thought, or spoil the class concentration that a teacher may have spent a considerable time establishing. Many teachers will say that these minor interruptions are the bane of their lives, because they happen so frequently, so regularly and often so unnecessarily.

We were asked to study this problem if it were possible to do so, and our observers duly made a note of every occasion during class-time when the teacher received a message or was otherwise interrupted from outside the classroom. In Chapter 5, in discussing the teacher's work during teaching sessions, we mentioned in passing that the teacher was inter-rupted about six times every day, which meant that any single session would be interrupted at least once and possibly twice. Further inspection of the records revealed large variations in these figures – ranging from no interruptions on some days to 15 on others. Sometimes, of course, a high proportion of interruptions was determined by a special happening on the day of observation – e.g. a concert rehearsal that involved messages being sent round the school frequently. Nevertheless, special events apart, one cannot help wondering whether the differences in frequency of inter-ruption were reflecting differences in school management and organ-ization. We did not have sufficient data to investigate these differences in frequency further, but we were able to make a rough analysis of the *reasons* for interruptions.

During the Autumn term, the observers were instructed to record where possible not only if an interruption occurred but any additional information concerning the interruption. We later classified the interruptions according to the reason for their occurring. (Because of practical difficulties, the observers were unable to record the reason for the interruption in about a fifth of the cases inspected, but we believe that those analysed were a representative selection, not only of the Autumn term but of interruptions throughout the year.) We present below and in Table 17.2 a breakdown of interruptions according to their type or reason: this analysis provides only a rough-and-ready guide – some types overlap a little, and in addition some instances of interruption contained a mixture of reasons.

TABLE 17.2 *Reasons for interrupting the teacher/class*

NATURE OF INTERRUPTION	% OF ANALYSED INTERRUPTIONS
Related to equipment	38
Related to school organization	18
Related to clerical items	15
Related to individual pupils	13
Related to distribution/collecting	6
Miscellaneous interruptions	10

(a) *Interruptions related to equipment*
Examples:

Pupil enters and asks observed teacher for item of equipment (e.g. pens, pencils, books, stationery, art or craft material, guillotine, film projector).

Pupil returns item borrowed . . .

(b) *Interruptions related to school organization*
Examples:

Another teacher enters to confer about swimming arrangements.

Head asks about arranging meetings with parents.

Pupil delivers message about: change in playtime; re-organization of lessons; lunchtime arrangements; time of netball match . . .

(c) *Interruptions related to clerical items*

Examples:

Pupil comes to collect attendance/dinner register.

Pupil returns register.

Secretary enters to query dinner totals.

Pupil asks for list of names/marks . . .

(*d*) *Interruptions related to individual pupils or groups*
Examples:

> Head asks (or sends note asking) for pupil(s) to see him.
>
> Secretary enters to tell pupil his mother is waiting to take him to doctor/dentist.
>
> Parent knocks and calls for pupil to go home.
>
> Head enters and asks teacher information about individual pupil's progress/behaviour/home background . . .

(*e*) *Interruptions related to distribution/collection of items*
Examples:

> Secretary enters with leaflets to be distributed to class.
>
> Pupil enters with notices for class to take home . . .

(*f*) *Miscellaneous interruptions*
Examples:

> Head brings visitor to see teacher/class.
>
> Caretaker enters to stoke boiler.
>
> Head looks in to see if heating working.

Comment on interruptions

While, after inspecting the reasons for interruptions, it is only too easy to generalize and conclude that the majority of these interruptions were unnecessary and that the head should have organized matters better, one must be a little cautious where individual cases are concerned. Comment on interruptions to the teacher's classroom work must take into account the context in which a particular school or teacher functions – limited facilities at the school, absence or shortage of teaching staff, dearth of equipment, lack of ancillary help, insufficient (or no) secretarial assistance, and so on. We must also add here the interesting and relevant point that, although many teachers may regard their head as the chief culprit, i.e. the person initiating most of the notices or messages the classroom teacher receives, inspection of our records shows that class teachers themselves were responsible for a large number of the interruptions caused to our observed teachers. Again, some of these may have been unavoidable interruptions and have to be seen in the context of the school situation.

We may sum up by saying that generalizations in this matter are not especially helpful. Our evidence leads us to conclude that, on the whole, there were an excessive number of apparently avoidable interruptions, and that if, as many teachers affirm, interruptions interfere with effective classroom teaching, then there is a case here for each school to study closely how it is affected by the problem and how it can deal with it, so that interference with the teacher's work (and thereby, the children's education) is reduced to an absolute minimum.

6 Field anthropologists and classroom teachers

PAUL J. BOHANNAN

(*Social Education*, Vol. 32, No. 2, February 1968, pp. 161–6)

There are three major areas in which anthropology is relevant in primary and secondary schools. First, of course, it is important as a subject matter. A great deal of anthropology is already taught in the schools. Often it is not called by its name, but Eskimos and Bushmen and Pygmies are standard fare in the primary grades. L. S. B. Leakey is a national hero in our junior high schools, and non-Western and world history courses are laced with anthropology. Much of this anthropology seriously needs upgrading to meet professional standards of relevance and accuracy and (ironically enough) to remove from it inaccuracies and romanticism such as those that have been introduced into American Indian studies by the Boy Scouts. But, on the other hand, some of it is already of pretty good quality – particularly the anthropology of early man and evolution.

Second, anthropology, better than any of the other social sciences, provides a method of investigation that is suitable for the study and evaluation of classroom procedures and cultures. Anthropologists, over the decades, have evolved a way of analysing and presenting small communities that can almost without alteration be switched to the study of schools and the cultural associations among classroom, community cultures, and the educational systems of our nation. It is, at the moment, becoming stylish for anthropologists to study schools. People from other disciplines are also studying classrooms and schools in the community, and are borrowing extensively from anthropological techniques when they do it. It is becoming obvious – and heartening – that we shall within the next few years see the efflorescence of a large body of data and no inconsiderable insight about the educational process in our own society, with a good bit of interesting comparative material. The school is, after all, one of the main 'institutions of cultural transmission' in modern societies; education is one of the most vital activities that any society must carry out. Finally we are getting around to investigating it directly.

The third point, however, is the one to which this article is devoted: the technique of anthropological field work offers great insight into some of the problems of teachers, both during their training and in their classrooms. I have found, to my great astonishment and delight, that teachers take to these ideas and techniques with almost no adaptation at all. It is very soon possible to develop in the teacher an awareness of social and cultural dynamics, as well as a mode of action which enables him to participate fully and vitally and at the same time to stand back far enough to see what is going on. It offers a proven device to control his emotions and his actions so that he stays in touch with the real world – with what is going on out there in the classroom.

I shall first give a brief description of what an anthropologist does in the field. I shall then review the seminar at Northwestern's School of Education in which eighteen M.A.T. candidates and I first investigated these ideas, and will then make some overt comparisons with the classroom teacher and a few concrete suggestions about how the teacher can use these techniques and ideas.

The cultural anthropologist in the field

Like the teacher, the field anthropologist does his job with his entire personality. His acceptance into the community, and his ultimate success or failure, depends almost as much on what he is as a person as on what he does as a trained professional. It is well to keep this idea in mind as we explore the job of the anthropologist.

The anthropologist, as ethnographer, is faced with the task of going into another culture and adjusting to it as he learns it. This learning is no mere question mongering – it means getting the other culture into his mind and his muscles, learning to speak its language as well as he can, and participating in the life of 'his community' to whatever degree his people and his own personality will allow. Then, even more difficult, he must return to his own culture and must devise ways of communicating in English, what he has learned in a foreign tongue and alien culture. And he must do it so that there is as little warping as possible of the values and ideas current in the culture he has studied – no mean task when all of the technical terms in English have themselves been developed to explain and adjust American and British cultures.

The first task for the field anthropologist is to learn the language. In the process, of course, he must learn new facts about his own language – about the strange ways in which he is accustomed to putting things to himself, and about the particular limitations and elasticities of English. Even more important than learning the words, he must learn to 'hear,' in the sense of understand in *their* terms, what it is that his informants are trying to tell him. If they do not answer his questions straight, it's three to one that the difficulty lies in the question and the way the ethnographer is asking it. In the course of learning the language, he must also learn new sets of gestures (and hence the literal 'feel' of that language may be much different) and new ways of evasions and new ways of hiding things from one's self. In short, he must learn new aspects and new deep meanings of his own 'body English' as well as of his own spoken English.

In this process, the anthropologist is constantly discovering himself as he investigates and records the data concerning the people he studies. It is no easy matter to get over *assuming* you know what is being said out there in the 'real world.' But you cannot really look at the real world of a foreign culture until you can see it in its own terms the very while you look at yourself looking at it.

Thus, both teachers and field anthropologists are in unparalleled situations for getting their own cultures straight in their own minds. They will discover, in the course of doing their work, that much of what had seemed common sense – ordinary background of ordinary social life, about which it had never before been necessary to think – is suddenly thrust into prominence and awareness.

In short, the teacher (like the anthropologist) must be made aware of his own values, his own unstated assumptions, his very bodily movements, if he is to learn the culture of his students. And the greater the difference between his own background and that of his students, the more aware of it he becomes – and hence, ironically, the clearer his job will be.

In short, if you are going to use your personality as the primary tool in your work, you have to learn something about your own personality and the cultural idiom in which it is accustomed to express itself. Only then are you in a position to modify or utilize your own techniques of learning and hence of teaching so that they do indeed serve the ends that you intend them to serve.

An anthropologist selects a people he is to study on the basis of two major considerations: his own capacity to live the kind of life these people live, and the problems which are currently paramount in his discipline. In this way, he will know that such-and-such a people or institution or situation is 'ready' to be studied, and that he can likely make a significant contribution to the knowledge in the field. Both these considerations are important.

It is necessary first to have an overt and intellectual goal in mind – that is, for the field anthropologist to learn something about the way a specific human group, whatever it may be, faces some of the fundamental problems of human living. It may be a problem in law and the way in which conflict is either settled or handled in the absence of settlement. It may be a problem in economy, and the way in which provisioning is taken care of in the absence of familiar institutions such as markets. It may, indeed, be a problem in cultural transmission, and the way in which present-day schools drive a wedge between generations and turn some of the children into near schizophrenics because of the double messages that they receive at home and at school. The consideration is always that the discipline has the conceptual equipment to confront a problem, but needs more facts and ideas to solve it, and that the individual practitioner has the requisite imagination and nerve to turn new ideas and new data to the benefit of the discipline.

However, there is another matter here: every individual field worker goes to the field with a developed and entire personality and mode of life. He obviously cannot make himself entirely over. Therefore, he must select a people whose temperament and mode of life he finds bearable. Not admirable, necessarily; not even pleasant. But bearable. After all, a field worker is going to be living with these people for a period of from one to three years, and if he did not find them at least minimally congenial, it would be absolutely impossible for him to do his job. Yet, if the anthropologist works among his own people, he is not going to have to alter the frame of reference of his very life – and it is this very alteration that leads to anthropological insight.

Therefore, the first requirement for an anthropologist is to find a place to work in which he is not grossly uncomfortable, but with which he is not overly familiar either. Now, this seems to me to be precisely the situation of any neophyte[16] teacher – particularly those who have chosen to work among the various ethnic groups in our country that are different from the one in which they have grown up. It is especially true of American middle-class teachers who, in line with the commitment to middle class values of helping others, have chosen to face the ethnic groups of the inner cities.

An anthropologist cannot use interpreters as a short cut for learning the language. If he does, he is not going to get to the heart of the meaning that these people attach to their institutions for living. He cannot both understand what they are about and allow himself the luxury of somebody else's doing his analysis and telling him how to behave (although if other people have been there before him, some of their hints may be useful – but they may be also worse than useless).

Again, I think the parallel is evident: the teacher cannot depend on somebody else, either his own teachers, or his principal, or anybody else, to tell him how to do this job. He must himself learn to communicate with his charges. The problem of communication may stem from no more than a difference in age. (I was acutely aware when I first faced a ninth grade of middle-class Americans that I, a middle-class American, had not dealt with 14-year olds since I was 14, and that the world had changed a lot since then.) However, in the present day in which we are trying to upgrade the schools of our inner cities and to educate a greater range of Americans to ever more demanding social roles, I venture that a large proportion of teachers find themselves face to face with people whose language they do not understand – in some cases because it may not be English, in others because it may not be the standard dialect of English, in still others because there may be secret languages or other secret modes of communication among students who zealously keep the teacher from understanding their private means of communicating.

The anthropologist – and the teacher – must also discover the degree to which he or she can be taken into the community that is the subject of

---

[16] A teacher beginning his or her career.

study. In some African communities every anthropologist is required to live as a chief because the people will not accept him on any other basis. In some American communities every teacher is required to present himself as a middle-class arbiter of morality because the students and the community will not accept him on any other basis. You must learn to work within an ascribed status, perhaps trying to change it a little, but more importantly, understanding the constrictions that it puts on your activities and your opportunity to learn.

In some African communities, the people are delighted when an anthropologist wants to live among them, in superficial ways at least, as they themselves live. In the same way, in some American communities some teachers will be welcomed into strange ethnic groups, but this experience, I judge, is exceptional. I think it is unlikely that most teachers will find themselves allowed to speak the local dialect, even if they learn to understand it. Middle-class teachers in lower-class Negro schools are faced with having to learn to understand a kind of English which they are never allowed, by their students, to use. They have to be circumspect enough to discover the limitations (either from self or from community) in living with and utilizing the culture of the people they teach or study.

Learning a language can be a tricky matter because no two languages structure the sense world in precisely the same way. When, as children, our five senses are culturally educated, we also learn that language in terms of which we shall for the rest of our lives cut up our perceptions in order to communicate about them. When we learn only one language, the result is necessarily a monoglot's view of culture and the whole world.

Therefore, in the process of learning a new language, an anthropologist begins to know overtly what he has formerly perceived only covertly: a specific organization to his cultural and social world, a palette of color, as it were, with which life in his particular latitudes is always presented and perceived. This kind of self-knowledge is the essence of field anthropology – and, I suggest, of successful teaching.

Something else happens too: we discover not just the way we see the world, but we also discover some of our feelings about it – about morality, about cleanliness and godliness, about money, and about ambition. We may thereupon become indignant, angry, frightened. The 'way out' of these feelings is, for the untrained, to blame the other guy, and belittle his culture and his values. This is one way – but a naive way – of saving your own value system, making it unnecessary for you to question your own assumptions and your own feelings.

This set of threats to the individual is usually called 'culture shock,' especially in its more acute form. Culture shock may occur to anyone when he finds his feelings threatened by matters he does not understand, and his actions made insecure by social situations in which he cannot make accurate predictions. Culture shock is a result of having to face situations in which you do not know what you are expected to do next, and hence any action you take may lead to misfortune or disaster. It is a kind of psychic deprivation, and can lead to serious consequences if you do not know how to deal with it, and yet cannot run away.

Let me give two examples of culture shock – both from my own life. One of these occurred in the Ivory Coast, long after I knew about culture shock – and indeed, only a few days after I gave a series of lectures on it. I proceeded immediately from an Eastern university in the United States, where I had been giving my lectures to a group of students who were proceeding overseas, to a conference in Abidjan. Everything went swimmingly until the weekend. I had accepted an invitation from an African colleague in the conference for Sunday, an invitation that I thought I ought for my own edification to accept, but which I was quite unenthusiastic about. A few hours later I felt I had to turn down another invitation from a group of French participants to spend Sunday with them at the beach swimming and picnicking. Then, on Sunday, I was stood up by the African. Now, I know perfectly well that such behaviour on the part of the African was not, by his standards, anywhere nearly as rude – indeed, insufferable – as it was by mine. Something else had come up, and it would have been extremely awkward for him to have notified me. However, when I realized what had happened, I went to my hotel room, pulled the blinds, and went to bed. I was emancipated enough not to blame him – I blamed his 'lousy culture.'

Within a few minutes, fortunately for me, I realized what I was doing – and recalled that I had only a few days before told my audience that if you are lonely or angry or home-sick or feel ill-used, you had better ask yourself, 'Buddy, what's biting you? What are you trying to get by with?' I had, to cover my own disappointment and to keep from being annoyed at my own 'virtue' in keeping the standards of my own culture about invitations, labeled *his* culture inferior. I dressed again, pulled up the shades, went out and found some people, and had a good day.

The other example is not so trivial. When I had been among the Tiv of Nigeria for about ten months, I hired a young man Tiv as my servant – what was called a 'steward' in Nigerian English. He was not a good steward. However, he could read and write in Tiv, and he took an immense interest in my work. I subsequently learned that the interest arose because he had been brought up by white missionaries and needed, like me, to learn his own culture intellectually and as an adult rather than as a by-product of being a child. He began to write text for me in the Tiv language and to help me with my ethnographic investigations in many other ways. I soon realized that I had a very important assistant here. I turned him into my 'scribe' and hired another steward. He and I became good friends, and we worked together several hours almost every day.

One evening, he came back from the river where he had been bathing and swimming. I asked him casually if anything was going on, and in a casual way he replied that a man had drowned in the river. I discovered through questioning that the man was a stranger who could not swim, and had stepped off a drop-off a few feet from the bank. Nobody had tried to save him. I knew my scribe to be a strong swimmer. 'Didn't *you* go after him?' I demanded. 'He wasn't mine,' was the laconic answer.

This incident upset me. I found that one of my most basic values had been flouted: the worth of individual human life. It took me several days to realize that this was not one of *his* basic values, and that in fact I had shocked *him* a few weeks before when he had learned that I had not seen my parents for four years, or my brother for seven, which to him showed absolutely appalling neglect. It took me several days to learn to like him again.

It is out of just such events that culture shock is made, and it is out of just such experiences that one comes upon the 'cure' for it: learning what one's own values are, then either abandoning them or else making an intellectual commitment as well as an emotional commitment to them, so that they need never turn up again merely as raw feelings. I do not mean that you cease to feel strongly about such things. I only suggest that you know which things you feel strongly about and then govern yourself sensibly when you are in some other ethnic group.

Thus, it is out of culture shock that the anthropologist gets the most important part of his understanding of his data, and learns to do his job better.

In fact, the anthropologist becomes the medium in which the two sets of cultural values, those of his mother culture and those of the subject culture, are brought into focus. The next few years of his life are to be spent in trying to translate into English, for communication to his colleagues the very values that he learned in order to get along with and to understand the culture and the communications of his informants.

It seems to me that many middle-class American teachers are in a 'field situation.'

A seminar for teachers in anthropological method

In the spring of 1967, I ran a seminar at North-western for 18 M.A.T. candidates, all of whom were teaching in ethnic groups other than their own. One of the candidates was a young man from middle-class small-town New England who had chosen to go into lower-class Negro schools of Chicago, another was a Wisconsin Lutheran girl who was teaching in a school made up almost entirely of second- and third-generation Eastern European Jews. Some of the other candidates were teaching Puerto Ricans, others were teaching new arrivals from southern Europe. Some were teaching in Chicago communities made up of a combination of Appalachian whites and American Indians; still others in schools that were operated especially for delinquent rejects from the public schools;

two were teaching in the psychiatric ward of a city hospital. All of them had in common that they could not merely call upon the culture of their youth and of their college days to see them through their present situations.

After a short introduction to the basic concepts of cultural anthropology – the way in which social relationships structure themselves, and the way in which any people in communication need, and daily re-create, a culture for their interaction – we began a series of reports about the kind of problems that they faced in their daily work. Some rather astonishing results were soon apparent.

Whereas they had formerly been asking such remote and philosopical questions as whether their task was to change the culture of the groups they were teaching to some sort of middle-class WASP[17] amalgam, they began to realize that this was not the immediate point. Except for the new arrivals, almost all of the various ethnic groups in the United States already knew middle-class WASP culture. They learn it on television, in magazine ads and comic books, on the city streets. Some of them actively– hostilely – reject it. Some of them are uncomfortable because they do not know what unimagined doom their trying to emulate it might bring about. The point is not whether you are going to teach them middle-class culture – obviously, you are. It is one of the cultures – and the dominant one – that is here to be dealt with.

The question is not whether you are going to teach it to them, but rather how you understand what their difficulties with it are, and the fact that two cultures are seldom an either/or proposition. When you discover this, you and they can decide in concert whether you are actively engaged in teaching it to them or whether they are going to reject it. You know where you stand – and you have not only communicated across a cultural barrier, you have gone a long way toward explaining that cultural barrier to them.

The seminar considered ways and means that mathematics can be taught to youngsters who do not see its function in their daily lives; we talked about how to teach literature in such a way that cultural differences become the essential point rather than the block to understanding. We talked about problems in teaching history and science and social studies – and in every case we discovered that the secret was an additive element: the inclusion of cultural differences in understanding and using such subjects. We even began doing a comparative study of roadblocks that different ethnic groups put up against good study habits. There are vast pressures in some lower-class groups against studying, and if a child studies, he may have to do it on the sly. In upper-middle-class third-generation European-Jewish children, the problem was how to make

<hr />

[17] White, Anglo-Saxon, Protestant (Culture).

them behave in study hall – until it was discovered that they refused to study in study hall for good reason: if they did not do their studying at home, their parents called the teachers demanding larger homework assignments.

What we really accomplished in this seminar was that, for these teachers at least, there came to be an awareness that communication is affected by culture, and that *it is the teacher* (just as it is the field anthropologist) *who must make the major adjustment*. Only in that way can any real appreciation of the overt situation be learned. And only then can any real program of change and upgrading be instituted: on the basis of knowledge not only of facts but of the internal attitudes of the students. And, most important of all, of the teacher.

We also discussed the attitude of middle-class Americans to the problem of power. We discovered that most of the neophyte teachers had never before in their lives been in a position of power, and as a consequence they were not only worried about the way in which their exercise of authority would be received in their student's ethnic groups, but they had never adjusted to an image of themselves as powerful people in terms of their own values. They began to realized that the power of every authority figure must be limited. We began to ask, 'What is worth enforcing in this particular situation?' Discipline? This problem turned out not to be especially difficult for most of these student teachers. Their problems of discipline were reduced vastly when they understood that listening behavior and attention are shown in different ways in our different subcultural groups. Quiet in the classroom? In most cases, it was necessary to placate the principal, but not necessary in the teaching process. Picking up scrap paper off the floor? Except for one young lady who decided she would demand it as an eccentricity of her own, we decided that we would not spend any of our authority on *that*.

In short, what matters? What is worth making a fuss about if you are to do the teaching job? I know that many school administrators take quite a different view of this – but I ask them, too, to get in the act. What is worrying *you* about this situation? What is really worth taking a stand on? Is it important in the educational process, or is it just your middle-class background showing?

Teachers in the class room

I decided as a result of this seminar that such training is almost essential to the training of teachers who will be working 'cross-culturally'. I have no doubt that it will allow them more profitably to work in and live in the communities of their students. Such teachers can, I trust and hope, avoid in large measure that greatest of personal and social tragedies in our schools – the teacher who, under constant threat of cultural strangeness, either becomes so authoritarian that education is impossible, or so

apathetic that education seems scarcely desirable, or so angry that education seems 'too good for them'. It is teachers in this situation who have,
quite understandably, led educational critics and civil rights leaders to
believe that lower-class schools are the worst staffed (when, in fact, many
people in them began as hand-picked experts and even volunteers).
Apathy and anger are the great protectors of the self. When all else fails,
they still protect.

There are a few simple questions that must consciously and repeatedly
be asked: Why am I angry? Why am I homesick? Why am I discouraged?
Why am I hostile? Why am I afraid?

The answers to these questions can almost always be found in the fact
that your expectations have not been fulfilled, that you are left high and
dry, not knowing where to turn or how to behave, that you have 'failed'.

And, of necessity, that leads to the next set of questions: What are
these people doing and saying *in their terms*? What are their purposes,
their underlying and unstated value positions? What do they want? And
finally: Why are *they* angry and afraid?

From the answers to these questions can come, in many cases at least,
and by some teachers, a firm basis for achieving the cross-cultural communication whose absence is one of the primary plagues in our schools
today.

Teachers are, to repeat, in some ways like field anthropologists: since
they work with their entire personalities, and since their fundamental
problem is one of cross-cultural communication, and since their feelings
are as important a cue as their intellects to discovery of hidden cultural
differences, some training is necessary if they are to avoid the destructive
emotions which make impossible the very job they set out to do. Field
anthropologists have faced these problems; some have found solutions
to some of them from which, it is apparent, teachers can profit.

7 Cherokee school society and the intercultural classroom

ROBERT V. DUMONT JR. AND MURRAY L. WAX
(*Human Organization*, Vol. 28, No. 3, Fall 1969,
pp. 217–26)

Indian education is one of those phrases whose meaning is not the sum
of its component words. Notoriously, 'education' is an ambiguous word
used to justify, idealize, or to criticize a variety of relationships. In the
context where the pupils are members of a lower caste or ethnically subordinated group, education has come to denominate a unidirectional
process by which missionaries – or others impelled by motives of duty,
reform, charity, and self-sacrifice – attempt to uplift and civilize the

disadvantaged and barbarian. Education then is a process imposed upon a target population in order to shape and stamp them into becoming dutiful citizens, responsible employees, or good Christians.[18]

In the modern federal and public school systems serving Indian children, there is less of the specifically religious quality; but the active presence of the missionizing tradition, however secularized, is still felt. To appreciate this fully, we must remind ourselves that the purpose of education presented to, and often enforced upon, the American Indians has been nothing less than the transformation of their traditional cultures and the total reorganization of their societies.[19] By denominating this as *unidirectional*, we mean to emphasize that the far-reaching transformations which have been occurring spontaneously among Indian peoples are neglected in the judgments of the reforming educators.[20] As a major contemporary instance, we need but turn to the first few pages of a recent book, representing the work of a committee of a high repute. The initial paragraph states that the goal of public policy should be 'making the Indian a self-respecting and useful American citizen' and that this requires 'restoring his pride of origin and faith in himself', while on the following page we find that very origin being derogated and distorted with the left-handed remark that, 'It would be unwise to dismiss all that is in the traditional Indian culture as being necessarily a barrier to change'.[21] The mythic image of an unchanging traditional Indian culture does not bear discussion here. Rather, we direct attention to the fact that such a remark could be advanced as the theme of a contemporary book about Indians, and that this book then received favorable reviews both from liberals involved in Indian affairs and from the national Indian interest organizations. Clearly, such reviewers take it for granted that Indian education should be unidirectional – e.g., none seemed to think it noteworthy that the last chapter of the book is on 'Policies Which

---

[18] Cf. Rosalie H. Wax and Murray L. Wax, 'American Indian Education for What?', *Midcontinent America Studies Journal*, Vol. 6, No. 2, 1965, pp. 164–170, reprinted in Stuart Levine and Nancy O. Lurie (eds.), *The American Indian Today*, Everett Edwards, Inc., Deland, Florida, 1968, pp. 163–169.

[19] For an enlightening account of the mission schools for American Indians, see the chapter, 'Nurseries of Morality,' in Robert F. Berkhofer, Jr., *Salvation and the Savage: An Analysis of Protestant Missions and American Indian Response, 1787–1826*, University of Kentucky Press, Lexington, Kentucky, 1965, pp. 20–43.

[20] Unfortunately, some of the anthropological textbooks on American Indians are guilty of the same static imagery, as they present particular tribes in 'the ethnographic present.' Conspicuous and happy exceptions are such books as Edward H. Spicer, *Cycles of Conquest*, University of Arizona Press, Tucson, Arizona, 1962, and Fred Eggan, *The American Indian*, Aldine Press, Chicago, *Illinois*, 1966. Cf. Murray L. Wax, 'The White Man's Burdensome "Business". A Review Essay on the Change and Constancy of Literature on the American Indians,' *Social Problems*, Vol. 16, No. 1, 1968, pp. 106–113.

[21] *The Indian: America's Unfinished Business*, compiled by William A. Brophy and Sophie D. Aberle, University of Oklahoma Press, Norman, Oklahoma, 1966, pp. 3–4.

Impede Indian Assimilation', the implication of that title being that the necessary goal is total ethnic and cultural dissolution.

An alternate way of perceiving the unidirectionality which characterizes 'Indian education' is to note the curious divisions of labor bifurcating the process of cultural exchange with Indian peoples. That is, missionaries and educators have devoted themselves to instructing the Indians but not to learning from or being influenced by them; whereas ethnographers have devoted themselves to learning from the Indians but not to teaching or influencing them. Thus, the ethnographers valued the learning of the native languages, while the schoolmasters and missionaries only seldom bothered to learn them, even when the native language was the primary tongue of their Indian pupils and the primary domestic and ceremonial medium of the community in which they were labouring.[22]

Because Indian educational programs have been unidirectionally organized, deliberately ignoring native languages and traditions, they have had to proceed more via duress than suasion. Today the duress is in the laws of compulsory attendance, as enforced by an appropriate officer; but the climax of traditional 'Indian education' was the forcible seizing or kidnapping of Indian children by agents of the U.S. government. These children were then incarcerated in boarding establishments whose programs were designed to shape them within the molds of the conquering society. Yet the irony of this crude and brutal effort was that, while the mass of children underwent profound changes, their very aggregation provided them with the need and opportunity to cohere and resist. Like the inmates of any total institution, Indian pupils developed their own norms and values, which were neither those of their Indian elders nor those of their non-Indian instructors. This process of autonomous development has continued to distinguish much of Indian conduct in relation to modern programs and schools, including the classroom we will be reviewing.[23]

---

[22] While missionaries have always included a small number of individuals who have patiently tried to understand the language and culture of their alien flock, and while some few missionaries have been excellent ethnographers, the majority, particularly on the North American continent, have had quite the opposite attitude. Today, missionary activity on the world scene has become increasingly sophisticated and culturally humble (as evidenced by *Practical Anthropology*), yet it is noteworthy how slowly this has affected labors among American Indians. Despite a century (or even several!) of mission activity among some tribes, the church in many instances remains a mission, detached from tribal influence or control, and the clergyman continues to be a person who is culturally alien and socially isolated and who regards his task as preaching but not learning.

[23] An excellent brief summary and bibliography of the history of research on Indian education is found in the presentation by Philleo Nash, *Proceedings* of the National Research Conference on American Indian Education, edited by Herbert A. Aurbach, Kalamazoo, Michigan, The Society for the Study of Social Problems, 1967, pp. 6–30. In order to discuss the history of Indian education research, Nash had to deal with some of the

Tribal Cherokee communities

The consequence of the various reformative and educational programs aimed at the Indian peoples has been not to eliminate the target societies but, paradoxically, to encourage an evolution which has sheltered an ethnic and distinct identity, so that today there remain a relatively large number of persons, identified as Indians, and dwelling together in enclaved, ethnically and culturally distinctive communities. The Tribal Cherokee of contemporary northeastern Oklahoma are not untypical.[24] Like other Indian communities, they have lost to federal, state, and local agencies the greater measure of their political autonomy. Many contemporary Indian peoples do have 'Tribal Governments', but these do not correspond to traditional modes of social organization or proceed by traditional modes of deliberation and action. In the specific case of the Oklahoma Cherokee, for instance, the Tribal Government is a non-elected, non-representative, and self-perpetuating clique, headed by individuals of great wealth and political power, while the Tribal Cherokee are among the poorest denizens of a depressed region, whose indigenous associations are denied recognition by the Bureau of Indian Affairs.

The Cherokee of Oklahoma once practised an intensive and skilled subsistence agriculture, which has all but disappeared as the Indians have lost their lands and been denied the opportunity to practise traditional forms of land tenure. The rural lands are now used principally for cattle ranching (often practised on a very large scale) and for tourism and a few

(Ftn. 23 cont.)

major changes of policy as well. The Conference *Proceedings* also contain a summary review by William H. Kelly of current research on Indian education and other helpful discussions and bibliographies. See also Willard W. Beatty, 'Twenty Years of Indian Education,' in David A. Baerreis (ed.), *The Indian in Modern America*, State Historical Society of Wisconsin, Madison, Wisconsin, 1956, pp. 16–49; Evelyn C. Adams, *American Indian Education*, King Crowns Press, New York, 1946; Harold E. Fey and D'Arcy McNickle, *Indians and Other Americans*, Harper, New York, 1959, Chapter 12. And of course the Meriam Report included an intensive assessment of the goals and achievements of Indian education: Lewis Meriam and Associates, *The Problem of Indian Administration*, Johns Hopkins Press, Baltimore, Maryland, 1928, especially pp. 346–429.

[24] We take the term 'Tribal Cherokee' from the research reports of Albert Wahrhaftig, which, in addition to whatever information may be inferred from the tables of the U.S. Census, constitute the best recent source on the condition of the Cherokee of Oklahoma. See, e.g., his 'Social and Economic Characteristic of the Cherokee Population of Eastern Oklahoma', and 'The Tribal Cherokee Population of Eastern Oklahoma,' both produced under sponsorship of the Carnegie Cross-cultural Education Project of the University of Chicago, 1965 (mimeographed); and 'Community and the Caretakers,' *New University Thought*, Vol. 4, No. 4, 1966/7, pp. 54–76. See also, Murray L. Wax, 'Economy, Ecology, and Educational Achievement,' Indian Education Research Project of the University of Kansas, Lawrence, Kansas, 1967 (mimeographed), and Angie Debo, *The Five Civilized Tribes of Oklahoma: Report on Social and Economic Conditions*, Indian Rights Association, Philadelphia, Pa., 1951.

local industries (e.g., plant nurseries, chicken processing), or crops such as strawberries, which require a cheap and docile labor supply. Until the recent building of dams and paved highways and the concomitant attempt to develop the region as a vacationland, the Tribal Cherokee were able to supplement their diet with occasional game or fish, but they now find themselves harassed by state game and fish regulations, and subjected to the competition of weekend and vacation sportsmen.

Like the other Indian societies of North America, the Cherokee have been goaded along a continuum that led from being autonomous societies to being a 'domestic dependent nation' and thence to being an ethnically subordinated people in a caste-like status. In Oklahoma there is a distinctive noncaste peculiarity, since a vast majority of the population proudly claim to be of 'Indian descent' as this signifies a lineage deriving from the earliest settlers. To be 'of Cherokee descent' is, therefore, a mark of distinction, particularly in the northeast of Oklahoma, where this connotes such historic events as 'Civilized Tribes' and the 'Trial of Tears'.[25] Yet, paradoxically, there exist others whose claim to Indianness is undeniable, but whose mode of life is offensive to the middle class. The term 'Indian' tends to be used to denote those who are considered idle, irresponsible, uneducated, and a burden to the decent and taxpaying element of the area. Within northeastern Oklahoma, these 'Indians' are the Tribal Cherokees, and their communities are marked by high rates of unemployment, pitifully low cash incomes, and a disproportionate representation on relief agency rolls. Perhaps the major respect in which the Cherokee Indians differ from groups like the Sioux of Pine Ridge is that the latter, being situated on a well-known federal reservation, are the recipients of myriads of programs from a multiplicity of federal,

---

[25] Responding to contact and intermarriage with the European invaders, the Cherokee were one of several tribes noteworthy during the 18th century for their adoption of foreign techniques. By 1827 they had organized themselves as a Cherokee Nation, complete with an elective bicameral legislature and a national superior court. Meantime, Sequoyah had been perfecting his syllabary, and in 1828 there began the publication of *The Cherokee Phoenix*, a bilingual weekly. Developments of this character led to the Cherokee and several neighboring tribes of the south-eastern U.S. being called, 'The Civilized Tribes', nevertheless, this did not protect them from the greed of the white settlers, particularly in Georgia. When the Indian nations would not cede their lands peaceably, Andrew Jackson employed federal troops to herd the Indian peoples westward into the region which subsequently was to become Oklahoma. There the survivors of the terrible journey ('The Trail of Tears') incorporated themselves once again as a Cherokee Nation and remained such until dissolved by act of Congress early in the present century. Today, books, museums, and pageants commemorate these events and highlight for the tourists the high-cultural aspects of upper-status life in the Cherokee Nation. Judged by that historical standard, the life of contemporary Tribal Cherokee constitutes a blot on a record otherwise cherished by Oklahomans of Cherokee descent.

private, and local agencies, whereas the Cherokee are still mainly the targets of welfare workers, sheriffs, and agressive entrepreneurs.[26]

In this essay we wish to focus on the schools attended by Indian children, in the cases where they are the preponderant element of the school population. This condition is realized not only on reservations, where the federal government operates a special school system under the administration of the Bureau of Indian Affairs, but also in other regions by virtue of covert systems of segregation. As in the case of Negro/white segregation, the basis is usually ecological. Thus, in northeastern Oklahoma the rural concentrations of Tribal Cherokee along the stream beds in the hill country predispose toward a segregated system at the elementary levels. But the guiding principle is social, so that there is reverse busing of Tribal Cherokee children living in towns and of middle-class white children living in the countryside. Within the rural elementary schools, the Indian children confront educators who are ethnically and linguistically alien, even when they appear to be neighbors (of Cherokee or non-Cherokee descent) from an adjacent or similar geographic area.

Such classrooms may be denominated as 'cross-cultural', although the ingredients contributed by each party seem to be weighted against the Indian pupils. The nature and layout of the school campus, the structure and spatial divisions of the school buildings, the very chairs and their array, all these are products of the greater society and its culture – indeed, they may at first glance seem so conventional that they fail to register with the academic observer the significance of their presence within a cross-cultural transaction. Equally conventional, and almost more difficult to apprehend as significant, is the temporal structure: the school period; the school day; and the school calendar. The spatial and temporal grid by which the lives of the Indian pupils are organized is foreign to their native traditions, manifesting as it does the symbolic structure of the society which has encompassed them.

The observer thus anticipates that the classroom will be the arena for an unequal clash of cultures. Since the parental society is fenced out of the school, whatever distinctive traditions have been transmitted to their children will now be 'taught out' of them; and the wealth, power, and technical supremacy of the greater society will smash and engulf these traditionalized folk. Forced to attend school, the Indian children there must face educators who derive their financial support, their training and ideology, their professional affiliation and bureaucratic status, from a complex of agencies and institutions based far outside the local Indian

---

[26] Cf. Murray L. Wax and Rosalie H. Wax, 'The enemies of the people,' in Howard S. Becker, et al. (eds.), Institutions and the Person: Essays Presented to Everett C. Hughes, Aldine Press, Chicago, Illinois, 1968, pp. 101–118.

community. The process is designed to be unidirectional; the children are to be 'educated' and the Indian communities thus to be transformed. Meanwhile, neither the educator nor the agencies for which he is a representative are presumed to be altered – at least by the learning process.

Cherokees in the classroom

The classrooms where Indian students and a white teacher create a complex and shifting sequence of interactions exhibit as many varieties of reality and illusion as there are possible observers. One such illusion – in the eyes of the white educator – is that the Cherokee are model pupils. Within their homes they have learned that restraint and caution is the proper mode of relating to others; therefore in the classroom the teacher finds it unnecessary to enforce discipline. As early as the second grade, the children sit with perfect posture, absorbed in their readers, rarely talking – and then only in the softest of tones – and never fidgeting. Even when they are marking time, unable to understand what is occurring within the classroom, or bored by what they are able to understand, they make themselves unobtrusive while keeping one ear attuned to the educational interchange. They respect competence in scholastic work, and their voluntary activities both in and out of school are organized surprisingly often and with great intensity about such skills. Eager to learn, they devote long periods of time to their assignments, while older and more experienced students instruct their siblings in the more advanced arithmetic they will be encountering at higher grade levels.

To the alien observer (whether local teacher or otherwise), the Cherokee children seem to love to 'play school'. The senior author, for example, recalls talking during one recess period with an elderly white woman who had devoted many years to teaching in a one-room school situated in an isolated rural Cherokee community and who now was responsible for the intermediate grades in a more consolidated enterprise that still was predominantly Cherokee. 'You just have to watch these children,' she said. 'If you don't pay no mind, they'll stay in all recess. They like to play school.' And, as if to illustrate her point, she excused herself, went back into the school building, and returned with a straggle of children. 'They told me they had work they wanted to do, but it is too nice for them to stay inside. ... You know, I forgot how noisy students were until I went to [the County Seat] for a teacher's meeting. It's time for me to ring the bell now. If I don't, they will come around and remind me pretty soon.'

Given the seeming dedication of her pupils, the naive observer might have judged this woman an exceedingly skilled and effective teacher. Yet in reality, she was a rather poor teacher, and at the time of graduation the pupils of her one-room school knew scarcely any English – a fact so well known that parents said of her, 'She don't teach them anything!'

Like many of her white colleagues, this woman was interpreting Cherokee conduct from within her own culture, as is evident in her description of the intensive involvement of her pupils in learning tasks as 'playing school'. In kindred fashion, other teachers describe the silence of the students as timidity or shyness, and their control and restraint as docility. Most teachers are unable to perceive more than their own phase of the complex reality which occurs within their classrooms because they are too firmly set within their own traditions, being the products of rural towns and small state teachers' colleges, and now working within and limited by a tightly-structured institutional context. Certainly, one benefit of teaching Indians in rural schools is that the educators are sheltered from observation and criticism. Except for their own consciences and professional ideologies, no one cares about, guides or supervises their performance, and little pressure is exerted to encourage them to enlarge their awareness of classroom realities.

Even for ourselves – who have had much experience in observing Indian classrooms – many hours of patient and careful watching were required, plus the development of some intimacy with the local community, before we began to appreciate the complexities of interaction within the Cherokee schoolroom. The shape assumed by the clash of cultures was a subtle one. At first, it could be appreciated most easily in the frustration of the teachers; the war within the classrooms was so cold that its daily battles were not evident, except at the close of the day as the teachers assessed their lack of pedagogical accomplishment. Those teachers who defined their mission as a 'teaching out' of native traditions were failing to make any headway; and some of these good people had come to doubt their ability to work with such difficult and retiring children (actually, as we soon discovered, their classes contained a fair share of youngsters who were eager, alert, intelligent, and industrious). A few teachers had resigned themselves to marking time, while surrendering all notions of genuine instruction.

As these phenomena began to impress themselves upon us, we began to discern in these classrooms an active social entity that we came to call 'The Cherokee School Society'. Later still, we were surprised to discover in other classrooms, which we came to call 'Intercultural Classrooms', that this Society remained latent and that instead the teacher and students were constructing intercultural bridges for communication and instruction (these will be discussed in the next section).

In order to comprehend the complexity of classroom interaction, we need to remind ourselves that the children who perform here as pupils have been socialized (or encultured) within the world of the Tribal Cherokee as fully and extensively as have any children of their age in other communities. In short, we must disregard the material poverty of the Tribal Cherokee families and their lower-class status and avoid any of the cant about 'cultural deprivation' or 'cultural disadvantage'. These children are culturally alien, and for the outsider (whether educator or social researcher) to enter into their universe is as demanding as the mastering of an utterly foreign tongue. In the compass of a brief article, we can do no more than indicate a few of the more striking evidences of this distinctive cultural background.

Even in first grade, Cherokee children exhibit a remarkable propensity for precision and thoroughness. Asked to arrange a set of colored match-sticks into a pyramidal form, the children became so thoroughly involved in maintaining an impeccable vertical and horizontal alignment that they were oblivious to the number learning which they are supposed to acquire via this digital exercise. These six-year-olds do not resolve the task by leaving it at the level of achievement for which their physical dexterity would suffice, but continue to manipulate the sticks in a patient effort to create order beyond the limitations of the material and their own skills. As they mature, the Cherokee students continue this patient and determined ordering of the world, but as a congregate activity that is more often directed at social than physical relationships. At times, this orientation is manifested in an effort toward a precision in social affairs that is startling to witness in persons so young (here, sixth graders):

> The teacher has asked about the kinds of things which early pioneers would say to each other in the evening around the campfire as they were traveling.
> Jane: 'Save your food.'
> Teacher: 'That's preaching.'
> Jane and Sally (together): 'No.'
> Jane: 'That is just to tell you.' (The tone of voice makes her sound just like a teacher.)
> The teacher agrees, and his acquiescent tone makes him sound like the student. He continues, 'They would get you in a room. . . .'
> Jane interrupts: 'Not in a room.'
> Teacher: 'In around a campfire then.' He continues by asking if everyone would be given a chance to speak or just representatives.
> Dick: 'That would take all night; they might forget.' Jane and Sally agree that representatives would be the right way.

The foregoing is as significant for the form of the interaction, as it is revealing of the students' concern for the precise reconstruction of a historical event. The students have wrought a reversal of roles, so that *their* standards of precision and *their* notions of social intercourse emerge as normative for the discussion.

Although this kind of exchange may be rare – actually it is typical only of the Intercultural Classroom – we have cited it here, as reflecting many of the norms of Cherokee students. As healthy children, they are oriented toward the world of their elders, and they see their adult goal as participating in the Cherokee community of their parents. In this sense, the art of relating to other persons so that learning, or other cooperative efforts, may proceed fruitfully and without friction becomes more important to them than the mastery of particular scholastic tasks, whose relevance in any case may be dubious. In the matrix of the classroom they learn to sustain, order, and control the relationships of a Cherokee community; in so doing they are proceeding toward adult maturity and responsibility. According to these norms, the educational exchange is voluntary for both students and teachers and is governed by a mutual respect.

In any educational transaction, the Cherokee School Society is actively judging the competence of the teacher and allowing him a corresponding function as leader. Their collective appraisal does not tolerate the authoritarian stance assumed by some educators ('You must learn this!') but rather facilitates the emergence of a situation in which the teacher leads because he knows ('I am teaching you this because you are indicating that you wish to learn . . .'). A consequence of this configuration (or, in the eyes of an unsympathetic observer, a symptom) is that the Cherokee students may organize themselves to resist certain categories of knowledge that the school administration has formally chosen to require of them.

We must bear in mind that within the Tribal Cherokee community, the reading or writing of English, calculating arithmetically, and even speaking English have minor employment and minimal utility. By the intermediate grades, the students perceive that, with no more than a marginal proficiency in spoken or written English, their elders are nonetheless leading satisfactory lives *as Cherokees*. Attempts to exhort them toward a high standard of English proficiency and a lengthy period of time-serving in school are likely to evoke a sophisticated negative reaction. After one such educational sermon, a ten-year-old boy bluntly pointed out to his teacher that a Cherokee adult, greatly admired within the local community – and senior kin to many of the pupils present – had only a fifth-grade education. When the teacher attempted to evade this rebuttal by suggesting that the students would, as adults, feel inferior because they lacked a lengthy education and could not speak good English, the pupils were again able to rebut. To the teacher's challenge, 'Who would you talk to?' the same boy responded, 'To other Cherokee!'

Orienting themselves toward the community of their elders, the Cherokee students respond to the pressures of the alien educators by organizing themselves as The Cherokee School Society. As the teacher molds the outer forms of class procedure, the children exploit his obtuseness as a white alien to construct the terms on which they will act as students. But, while among the Oglala Sioux this transformation is effected with a wondrous boldness and insouciance,[27] here among the Cherokee it is with an exquisite social sensibility. A gesture, an inflection

---

[27] Cf. Murray L. Wax, Rosalie H. Wax, and Robert V. Dumont, Jr., *Formal Education in an American Indian Community*, The Society for the Study of Social Problems, Kalamazoo, Michigan, 1964, Chapter 6.

in voice, a movement of the eye is as meaningful as a large volume of words would be for their white peers. By the upper elementary grades, the result is a multiple reality according to which the adolescent Cherokee appear now as quiet and shy, or again as stoical and calm, or yet again (apparent only after prolonged observation) as engaged in the most intricate web of sociable interaction. Such delicacy of intercourse, so refined a sensibility, reflects and requires a precision of movement, a neat and exact ordering of the universe.

Interestingly, the Cherokee School Society does not reject the curricular tasks formulated by the alien educational administrators. In fact, the pupils proceed with their usual patient intensity to labor at assignments that can have no bearing on their tradition or experience. The fact that they are unable to relate these materials meaningfully to life within the Cherokee community acts as an increasing barrier to their mastery of them. In particular, the fact that most students have acquired no more than rudimentary proficiency in spoken English means that the involved patterns of the printed language in the advanced texts are beyond their most diligent endeavors; neither the language nor the topics can be deciphered.

So far, we have emphasized that the Cherokee students are interested in learning and that, from the viewpoint of the educator, they are docile pupils. Yet the cultural differences noted, and the basic social separateness and lack of communication, ensure that conflicts will develop and become more intensive as the students mature. The school cannot proceed along the trackways established by educational authority, nor can it be switched by the students into becoming an adjunct of the rural Cherokee community. Hence, as the children mature, the tension within the schoolroom becomes more extreme. Since the participants are one adult and many children, and since the latter are imbued with a cultural standard of nonviolence and passive resistance, open confrontations do not occur. Instead, what typically happens is that, by the seventh and eighth grades the students have surrounded themselves with a wall of silence impenetrable by the outsider, while sheltering a rich emotional communion among themselves. The silence is positive, not simply negative or withdrawing, and it shelters them so that, among other things, they can pursue their scholastic interests in their own style and pace. By their silence they exercise control over the teacher and maneuver him toward a mode of participation that meets their standards, as the following instance illustrates:

> Teacher: 'Who was Dwight David Eisenhower?
> Silence.
> Teacher: 'Have you heard of him, Joan?' She moves her eyes from his stare and smiles briefly.
> Very quickly, the teacher jumps to the next person. There is something in his voice that is light and not deadly serious or moralistic in the way that is

customary of him. He is just having fun, and this comes through so that the kids have picked it up. They respond to the tone, not to the question, 'Alice?'

Alice leans back in her chair; her blank stare into space has disappeared, and her eyes are averted. She blushes. Now, she grins.

The teacher does not wait, 'Wayne?'

Wayne is sitting straight, and his face wears a cockeyed smile that says he knows something. He says nothing.

Seeing the foxy grin, the teacher shifts again, 'Wayne, you know?' This is a question and that makes all the difference. There is no challenge, no game-playing, and the interrogation mark challenges Wayne's competency. But Wayne maintains the foxy grin and shakes his head, negative.

Quickly, the teacher calls on another, 'Jake?' He bends his head down and grins but says nothing.

Teacher (in authoritative tone): 'Nancy, tell me,' But she says nothing, keeping her head lowered, although usually she answers when called upon. The teacher switches tones again, so that what he is asking of Nancy has become a command. Perhaps he catches this, for he switches again to the lighter tone, and says; 'Tell me, Debra.'

The only one in the room who doesn't speak Cherokee, Debra answers in a flat voice: 'President.'

As soon as the answer is given, there are many covert smiles, and Alice blushes. They all knew who he was.

To most educators and observers, such an incident is perplexing. Who within that classroom really is exercising authority? Are the students deficient in their comprehension either of English or of the subject matter? Are they, perhaps, flexing their social muscles and mocking the teacher – because they don't like the lesson, they don't like him to act as he is acting, or why? For the Cherokee School Society has created within the formal confines of the institutional classroom another social edifice, their own 'classroom', so that at times there appears to be not simply a clash of cultural traditions but a cold war between rival definitions of the classroom. Such tension is not proper within Cherokee tradition, since the Tribal Cherokee value harmonious social relationships and frown upon social conflict,[28] Moderate disagreement is resolved by prolonged discussion interspersed, wherever possible, by joking and jesting, while severe disagreement leads to withdrawal from the conflict-inducing situation. Given the compulsory nature of school attendance, however, the students cannot withdraw from the classroom, much as they might wish to, and the teacher can withdraw only by losing his job and his income. Thus, an unmanageable tension may develop if the teacher is unable to recognize the Cherokee pupils as his peers who, through open discussion,

---

[28] See the discussions of the 'The Harmony Ethic,' in John Gulick, *Cherokees at the Crossroads*, Institute for Research in Social Science, the University of North Carolina, Chapel Hill, N.C., 1960, pp. 135–139 *et passim*.

may share with him in the decisions as to the organizing and operating of the school.

The unresolved conflict of cultural differences typifies these class-rooms. Within them, there is little pedagogy, much silence, and an atmosphere that is apprehended by Indians (or observers of kindred sensibility) as ominous with tension. The following incident, participated in by Dumont, exhibits all these features in miniature:

> The classroom was small and the teacher had begun to relate a joke to Dumont. Not far away were seated four teenage Cherokee, and the teacher decided to include them within the range of his ebullience: 'Boys, I want to tell you a joke. . . .' It was one of those that played upon the stoical endurance of Indians in adapting to the whimsical wishes of whites, and to narrate it in the classroom context was highly ironic. The plot and phrasing were simple, and easily apprehended by the students. But when the teacher had finished, they merely continued looking toward him, with their eyes focused, not upon him, but fixed at some point above or to the side of his eyes. As he awaited their laughter, their expressions did not alter but they continued to stare at the same fixed point and then gradually lowered their heads to their work.

The Cherokee School Society maintains a rigid law of balance that says, in effect, we will change when the teacher changes. If the teacher be-comes involved in appreciating the ways of his students, then they will respond with an interest in his ways. Needless to say, the older the students become, the higher their grade-level, the less is the likelihood that this reciprocity will be initiated by their educators. There is thus a deep tragedy, for it is the students who lose and suffer the most. Yet the School Society is their technique for protecting themselves in order to endure the alien intrusiveness of the teacher and the discourtesy and barbarity of the school. Occasionally, observer and students experience a happier interlude, for some teachers are able to enter into a real intercultural exchange. Unfortunately, they are as rare as they are remarkable. And they are sometimes unaware of their truly prodigious achievements in establishing what we term the Intercultural Classroom.

The intercultural classroom

Within the Intercultural Classroom, Tribal Cherokee students do such remarkable things as engaging in lengthy conversations with the teacher about academic subjects. For this to occur, the teacher must be respon-sive to the distinctive norms and expectations of the students; but, strikingly, he need not abide by these nor accept norms as long as he is able to persuade the students of his willingness to learn about them and to accommodate to them. This attitude places the teacher on a plane of parity such that he must learn from his students the most rudimentary

Cherokee cultural prescriptions. Naturally, both parties experience conflicts in this reshuffling of teacher/learner roles. Certainly, such interaction is not what the teacher has been trained so sustain. Yet there arise structured devices for reducing these conflicts.

For instance, to bridge the social breaches that are always opening, the Cherokee students urge forward one of their members – not always the same person – to mediate and harmonize. Then if the teacher, by an unconscious presumption, disrupts the harmonious flow of class activity, it is the mediator whose deft maneuver reduces the intensity of the tension and relaxes the participants. In a sense, what the mediator does is to restore parity between teacher and students by removing the nimbus of authority from the teacher, thus allowing the students to work out with the teacher a compromise which redirects class activities and so permits them to regain their proper tempo. The teacher is freed to pursue the subject matter, but as scholastic assistant rather than classroom tyrant. With this in mind, let us examine the sequence of events which ended in a conversational repartee already quoted:

> They are reading about important men in history and have just finished with a section about adult educators.
> Teacher: (Referring to the observers.) 'We have two distinguished educators here. Does this make you feel proud?'
> It is quiet for the first time in the room. It is likely that the students are all thinking, how could we be proud of educators! As observer, I am uneasy and expectant; I wonder who will break the silence and how he will handle the delicate situation.
> John: 'I don't like schools myself.' (!)
> Teacher: 'Would you quit school if you could?' (He's asking for it!)
> John (a firm answer): 'Yes.'
> Teacher: 'Suppose that your dad came and said you could quit, but he brought you a shovel and said, "Dig a ditch from here to Brown's house,' since you weren't going to school.'
> John: 'Okay.'
> Another student: 'He might learn something.'
> Everyone finds this humorous; the class is in good spirits and is moving along.
> John, too, is quick to reply: 'Might strike gold.' The topic has been discussed earlier in class. (The interaction develops and others become involved, including the more reticent students.)

Here it is John who has played, and most successfully, the role of mediator. The teacher had ventured into a delicate area that had the potential of disrupting the classroom atmosphere. The responding silence was a token of the social peril, and John, who so often among his peers had assumed the mediating role, moved forward first, boldly countering with a declaration as strong as the teacher's. As a consequence, he redefined the structure of the interaction and became the initiator of the exchange, while the teacher merely sustained it. A cultural bridge was thereby constructed, accessible alike to students and teacher; and John's 'Okay' is his consent to the conditions of the structure.

The mediating role becomes less necessary as the teacher grows more attuned to the interactional norms of Indian society; it becomes more difficult (if more essential) if the teacher insists on maintaining a tyrannical control over the classroom. Yet, even as the teacher is attuned, some function is reserved for a mediator, for the teacher tends to proceed in terms of work to be done by an abstract student, while the mediator explores how the task can be redefined within the framework of the Cherokee student. His is a work of adaptation, and insofar as he is successful, the classroom becomes *intercultural* – a locus where persons of different cultural traditions can engage in mutually beneficial transactions without affront to either party.

What must the teacher do to foster the emergence of an intercultural classroom within the cross-cultural situation? The answer would require another essay at least as long as the present one, but it may be helpful to quote the remarks of one teacher in the region:

> 'I can't follow a lesson plan, and I just go along by ear. I've taught Cherokee students for six years in high school, and this is my first [year] in elementary school.' Referring, then to his experiences as a high school coach, he continued, 'The thing you have to do, if you get a team, is that you got to get them to cooperate. . . .'

At first glance, this appears at odds with our earlier assertions about the spontaneous emergence of the Cherokee School Society, not to mention contradictory to the conventional notions that Indians will not compete with each other. But what he is explaining is that unless the teacher chooses to recognize the social nature of the classroom and to work toward integrating his teaching with that life, he will not be able to elicit active learning experiences from his pupils. Or, to put it negatively, if the teacher does not work with his Indian students as a social group, their union will be directed toward other goals. Yet the teacher can secure their response only if he 'gets them' to cooperate; he cannot 'make them' do so.

Conclusion

The foregoing report provides the basis for judgments and hypotheses on a variety of levels. On the practical level, it would seem that ethnic integration is not an essential precondition for satisfactory education of groups from a low socio-economic background. The Tribal Cherokee certainly are impoverished and poorly educated. Nevertheless, we would predict that the consolidation of rural schools into larger, better-staffed, and better-equipped schools in northeastern Oklahoma may actually lead to deterioration rather than improvement of the educational condition.

Given the ethos of the Tribal Cherokee, consolidation may mean the irremediable loss of many opportunities for assisting their children educationally.

On the methodological level, we are reminded of how sociologically valuable it is for researchers to focus on the frontier situation 'where peoples meet'.[29] The resulting accommodations, adaptations, and divisions of labor are an enlightening and fascinating phenomenon, which especially deserve to be studied as a corrective to those theoretical systems which regard the national society as an integrated social system. On the methodological level also, our study illustrates anew the value of ethnographic observations of classroom activities. Basic and simple as it may seem, and unpretentious in the face of modern testing procedures, direct observation still has much to teach us.[30]

Finally, on the substantive level, the research reported here cautions against the erosion of our conceptual armamentarium when researchers allow their research problems to be defined by educational administrators. When that happens, the educational situation of peoples such as the Indians tends to be conceived in terms of individual pupils and their 'cultural deprivation'. The researcher then is asked to assist the administration in raising these disadvantaged individuals to the point where they can compete in school in the same fashion as do white middle-class children. Our research is a reminder that such styles of conceptualization neglect the social nature of the classrooms and the social ties among the pupils. They also neglect the tension between teacher and pupils as a social group, and the struggles that occur when the teacher presses for individualistic achievement at the expense of group solidarity.[31]

---

[29] Everett C. Hughes and Helen M. Hughes, *Where Peoples Meet: Ethnic and Racial Frontiers*, The Free Press, Glencoe, Illinois, 1952.

[30] Consider for example, the impact and contribution of such recent books which rely either on direct observation or participation observation of classrooms as John Holt, *How Children Fail*, Delta, New York, 1964; Harry F. Wolcott, *A Kwakiutl Village and School*, Holt, Rinehart and Winston, New York, 1967; Wax, Wax, and Dumont, op. cit.; Estelle Fuchs, *Pickets at the Gates*, The Free Press, New York, 1966; G. Alexander Moore, *Realities of the Urban Classroom: Observations in Elementary Schools*, Doubleday Anchor, New York, 1967; Elizabeth M. Eddy, *Walk the White Line*, Doubleday Anchor, New York, 1967.

[31] Such phenomena were clearly noted by Willard Waller in his *Sociology of Teaching*, first published in 1932, reprinted by Science Editions, John Wiley, New York, 1965. It is unfortunate to see the neglect of such elementary sociological considerations in much of the more recent literature of the 'sociology of education.'

Some issues arising from the readings

Preliminary comments

In this section we discuss three questions which arise from the selected readings. Firstly, the factors which may influence the practical judgements that classroom teachers have to make. Secondly, some of the consequences of value issues for education. Finally, some of the evidence for, and consequences of, high expectations about what education can achieve.

Factors which may influence the practical judgements of classroom teachers

A central issue in the sociology of education is the manner in which economic, social, and political factors influence and constrain what happens in educational systems, schools, and classrooms.[1] All we attempt here is to look at three factors which may influence the context in which teachers have to make decisions at classroom and school level. The three factors are: the physical plant available; interactional factors within the school; and time. This brief discussion provides concrete examples for some of the points raised in Section 1.[2]

1. Physical plant available

The physical plant of the school can be examined from two standpoints.[3]

[1] For some general discussions see Olive Banks, *The Sociology of Education* (Batsford, 1968); D. F. Swift, *The Sociology of Education* (Routledge & Kegan Paul, 1969). For some case studies see Burton R. Clark, *The Open Door College* (New York: McGraw-Hill, 1960); William Taylor, *The Secondary Modern School* (Faber, 1963); Julienne Ford, *Social Class and the Comprehensive School* (Routledge & Kegan Paul, 1969).

[2] See pp. 1–24. We would like to acknowledge the great help given to us by W. Brian Davies, Department of the Sociology of Education, London Institute of Education, by his comments on the structure of an earlier draft.

[3] We would like to acknowledge the help given to us over this section by Ray Derricott,

(*i*) The external facade which the school presents to its environment. This may influence what people take the school to represent and how they are disposed towards it. Factors which may be important include: the visibility of the entrance to the school; the physical structure of the entrance area, and implicit and explicit signs to be found there; and the extent to which what is going on in the school can be seen by those outside.[4]

(*ii*) The internal structure of the school and the educational furniture it contains. For the classroom teacher important factors here would include: the type, size, and shape of the room in which he teaches, and the consequences of these physical factors for teaching method; visual aids, accessories, and other forms of equipment, which are available *and which can be used*; books and related materials;[5] the seating available for students and its relationship to numbers in the class; temperature in winter and summer, and whether windows open and close; the immediate physical surroundings to the classroom and the level of noise, visual distraction, etc. As MacDonald and Rudduck suggest à propos of curriculum development projects: 'In organizational backing, it is the little things, such as plugs for the tape-recorders, and shelving for materials which can mean a lot. Lack of foresight here can have absurdly far-

---

(Ftn. 3 cont.)
Deputy Director of the Schools Council Project, History, Geography and Social Science 8–13, at the University of Liverpool, School of Education.

[4]There is a very considerable literature on this area. We simply wish to raise the issue of the importance of buildings. For further information see: the Building Bulletins published by the Department of Education and Science and the various architectural journals, such as the *R.I.B.A. Journal.* A list of Building Bulletins can be found in J. E. Vaughan and Michael Argles, *British Government Publications Concerning Education: an Introductory Guide* (School of Education, University of Liverpool, 1969) (Copies available from School of Education Library.) See also P. Manning, ed., *The Primary School: an Environment for Education* (Pilkington Research Unit, Department of Building Science, University of Liverpool, 1967); and M. Seaborne, *Primary School Design* (Routledge & Kegan Paul, 1971). For a case study see Louis M. Smith and Pat M. Keith, *Anatomy of Educational Innovation: an Organizational Analysis of an Elementary School* (New York: John Wiley, 1971), particularly pp. 171–208. For a comment on the effect that 'learning by experience' has had on materials, methods and school architecture see R. F. Dearden, *The Philosophy of Primary Education* (Routledge & Kegan Paul, 1968), p. 107.

[5]How much is spent on books in the Junior School, may be as important a question as how teachers are trained to teach children to read. On books used in school see Hillel Black, 'What our children read', in G. Smith and C. Kniker, eds., *Myth and Reality: a reader in Educational Foundations* (Boston: Allyn and Bacon, 1972), pp. 84–112, particularly pp. 89–91 on Darwin's theory of Evolution. Jeannette Henry, 'Our inaccurate textbooks', pp. 503–8 in N. Yetman and C. Steele, ed. *Majority and Minority: the dynamics of racial and ethnic relations* (Boston: Allyn and Bacon, 1971); Michael V. Belok, 'Schoolbooks' images of India and Indians – change and permanency', *International Review of History and Political Science* Vol. 5, No. 1 (February 1968), pp. 111–21. For a sociological approach to textbooks see C. Wright Mills, 'The professional ideology of social pathologists', in *Power, Politics and People*, ed. Irving Louis Horowitz (Oxford University Press, 1967), pp. 525–52.

reaching effects ... Enthusiasm is no substitute for adequate resource support.'[6]

The considerable variety of 'physical plant' provision in *The Teacher's Day* study has been noted. Hilsum and Cane conclude that: 'Although the overall impression of buildings and equipment was favourable, we would be less than objective if we did not describe the difficulties. Forty-seven of the 66 schools were said by their heads to have deficiences of accommodation that affected the teaching day. About one quarter of the schools reported severe limitations of space. In such schools, teachers were observed working with large classes in rooms that were too small for movement and circulation, with little or no provision for storage and work surfaces. Some had awkward shapes, being long and narrow, and others had a low ceiling or tiered steps, or were poorly heated, lighted and ventilated ... owing to pressure on accommodation, groups of pupils were being taught in corridors, entrance halls, canteens, medical rooms and large halls. One teacher with a class in the hall had to adjust her plans for the whole day around the use other teachers wanted to make of the hall; there was constant moving of tables and chairs, and interruptions from head, secretary and others moving through the hall; and the teacher had to keep books etc., in boxes.'[7] Each of these factors inpinges upon the context in which teachers have to make decisions about what to do.

Three additional points can be made about the physical plant factor in schools. Firstly, it is important that additional research is conducted on how the physical structure of schools impinges on classroom teachers and the children that they teach. As Bennett and Bennett state, 'In order to analyse the specific relationships which obtain between physical environment and social behavior, it is necessary to establish *precisely* which elements of the environment or scene may affect human conduct.'[8]

Secondly, building technology and costs are significant constraints on what kinds of physical structures can be built. The architect has to

[6] B. MacDonald and J. Rudduck, 'Curriculum research and development projects: barriers to success', *British Journal of Educational Psychology*, Vol. 41, No. 2 (June 1971), p. 152. Note also the comments of M. D. Shipman, 'The role of the teacher in innovating schools', paper read to the Organization for Economic Cooperation and Development, Paris, 1971, p. 9, 'The teachers were faced with the organization of enquiry-based, integrated studies using team teaching in schools that continued with traditional methods for the major part of the time. It was not just difficult to find the right sized spaces for teaching whole year groups instead of individual classes. Individual and small group work demanded a series of different sized spaces in schools which had been designed for one teacher with one class in one room.'

[7] Hilsum and Cane, op. cit., p. 33. See also pp. 34–5. Not used in our selection.

[8] D. Bennett and J. Bennett, 'Making the scene', pp. 86–7 in the Open University Reader, *School and Society*, ed. B. R. Cosin et al. (Routledge & Kegan Paul, in association with the Open University, 1971). Our italics.

attempt to resolve the conflict between the relative permanence of buildings (both internally and externally) and the uncertainty about what ought to go on in schools. He has to do this within a fixed budget and a given technology.

Thirdly, historical/empirical accounts of the social and political processes through which certain sorts of building structures (for example 'open plan' in the primary school) came to occupy their place in education, would make useful additions to the knowledge we have. Facts about the proponent groups[9] behind movements for architectural change, and the consequences of architectural change for educational practice, would also be important areas of inquiry. Some contemporary educational ideologies[10] presuppose a physical and architectural environment which is not found in many schools, and there appears to be little evidence about the consequences of implementing educational practices in situations significantly different from those prescribed by the advocates of change.

2. Interactional factors within the school

An important factor within the school will be the decision, or non-decision making process,[11] that is, the organizational procedures used within the school to make decisions about what should be done, or those procedures whose latent function ensures that the majority of the staff do not share in decision making. Status factors may be crucial. As Musgrove argues, 'A strong sense of hierarchy, whether in a classroom or a staff meeting, is likely to interfere with the efficiency of problem-solving. Sharp status differences interfere with the free flow of communication and impair the error-correcting functions of interaction: no one likes to correct his senior's errors and to present him with necessary and relevant information which he may find unpalatable. There is no dearth of good experimental evidence that groups in which differences of status are pronounced are relatively inefficient in solving

[9] See Volume II, p. 60 for a discussion of this concept. On open plan schools it would be useful to have more evidence about (*i*) the relationship between building costs and the popularity of this form of structure with the Department of Education and Science and local authorities; (*ii*) a detailed historical/sociological account of what might be called the 'ideological rationalization' for this sort of building (some points are made about this in volume II, p. 114.

[10] See Volume II, pp. 55–117 for a discussion of this concept. For an attempt to link the Plowden Report to architecture, see 'St. Thomas of Canterbury R.C. Primary School, Cheetham, Manchester: an educational brief for the guidance of the architects', prepared by a Joint Advisory Panel and published by Manchester Education Committee (1969).

[11] P. Bachrach and M. S. Baratz, 'Decisions and non-decisions: an analytical framework', *American Political Science Review*, Vol. 57, No. 3 (1963).

problems.'[12] As we argue later in this section, the Gross study suggests that a major cause of failure to implement the innovation they studied, was lack of feedback between those initiating the change and those attempting to carry it out.[13]

A teacher coming to work in a new school for the first time, is entering a complex social situation, where a large number of decisions, or non-decisions, will already have been taken – for example, on staff selection; on curricula; on the matching of individual teachers with particular groups of children; on organizational matters such as streaming or mixed ability grouping and the criteria to be used for placing children in groups; on timetabling; on allocation of resources between departments, and within departments; and on the status and power of ancillary staff over classroom activities. It is the un-intended,[14] as well as the intended consequences of these decisions which influence the contexts in which teachers work.

3. Time

This factor is likely to be important to the classroom teacher for two reasons. Firstly, the initial practical judgements which the teacher makes (about, say, discipline or what to teach) will structure the con-text in which later decisions have to be taken.[15] Secondly, classroom teachers usually have to work for about two hundred days out of the year,[16] and they may, therefore, develop a perspective on teaching not primarily concerned with the detailed preparation of five or six brilliant lessons, but rather with how to cope with the demands of the job, day after day, and week after week. The time-scale may be, not only what to teach today, but how to survive a three-month term.[17] As MacDonald

---

[12] F. Musgrove, 'Faith and scepticism in English education', Inaugural lecture, Bradford Institute of Technology (1966), p. 11. See also further statements of Musgrove's position in *Patterns of Power and Authority in English Education* (Methuen, 1971); and 'The future of the teaching profession', *Journal of Curriculum Studies* (May 1971).

[13] See p. 200.

[14] On the unintended consequences of human action see Section 1, p. 60. For some empirical studies of the unintended consequences of decisions in educational organiza-tion see: A. Cicourel and J. Kitsuse, *The Educational Decision Makers* (Bobbs-Merrill, 1963); D. Hargreaves, *Social Relations in a Secondary School*, op. cit.; B. R. Clark, *The Open Door College*, op. cit.; C. Lacey, *Hightown Grammar* (Manchester University Press, 1970).

[15] See, for example, the interesting discussion in W. Waller, *The Sociology of Teaching* (New York: Russell & Russell, 1961), pp. 301–10.

[16] Hilsum and Cane, op. cit., p. 22.

[17] Cf. John Webb, 'The sociology of a school', *British Journal of Sociology*, Vol. 13, No. 3, pp. 264–72. On p. 267 he says that, 'In the typical teacher ... fatigue tends to be residual. That is, it is not significantly dispelled by the normal rest or recreation periods (a night's sleep or a weekend's relaxation) and is therefore cumulative. It was discovered in industrial studies, and perhaps particularly characterizes those jobs that are very noisy and tedious. As well as being physiological, residual fatigue functions psychologically

and Rudduck suggest, 'In practice, teachers generally are so concerned with system maintenance that their energy is spent in running to keep up with the *status quo*. Innovation needs time: time for teachers to familiarise themselves with any new teaching materials; time to reflect individually and with colleagues on new experiences.'[18] Shipman notes a similar problem when he concludes that in the Keele Integrated Studies Project 'The most frequently mentioned and most pressing factor increasing the stress on the teachers was the time and energy involved'[19] in the project. It would be valuable to have additional data on how teachers modify the 'time perspective' which they derive from the training process.

Values and classroom teachers

We discuss here a number of issues from the readings by Bohannan and Dumont and Wax; each issue forms part of the social contexts in which teachers have to make practical judgements and adds to the complexity of those judgements.

1. Educational categories and the classroom teacher[20]

Dumont and Wax discuss some of the problems[21] that arise when an

---

(Ftn. 17 cont.)
so as to impair a person's best qualities, like the ability to look at his task with enough detachment to consider whether he is using the right tools, and is on the right track.' It would be nice to have evidence on teachers' fatigue. For a sociological approach to time and timetables, which could provide ideas for investigating teachers' perspectives, see Julius A. Roth, *Timetables: Structuring the Passage of Time in Hospital Treatment and other Careers* (Indianapolis: Bobbs-Merrill, 1963). See also Roger Dale, 'The use of time in school', Unit 7 of Course E. 282, 'School and Society' (Open University Press, 1972).
[18] MacDonald and Rudduck, op. cit., p. 152.
[19] M. D. Shipman, op. cit. (1971), p. 8. Note also pp. 9–10 where Shipman states that a 'group of teachers were having to stay after school beyond the time when their colleagues had departed and were having to return to school in vacation time to prepare work in integrated studies.' Note also the comments of Robert A. Stebbins, 'The meaning of disorderly behavior: teacher definitions of a classroom situation', *Sociology of Education*, Vol. 44 (Spring 1970), that, 'The teacher has no chance to meet each routine situation with the amount of contemplation characteristic of many unique definitions; if he took the time necessary to do so, he would fail in his aim to educate large groups of pupils', (p. 234).
[20] Implicit in this section are matters of considerable difficulty, in particular the relationship between the individual level of analysis and the sociological. We are grateful to Professor Olive Banks, University of Leicester, for detailed comments on an earlier draft. We have also benefited from numerous discussions with our colleague David Thomas on the general theme of educational categories.
[21] For some approaches at the level of the classroom see John W. Friesen, 'Four approaches to value teaching', *Kansas Studies in Education*, Vol. 22, No. 1 (Spring 1972), pp. 16–24.

attempt is made to integrate the 'children of Cherokee Indians' into American society, as that society is perceived by certain school teachers. Bohannan mentions schools for 'lower-class Negroes', schools for 'second- and third-generation Eastern European Jews' and for some other categories of children.[22] Each of these articles therefore provides examples of 'educational categories'. By 'educational category' is meant a way of classifying children, which is believed to be relevant when deciding what sort of education they should be given. One result of being put into such categories may be an improvement in the quality of the education which children receive.[23] Another may be that children are given a special kind of education provided by specially trained teachers, or that children in certain categories are educated in isolation from other children.

In the British educational system there are a number of such categories, some derived from social sciences (particularly from the concepts 'social class' and 'intelligence'), some from educational reports, and from other areas.[24] Examples of educational categories, in current use, include 'working-class children', 'middle-class children', 'children under social handicap', 'the down-town talented', 'gifted children', 'Newsom children' and many others.

The use of educational categories gives rise to a number of problems:

(*i*) What sociological, psychological, or anthropological evidence is available to validate the use of such categories?

(*ii*) What would represent a reasonable amount of evidence to argue, prima facie, that children from a particular sub-culture[25] ought to be treated, educationally, in some special kind of way?

(*iii*) What procedures are available to ensure that children in particular categories are identified accurately?

(*iv*) What evidence do we have about how teachers use educational categories in classroom interaction, and what kinds of information do

---

[22] Bohannan, op. cit., this book pp. 155–56.

[23] Or at least teachers and others may believe this to be the case.

[24] See on this, A. Yates, *Grouping in Education* (New York: John Wiley, 1966), particularly pp. 125–39. In the past the value assumptions behind such categories were often more explicit: Mary Carpenter's book, for example, was called *Reformatory Schools, for the Children of the Perishing and Dangerous Classes, and for Juvenile Offenders* (1851), Woburn Press Reprint Series.

[25] On the notion of 'sub-culture' see E. C. Hughes, H. Becker and B. Geer, 'Student culture and academic effort', pp. 372–85 in R. Bell and H. Stub, *The Sociology of Education: a Sourcebook* (Homewood, Illinois: Dorsey Press, 1968). See especially pp. 377–8. For a useful discussion of 'sub-culture' see 'Campus cultures, role orientations and social types', Charles D. Bolton and Kenneth C. W. Kammeyer, being selection 26 of *College and Student*, ed. K. Feldman (New York: Pergamon Press, 1972). See especially pp. 381–5.

teachers consider that these categories provide about *individual* children?[26]
Cicourel and Kitsuse group the 'adolescent problems' which arise within
schools, under three headings and provide examples of the categories
used under each heading. Firstly, those relating to the students' academic
activities, with categories like 'academic problem', 'over-achievers',
'opportunity students'. Teaching children to read, for example, would
produce a series of success and failure categories. Secondly, those pertain-
ing to breaking the rules of conduct, with categories like 'trouble-makers',
'delinquents'. Thirdly, those concerned with the emotional problems
of students, with labels like 'nervous', 'withdrawn and unsocial', and
'isolates'.[27] In their study *The Educational Decision-makers*, Cicourel
and Kitsuse argue that the student counsellors whom they were studying
developed ways of categorizing students. The categories that the counsellors used for students fell between 'common sense' type categories, and
'clinical' type categories which were derived from social science. They
give as examples of the former 'lazy', 'indifferent', 'wild', 'girl crazy',
and of the latter 'rejected', 'overly dependent', 'weak in ego strength',
or having an 'unresolved Oedipus problem'.[28] Further empirical studies of
how teachers use educational categories, how the categories relate to
'common sense knowledge' and 'social science', and how the teacher
training process contributes to the provision of categories, might
provide valuable additional data.

(v) What evidence is there that possible variations and complexities
within categories, are communicated to teachers when they are intro-

[26] For example, the current use of the phrase 'middle class' as a synonym for 'everything
is satisfactory educationally', and 'working class' for the contrary, may be an extreme oversimplification of the issues and problems involved. Are the educational outcomes of
social class that simple? Some educational (and sociological) discussions appear to be based
on an implicit psychology, which consists of two types of child, 'the working class' and
'the middle class'. The *educational* implications of a book like *Communities in Britain* by
Ronald Frankenberg (Penguin Books, 1966), do not appear to have been grasped.

[27] A. Cicourel and J. Kitsuse, 'The social organization of the high school and deviant
adolescent careers', p. 126 in E. Rubington and M. Weinberg eds., *Deviance: the inter-
actionist perspective* (New York: Macmillan, 1968).

[28] A. Cicourel and J. Kitsuse, op. cit. (1963), p. 82. In their article, 'The social organization of the high school and deviant adolescent careers', op. cit., Cicourel and Kitsuse
suggest that 'The organizational processing of students who are defined as "emotionally
disturbed" is likely to be more problematic than in the case of the "academic" or "conduct"
problems for several reasons. Unlike the classification of the student as an "academic
problem", there is relatively little organizational control over the competence of the
person who reports the behavior which is the occasion for initiating the process of classifying a student as "emotionally disturbed". Almost any person within the school as well
as outside of it may report that a student has been observed behaving in a "strange",
"bizarre" or "crazy" manner. Since the common-sense interpretation of such behavior
is relative to the observer, there may be considerable disagreement as to the "objectivity"
of the observer' (p. 134).

duced to a particular category?[29] Further, what evidence is there that the
limitations of categories to explain educational success or failure are
made explicit to teachers? A general comment on this is made by Cane
and Smithers who, in their study of reading in twelve infant schools,
conclude that they learnt to 'suspect too facile an explanation of reading
backwardness in terms of social class alone.' Many homes in poor urban
areas may provide a better atmosphere of encouragement to the child
than some in middle class professional areas. In this connection, we may
recall the research on environmental influences carried out by Wiseman
at Manchester: the strongest influences on achievement were parental
attitude towards education and degree of literacy in the home. These
factors can cut across patterns of income, occupation and social status.
It is a mistake, then, for teachers to make assumptions about children's
potential on the basis of class or income – a mistake which can lead to
distortions in actual achievement, for, while the home influence is
predominant, the school influence is by no means negligible.'[30] Similar
sorts of limitation may apply to the use of other educational categories.

Cicourel and Kitsuse argue that 'the behavioral content of a youth's
activities ... may not be as critical ... as the interpretations which are
placed upon it by others.'[31] They also raise a number of questions about
the process of categorization. What is the range of social types that
are used within particular organizations? What are 'the social processes
whereby adolescents come to be defined and classified as social types'?
What are the consequences of such processes of categorization 'for any
given adolescent's career' within particular organizations? Cicourel
and Kitsuse also point out that these social typings will be constantly
subject to change and that 'any given student may be the object of several
social type designations by the same teacher, by different teachers or by
other students. Consequently, it is possible for a student to have several
careers concurrently or consecutively within'[32] the same organization.

[29]On this area see D. Swift, 'Recent research in the sociology of education', D.E.S./
A.T.C.D.E. Conference on the Sociology of Education (1969). This paper raises the
important question of how sociology and psychology relate to each other. See also D. Swift,
'Educational psychology, sociology and the environment: a controversy at cross-purposes',
British Journal of Sociology, Vol. XVI, No. 4 (1965), pp. 336–41. For a social-psychological
view of 'stereotypes', see Peter Kelvin, *The Bases of Social Behavior* (Holt, Rinehart &
Winston, 1970), pp. 113–26.

[30]B. Cane and J. Smithers, *The Roots of Reading* (Slough: NFER, 1971), p. 81. Note
the need for considerable empirical evidence before statements could be made about the
values of groups of parents. Even then it would not be known whether an individual
child represented the 'normal' attitude or not.

[31]Cicourel and Kitsuse, (1968) op. cit., p. 132, footnote 12. They also stress the need to
'specify the behavioral regularities which are identified as relevant by personnel who
have day-to-day contract with adolescents.'

[32]Cicourel and Kitsuse, (1968) op. cit., p. 126. The teacher will also have notions of
'the good student' which would need to be investigated. See Cicourel and Kitsuse,
(1968), p. 126, footnote 6; Keddie, op. cit., p. 154; L. Cohen, 'Dogmatism and views of the
ideal pupil', *Educational Review*, Vol. 24 (November, 1971).

The precariousness of socially assigned identities, and their socially constructed nature, is made explicit by Breton who attempted, 'to explain the output of the school in terms of the structure and processes internal to the school as well as in terms of the character of its input.'[33] Breton concentrates on the stratification processes which are internal to the school and examines 'their effect on the educational plans of the students.'[34] He notes the following factors which he argues are relevant to the school stratification system: 'the structure of the curriculum as articulated in the set of programmes of study, the particular combination of programmes in the school, the rules and procedures for the evaluation of the student's performance, the marks he receives for his performance and the resultant class standing, the grouping of students on the basis of their ability. Less formal factors could also be considered as, for instance, the expectations of teachers and principals concerning the academic performance of certain categories of students.'[35] Breton concludes that his results, 'support the notion that an adolescent's class of destination is very much a function of the position he occupies in the school stratification system.'[36] Such a perspective stresses some of the major consequences that the use of educational categories generates, and suggests further ways in which they can be investigated empirically.

2. With whose values is the classroom teacher concerned?

The readings by Dumont and Wax and Bohannan both suggest that the teacher has to be sensitive to the values of the groups he teaches, and to his own values. In addition, he has to consider the values of other teachers in his school, the senior teachers, inspectors, and local education authorities. There may be confusion and conflicts within each or all of these groups. The teacher will need value criteria for selecting between the possibility conflicting demands of the role set.[37]

The classroom teachers' involvement with groups whose values may be in conflict with their own, may, as noted in the Bohannan article, lead to 'cultural shock'.[38] The conflict and tension may be so complex

[33] R. Breton, 'Academic stratification in secondary schools and the educational plans of students', *Canadian Review of Sociology and Social Anthropology*, Vol. 7, No. 1 (1970), p. 19.
[34] Ibid., p. 18.
[35] Ibid., p. 18–19.
[36] Breton, op. cit., p. 33. For an interesting discussion which raises further issues see Robert A. Scott, 'The construction of conceptions of stigma by professional experts', in *Deviance and Respectability*, ed. Jack Douglas (New York: Basic Books, 1970), pp. 255–90.
[37] See Kelvin, op. cit. pp. 139–67; N. Gross et al., *Explorations in Role Analysis: Studies of the School Superintendency Role* (New York: John Wiley, 1958); and A. Rose, 'Sociology and the study of values', *British Journal of Sociology*, Vol. 7 (1956).
[38] For a more detailed approach to this area see Philip K. Bock, ed., *Culture Shock: a Reader in Modern Cultural Anthropology* (New York: Alfred A. Knopf, 1970).

and subtle, as Dumont and Wax argue, that certain teachers may not even be aware of it. Moore defines cultural shock as 'the inevitable bewilderment and disorientation that faces anyone in new surroundings. The newcomer is walled in by people and actions he does not understand, since these people are acting according to orientations and understandings of their own culture, which are foreign to him and exclude him. The results of this shock are usually withdrawal and apathy – sometimes even slow anger and dismay.'[39] Moore gives as an example of extreme cultural shock in schools, the case of Mrs Auslander where, during one class, 'many of the children are hitting one another; a child will get up from his seat, go over to another child for no apparent reason and slap him in the face, or perhaps push him or strike his body before rushing back to his seat . . . One boy, Angel, runs over to Allen, throws him on the floor, and jumps on his back with both feet. Allen quite naturally screams and yells. The teacher screams too: "Get away from there!"'[40] Mrs Auslander spends most of the lesson 'putting written work on the board in the midst of all this bedlam.'[41] There is a similar, though less dramatic case, in the extract from *The Teacher's Day*, where Mrs D. had problems with the pupil John (p. 144).

One question which might be asked about the problem of 'cultural shock' in British schools is what factors, within diverse school settings, lead to emotional and cognitive stress among different teachers? The notion that *all* teachers find certain sorts of schools (for example, down-town schools) stressful is almost certainly an oversimplification. Student teachers need to gain insight into the sorts of school contexts they would be unable to cope with. It might be important for them to do this during training, rather than having to find out during their early years of employment.

3. How can signs of group values be read by teachers?

One common distinction made in this area is between non-verbal signs (such as posture, facial expression, movements, hair and clothes) and verbal responses and comments.[42] As we have noted in the Dumont and

[39] A. Moore, *Realities of the Urban Classroom: Observations in Elementary Schools* (New York: Doubleday Anchor, 1967), p. 3. See also p. 4 where he quotes from Wallace a 'three stage disaster syndrome'.

[40] Ibid., pp. 64–5.

[41] Ibid., p. 69. See E. Goffman, 'On cooling the mark out', in A. M. Rose ed., *Human Behavior and Social Processes* (Routledge & Kegan Paul, 1962). Note particularly the phrase 'There is no doubt that certain kinds of role success require certain kinds of moral failure', p. 487.

[42] The non-verbal area is currently under review by a group at the School of Education, University of Liverpool, under Professor W. A. L. Blyth. It is hoped that research proposals will result from the discussions. On this area see M. Argyle, 'Research on non-verbal communication', Oxford University, Department of Experimental Psychology (1971) (available from The National Lending Library).

Wax extract, for the Cherokee, 'A gesture, an inflection in voice, a movement of the eye is as meaningful as a large volume of words would be for their white peers.'[43] Himmelweit, discussing the teaching of sociology and psychology to social workers and teachers, argues that both these groups have to make decisions on the basis of insufficient evidence, with inadequate means and time, and therefore 'to deal with this situation, both social worker and teacher learn to make decisions by relying on cues, on norms they have built up; they learn to use one or two signs as guides to action.'[44] Davies makes a similar point when he states that teachers work with a small group or groups over a relatively long period of time during which they 'will have to reach a very large number of judgements concerning a variety of human and curricular material, on the basis of limited objective evidence.'[45] If, as seems likely, some teachers face a situation of conflict and tension Himmelweit's comments on social workers may also apply to them. She writes, 'The greater the uncertainty of the situation, the less prepared the individual for this uncertainty, the greater the need to produce order, even at the expense of distorting the facts.'[46] This could mean that the cues go completely unnoticed. It is likely that this area involves 'tacit knowledge',[47] that teachers will vary in their capacity to 'take in' the verbal and non-verbal signs within classrooms and organizations, and that this differential awareness will affect teachers' performance. Further research is required which might act as a basis for the development of practical skills in the education of teachers.

4. How does the teacher know that his reading of the signs is correct?

How does the teacher know that his reading of the signs of group values, represents an accurate understanding of the meaning attached to the signs

[43] Dumont and Wax, op. cit. (this book) pp. 167-8.

[44] H. Himmelweit, 'The teaching of social psychology to students of education and social work', in *The Sociological Review*, Monograph No. 4, ed. P. Halmos, University of Keele (July 1961), p. 82.

[45] W. Brian Davies, 'On the contribution of organizational analysis to the study of educational organizations', Paper read to The British Sociological Association, Annual Conference, Durham, England, April 1970, p. 19. Reprinted in Richard Brown, ed. *Knowledge, Education, and Cultural Change* (Tavistock Publications, 1973), pp. 249–95. See Robert A. Stebbins, 'The meaning of disorderly behavior: teacher definitions of a classroom situation', op. cit., especially the notion of 'habitual definition' p. 219. See in addition Emmet's discussion on p. 53 of this book, and the discussion of Emmet on p. 103.

[46] Himmelweit, op. cit., p. 83. See also J. L. Simmons, 'On maintaining deviant belief systems: a case study', *Social Problems*, Vol. 11 (1964), pp. 250–6, esp. pp. 252–3. The *educational* problem as Himmelweit (p. 87) points out is how to raise 'the student's threshold of tolerance for ambiguity'.

[47] See A. V. Cicourel, *The Social Organization of Juvenile Justice* (New York: John Wiley, 1968), p. 6; H. Garfinkel, 'Studies of the routine grounds of everyday activities', *Social Problems*, Vol. 11 (1964); and our discussion in Section 1, p. 113.

by the group involved?[48] Dumont and Wax, for example, suggest that the teachers in the classrooms they investigated did not understand the behaviour of the children and often misinterpreted it.

Fuchs[49] has some clear examples of this problem, where one teacher is faced with the question of what to do about the use of obscene language by children. Fuchs argues that the use of such language can be linguistic habit where the words are used so often they are meaningless; it can represent hostility and aggression towards the teacher; or it can be a sign of more serious psychological disturbance.[50] A possible consequence of the use of obscene language may be to manipulate the teacher into using violence to control the class although this is opposed to her stated values.[51] A further example is given by Fuchs[52] that for a Puerto Rican child silence can be a mark of respect, and yet teachers may interpret it as insolence and disobedience. The problem remains: how can these various attempts to understand what is going on in classrooms be tested and shown to be successful or unsuccessful?

5. What to do as a consequence of the above factors

Notwithstanding the complexity of the above factors, the classroom teacher still has to make practical judgements about what to do with the groups of children that he or she teaches day by day. The Dumont and Wax reading raises a number of crucial questions about this. Ought teachers to attempt to modify or change the values and culture of their pupils, or ought there to be a mutual process of change by teacher *and* students?[53] Do teachers and schools actually have the knowledge and

---

[48] On this see J. Peel, 'Understanding alien belief systems', *British Journal of Sociology*, Vol. 20, No. 1 (1969); P. Winch, 'Understanding a primitive society', *American Philosophical Quarterly*, No. 1 (1964); J. H. M. Beattie, 'Comment on understanding alien belief-systems', *British Journal of Sociology*, Vol. 21 (1970).

[49] E. Fuchs, *Teachers' Talk* (New York: Doubleday, Anchor Original, 1969). See pp. 52–3 where a teacher tries to wash out a boy's mouth with soap because of his language.

[50] Ibid pp. 55–6. See also her example of the game played by lower class Negro boys called 'The Dirty Dozen'. Fuchs argues that if teachers take part in such a game to be 'hep' this may be seen by the boys as highly inappropriate behaviour, pp. 56–7.

[51] See Leila Berg, *Risinghill: Death of a Comprehensive School* (Penguin Books, 1968). An empirical study of this school would have been a useful contribution to the literature.

[52] Fuchs, op. cit., p. 54.

[53] Note the reference by Abraham Edel in 'The contribution of philosophical anthropology to educational development', to Margaret Mead who, 'points out that the shift from learning what everyone agrees everyone would *want* to know, to teaching what some think others *should* know is a differentiating mark between most primitive education and modern complex schooling,' in G. Barrett, *Philosophy and Educational Development* (Harrap, 1966), p. 80. For an account of young people's views on school see *Schools Council Enquiry I: Young School Leavers* (HMSO, 1968). See, in particular, pp. 32–8 and pp. 56–62.

skills to change values and cultures?[54] What proportion of teachers are able to alter their value positions, by choice, as a result of what they learn through interaction with pupils? Put in more specific terms, should the teachers in the Dumont and Wax study try to change the values, aspirations, and skills of the Cherokee Indian children? What arguments can be put forward to demonstrate that the culture that the teachers had to offer was superior to the existing culture of the Cherokee children?[55] What is meant by 'superior' in this context? Did the teachers actually succeed in changing the Indian children or, if they failed, what was the cost of failure for the teachers and the children? If the teachers succeeded (in their terms) what was the cost of success for the teachers and for the children?[56] There is now a considerable 'anti-schooling' literature which raises questions of this sort?[57]

In Britain, the problem can be posed crudely as: (a) for some groups of children, the educational process consists of an attempt to initiate them into a culture which their parents and teachers to some extent share; (b) for other groups of children, the educational process consists of an attempt by teachers (in some cases partly supported by parents) to replace one culture with another, or to replace aspects of one cultural tradition[58] with aspects of another. Difficult value issues are involved when it is claimed that one culture is superior to another in all or some respects, or that all cultures are equally valid in all respects. It seems to us important to make explicit the nature of, and backing for, value judgements which are made, necessarily, as a result of these dilemmas.

All the above factors influence the context in which practical judgements and moral choices are made in schools. As Emmet pointed out, a

---

[54] See our discussion of the Gross study in this section, p. 196.

[55] Cf. R. F. Dearden, op. cit. (1968), p. 42, who writes, 'Finally there is the educator's special problem of his right to make value-judgements as to what is good *for others*, which presupposes the objectivity of his value judgements.'

[56] We are grateful to Joan Carr for pointing out to us that in some educational systems the cost of 'success' may be very great indeed. See on this the introduction to N. Keddie, (1973) op. cit

[57] See, for example, J. Holt, *How Children Fail* (1969); P. Goodman, *Compulsory Miseducation* (1971); E. Reimer, *School Is Dead: an Essay on Alternatives in Education* (1971); N. Postman and C. Weingartner, *Teaching as a Subversive Activity* (1971) – all Penguin Books. See also I. Illich, *The Deschooling of Society* (New York: Harper & Row, 1971). For useful collections of views relating to this area see John de Cecco, ed., *The Regeneration of the School* (New York: Holt, Rinehart & Winston, 1972), and Glenn Smith and Charles R. Kniker, *Myth and Reality*, op. cit.

[58] For a relevant discussion see Julia Evetts, *The Sociology of Educational Ideas* (Routledge & Kegan Paul, 1973). On page 66 she argues, 'It is increasingly obvious . . . that there is not one but many conceptions of education and evaluations of knowledge. If this is accepted, then it follows that we cannot distinguish between appropriate and deprived environments in terms of educability. *There will be as many appropriate environments as there are conceptions of education.*' Our italics. See also Section I pp. 73–92 of this book.

'sociological awareness of the logic of situations' need not 'lead to a deterministic view that any given decision *had* to be so and not otherwise. But it can discourage 'scapegoating' and 'conspiratorial' interpretations of situations which turn out badly.'[59] Further research is required on whether or not one unintended consequence of teacher training is that some teachers come to hold a non-contextual view[60] of the school, which enables them to develop unrealistic views of what they can achieve.[61]

Values and the study of educational organizations

These issues about values may have consequences for the empirical study of educational organizations. As Davies has asked, are there 'fundamental links between the ideologies held by educators (in respect of aims or goals and criteria for the evaluation of organizational success)' and the structure of educational organizations? We need to know the extent to which teachers' 'values, which may differ enormously, about children and knowledge, are determinative of school organization.'[62] It would, Davies continues, be quite unsatisfactory to allow exploration of organizational structure to rest at the level of values imputed to its members. We need to know how these values arose, why they persist, and how they relate to the role set and the demands of the job.[63]

What are required are empirical studies of educational organizations which cope at the conceptual and methodological levels with the inter-relationships between knowledge, values, organizational structure, and the individual level of analysis.[64] Pugh,[65] makes the point that organiza-

[59] See Emmet reprinted in this book p. 64.

[60] See, for example, B. Geer, 'Teaching' in *International Encyclopaedia of Social Science*, p. 563. For an empirical approach see D. S. Finlayson and L. Cohen, 'The teacher's role: a comparative study of the conceptions of college of education students and head teachers', *British Journal of Educational Psychology*, Vol. XXXVII, part 1 (February 1967), pp. 22–31.

[61] See page 190.

[62] Davies, op. cit., p. 22.

[63] Ibid. p. 22

[64] See, on teachers' knowledge, A. Hartnett and M. Naish, 'Teachers' knowledge – an exploratory essay', (in preparation). (*i*) In the first part of this essay we examine the broad problem areas with which classroom teachers are concerned, as follows. (*a*) The curricular problem – what to teach particular groups and individuals. (*b*) The pedagogic problem – how to teach groups and individuals. (*c*) The organizational/career problem – how to deal with head teachers, heads of department, inspectors, etc., and to cope with the implications of being a professional with a career structure. Both (*b*) and (*c*) involve what Schutz calls 'recipe knowledge'. Recipes for action, Schutz says, 'bring forth in typical situations typical results by typical means.' (See A. Schutz, 'The well-informed citizen: an essay on the social distribution of knowledge', *Social Research*, Vol. 13 (December, 1946), pp. 463–78. See also Joan Barker Lunn, *Streaming in the Primary School* (Slough N.F.E.R. 1970)., pp. 215–21.) (*d*) The assessment problem – procedures for deciding whether the pupil has successfully completed the learning intended under (*i*) (*a*). (For

tional theory ought to use both psychology and sociology to give 'a unified science of individual, group, and organizational behavior. The behavior itself at these three levels is intimately interrelated, and so, therefore, should be the study of it.' Pugh characterizes as significant limitations on 'all major sociological theories of organizational function-

(Ftn. 64 cont.)
other approaches see B. Bernstein, 'On the classification and framing of educational knowledge' and Geoffrey M. Esland, 'Teaching and learning as the organization of knowledge', pp. 47–69, and pp. 70–115 in M. F. D. Young, ed., *Knowledge and Control*, op. cit.) (e) Some teachers may believe, or be encouraged to believe, that they need rationales, explanations, justifications for what they do, or think that they do, under (i) (a)–(d) above. We call this the justificatory problem. (Cf. the discussion in Section 1 of this book on Oakeshott, pp. 109–10. See the Plowden Report, *Children and their Primary Schools* (HMSO, 1967), p. 186, paragraph 497, 'It was interesting that some of the head teachers who were considered by H.M. Inspectors to be most successful in practice were least able to formulate their aims clearly and convincingly.' See also B. Williams' comment, that it is sometimes too readily assumed that making people reflective about what they are doing, necessarily makes them better at doing it, 'Philosophy and imagination', *Times Educational Supplement* (28 April 1972, p. 19.)

(ii) In the second part of this essay we make some *preliminary* distinctions between knowledge, belief, values, skills, ideology, common-sense knowledge, recipe knowledge, and practical knowledge. We also explore some of the relationships between these terms. This leads to a discussion of some of the possible components in teachers' knowledge. (a) Theoretical knowledge which relates to subject competence, and to the problems that arise under the pedagogic, organizational/career, and assessment areas. (See above (i) (a)–(d).) (b) Theoretical knowledge as a justification for practice. For example, we ought to do x and y in the primary school, because research advocates it. (See above (i) (e).) (c) Educational ideologies. These relate to all of (i) above, and to (ii) (b). A distinction is drawn in the essay between the belief systems of *individuals*, and sociological and philosophical approaches to the concept of ideology. (See also Volume II of this book, and the paper by M. Naish, A. Hartnett and D. Finlayson, 'Ideological documents in education: some suggestions towards a definition', pp. 55–117.) (d) We discuss what we term the 'professional capital of teachers'. This is a general term for all the practical knowledge which teachers develop as a result of their experience in schools in dealing with the problems outlined in (i) above. Cf. the notion of 'operational philosophies', p. 360, of A. Strauss et al., *Psychiatric Ideologies and Institutions* (New York: Free Press, 1964).

(iii) In the final section of the essay some comparisons are made between school teaching and medicine as occupations, and as areas of practice. (a) Comparisons are made between the variety and complexity of value disputes in education, and those in medicine, over questions of means and ends. (See the quotation from Emmet, Section 1 of this book, p. 86.) (b) Comparisons are made between social science and philosophy, and the practice of education; and between natural science, and the practice of medicine. (This broadly covers a series of epistemological issues.) (c) Some comparisons are made between the professional socialization of doctors, and that of school teachers. Cf. Bloland who suggests that 'medical training would be more like teacher-training if two-thirds of the time were devoted to rephrasing and discussing the Hippocratic Oath.' H. Bloland, 'Sources of professional autonomy: the physician and the public school teacher', *Educational Forum*, Vol. 33, No. 3, (March 1964), p. 371. See also M. Naish and A. Hartnett 'What theory cannot do for teachers, *Education for Teaching*, (1975) op. cit.

[65] D. S. Pugh, 'Modern organizational theory: a psychological and sociological study', in F. Carver and T. Stergiouanni, eds, *Organizations and Human Behavior: Focus on Schools*, (New York: McGraw Hill, 1969), pp. 111–29, also in *Psychological Bulletin*, Vol. 66, 1966, pp. 235–51.

ing . . . an extremely naive treatment of human motivation combined with a neglect of individual differences which are characteristically devalued into "personal idiosyncracies". An organization is a system of functioning human beings who are different, and if the sociologist neglects these differences he is not leaving them out of account, he is saying that for the processes with which he is concerned, these differences are of no account – that is, they are equal to zero. This is a most important psychological statement . . . which requires empirical investigation rather than a priori assertion.' Pugh then suggests that 'psychological studies of leadership patterns in relation to personality and social skill training imply a very naive view of the relationship between personality and role behavior, combined with a neglect of structural differences in organizational position . . . leadership is exercised within different organizational structures, and if he neglects these differences the psychologist is not leaving them out of account, he is maintaining that for the processes with which he is concerned they are of no account. This is a very important sociological statement.'[66] This statement too, Pugh argues, requires empirical investigation. Such a perspective might be useful in the study of educational organizations, where there are differential conceptions of tasks, procedures, and evaluation among teachers and their pupils. Negotiations and arrangements between conflicting viewpoints might be crucial.[67] However, studies which looked at educational organizations and processes at the individual, group, and organizational levels simultaneously would raise questions which cut across the existing structure of academic disciplines. This would entail consequences for the professional socialization of social scientists in education; the organizational environments in which they work; and the funding of research projects.[68]

Expectations about what education can achieve

1. General problems

We have looked at some of the factors that teachers have to take cognizance of when deciding what to do, and at some of the value issues which

[66] Pugh, op. cit., pp. 112–13, in Carver and Stergiouanni.

[67] Davies, op. cit., pp. 6, 10 and 22. See also C. Perrow, *Organizational Analysis* (Tavistock Publications, 1970), especially Chapter 2; A. Strauss et al., *Psychiatric Ideologies and Institutions* op. cit., and the comments on this study in A. Hartnett, 'Professional ideologies in institutions: some methodological problems', University of London MA, 1969 (unpublished); R. G. Corwin, *Militant Professionalism: a Study of Organizational Conflict in High Schools* (New York: Appleton-Century-Crofts, 1970), especially pp. 17–39; J. Victor Baldridge, *Power and Conflict in the University* (New York: John Wiley, 1971).

[68] See 'Some issues arising from the readings' in Volume II, p. 170–1.

face them. We now discuss the expectations which might be held about what education does, can, or ought to be able to achieve.[69]

The following are examples of expectations about education: (a) comprehensive schools may be seen as ways of reducing class barriers and bringing about a more 'open' society; (b) 'nursery schools for all' might be viewed as a way of increasing the opportunities which exist for 'disadvantaged' social groups; (c) new universities might be set up to bring higher education to social groups who previously had been precluded from it; (d) immigrant and indigenous children might be taught in the same classrooms to reduce race prejudice; (e) white and black children might attend the same schools to help integrate the blacks; (f) a form of 'middle-class culture' might be taught to ethnic groups such as Indians in America, or the lower working class in the UK, in an attempt to bring them within the 'wider culture'; (g) in societies where there is violent political or religious conflict, education may be seen as a method of bringing peace; (h) education may be seen as playing an important part in bringing about industrialization.[70]

Many other examples could be provided—the readings by Dumont and Wax and Bohannan, contain concrete examples. Such expectations need to be examined against the background of the work which teachers actually do, and the contexts in which they work. It is sometimes dif-

[69] On expectations see Frank Musgrove and Philip H. Taylor, *Society and the Teacher's Role* (Routledge & Kegan Paul, 1969). For an American view see Jeremy D. Finn, 'Expectations and the educational environment', *Review of Educational Research*. Vol. 42, No. 3 (Summer, 1972), pp. 387–410.

[70] For a fascinating example of this see page 258, footnote 4, in D. Smith, 'Power ideology, and the transmission of knowledge: an exploratory essay', in E. Hopper, Ed. *Readings in the Theory of Educational Systems* (Hutchinson, 1971). Smith discusses the experiences of Michael Huberman who, 'in a brochure entitled "Reflections on the Democratization of Secondary and Higher Education" (UNESCO, 1970) ... challenged the assumption that a significant contribution is made by education systems (as at present organized) to democratization or economic growth. All but a few copies of his brochure were ordered to be destroyed by the UNESCO establishment. See, for example, *The Times Educational Supplement*, 21.8.70.' For some cross-cultural evidence on expectations held about education see U. Bronfenbrenner, *The Two Worlds of Childhood* (New York: Russel Sage Foundation, 1970), especially pp. 23–6 and the posters, pp. 39–48. See also Ivar Berg, *Education and Jobs: the Great Training Robbery* (New York: Praeger, 1970). For two historical approaches to the progressive education movement see Lawrence A. Cremin, *The Transformation of the School* (New York: Alfred A. Knopf, 1962) and David W. Swift, *Ideology and Change in the Public Schools* (Columbus, Ohio: Charles E. Merrill, 1971). For an interesting discussion on the role of schools in American society see Christopher Jencks et al., *Inequality* (New York: Basic Books, 1972). They conclude that, 'As long as egalitarians assume that public policy cannot contribute to economic equality directly but must proceed by ingenious manipulations of marginal institutions like the schools, progress will remain glacial,' (p. 265). On pre-school education see Maeve Denby, 'Pre-school—the cycle of opportunity', National Elfrida Rathbone Society (1973). On 'performance contracting' see H. J. Eysenck, 'Performance contracting: the theory that failed', *Times Educational Supplement* (19 January 1973), p. 4.

ficult to understand how the mundane, routine tasks which occupied good proportions of the teachers' working day in the Hilsum and Cane study,[71] relate to the great expectations held about education.

These expectations raise a number of important issues of which we discuss three. Firstly, educational programs, based on these expectations, take place in societies where power, wealth, and status are unequally distributed, and this constrains or limits what can occur in schools.[72] Such programmes would often involve considerable political and social change if they were to be successful. As Bantock has said, no one 'has yet worked out what it is feasible to expect [from schools] in a minimum space of ten years, working for approximately five and a half hours a day, five days a week, for forty weeks in the year – especially when so much of the out-of-school environment is distinctly anti-educational. There is thus no limit to the pretensions of some educationalists, though they usually lack any rigorous appreciation of the possibilities of their implementation. The talk is ambitious – but it lacks concreteness.'[73] Musgrove also argues that, 'It is probably dangerous for politicians and social reformers to have too great a faith in education. They are tempted to seek a solution to social problems in our schools when the answer lies elsewhere.'[74]

Secondly, a distinction requires to be drawn between discussions about education at the level of ideology,[75] and that of empirical inquiries into what is happening in schools as a consequence of policy decisions. In order to know whether or not expectations about education have been achieved, a great deal of complex empirical data would be required. Such data would be needed at the level of the classroom and the school, as well as at the level of the educational system. Such data would presuppose research which had a theoretical base from which questions could be asked about what happens to children, students, and teachers who work in, and pass through, schools and other educational organizations, as a result of their experiences in these organizations. Musgrove states that 'the education of a student arises from his relationship to a particular learning environment. We need to know far more

[71] See p. 139.

[72] This is a central problem in the sociology of education. See, for example, O. Banks, *The Sociology of Education*, op. cit. For a survey of some of the literature see Anthony Hartnett, ed., *The Sociology of Education: an Introductory Guide to the Literature*, op. cit.

[73] G. H. Bantock, 'Conflicts of values in teacher education', p. 126 in Colston Papers No. 20, *Towards a Policy for the Education of Teachers,* ed. W. Taylor (Butterworths, 1969). As Musgrove, *Patterns of Power and Authority in English education*, op. cit., suggests 'schools are underpowered in relation to the goals they try to attain' (p. 1), and 'teachers are relatively powerless because they have little to offer that their pupils urgently want' (p. 29).

[74] Musgrove, 'Faith and scepticism in English education', op. cit., p. 2.

[75] See Volume II, p. 56, on this concept.

than we do about the development of particular kinds of students in particular kinds of educational institutions. We have little systematic knowledge of the ways in which students develop: we have still less about the institutional framework which conditions their development ...'[76] Stenhouse places the problem in the context of the school when he writes, 'No one seems to be able to define an educational activity closely enough to realise it in the same form in a number of classrooms. One is continually faced with situations in which the form of educational activity produces a wide range of effects, differing significantly from classroom to classroom, both because of variations in teaching pattern and variation in the context of the school.' These variations include 'the authority structure and organization of the school ... the personalities of the teachers involved and ... the environmental background of the students.' These factors go to make up what Stenhouse calls 'the complex of variables that make the settings of individual schools.'[77]

Broudy has put the point that one consequence of this complexity of variables and outcomes in education, has been the attempt to limit what ought to be taught to those objectives which can be measured and tested. This has meant that research has been 'loath to seek answers to educational questions about broad outcomes of schooling as well as long-range outcomes of a course of instruction.'[78] Hyman stresses this point

---

[76] Musgrove, op. cit., (1966), p. 9. On this area see also P. Bourdieu, 'Systems of education and systems of thought', *International Social Science Journal*, Vol. 19, No. 3 (1967), and our discussion of Bourdieu on p. 153 in Volume II. For an interesting collection of research evidence and perspectives see *College and Student, Selected Readings in the Social Psychology of Higher Education*, ed. Kenneth A. Feldman, op. cit. See particularly Section 10, 'Difficulties in measuring and interpreting change and stability during college', by K. Feldman, p. 127–42.

[77] L. Stenhouse, 'Some limitations of the use of objectives in curriculum research and planning', *Paedagogica Europaea*, Vol. 6 (1970/71), p. 81. On the teaching of reading, see B. Cane and J. Smithers, op. cit.; on p. 81 they conclude: 'In short, we have shown that, even when the initial readiness of the children is taken into account, 12 schools in poor urban areas vary a great deal in the reading standards they have managed to achieve with their pupils.' MacDonald and Rudduck, op. cit., suggest that their article 'explores the problems of opting for an alternative plan [to that of some American curriculum development teams] which is sensitive to the diversity of educational settings and recognises the autonomy of decisions makers at different levels of the system', p. 148.

[78] H. Broudy, 'Can research escape the dogma of behavioral objectives?', *School Review*, Vol. 79 (November 1970), p. 44. See also Elliot W. Eisner, 'Educational objectives help or hindrance?', *School Review* (Autumn 1967), p. 250–60. Note especially his comments, 'that theory concerning educational objectives has not taken into account the particular relationship that holds between the subject matter being taught and the degree to which educational objectives can be predicted and specified' (p. 255). 'The assumption that objectives can be used as standards by which to measure achievement fails, I think, to distinguish adequately between the application of a standard and the making of a judgement' (p. 255). 'If educational objectives were really useful tools, teachers, I submit, would use them. If they do not, perhaps it is not because there is something wrong with the teachers but because there might be something wrong with the theory' (p. 253).

when he argues that since, 'teaching is a dynamic activity in which all the relationships among variables are never known and where unexpected things regularly emerge, it is impossible to specify all the outcomes ahead of time even if we cared to do so. A teacher may not only alter his objectives, but he may discover new ones to pursue during the act of teaching. What is more, the most desirable outcomes are often not those specified in advance as objectives. The most significant outcomes may be those that are not planned for nor fully anticipated when establishing objectives.'[79] This represents a further example of the unintended consequences of human action, and implies that educational processes can be characterized as those whose outcomes cannot be predicted with certainty.[80]

As we argue in Volume II,[81] similar sorts of factors may also apply at the level of national policy-making in education. Smith, for example, notes that: 'Institutional change may be directed by a wide variety of interests located at many points within a complex administrative structure, possibly producing results quite different from those envisaged in the original statement of public policy.' Smith suggests that the study by Burgess and Pratt has demonstrated, 'that a perilous and largely uncharted maze intervenes between public statements of policy in higher education and their implementation. Ministerial speeches on the need for more scientists, engineers and technicians have been made for over a hundred years.

---

[79] R. Hyman, 'Means-ends reasoning and the curriculum', *Teachers College Record*, Vol. 73, No. 3 (January 1972), p. 398. Hyman also suggests that 'it is reasonable to argue that teachers only fully know their objectives while teaching a lesson or after completing one' (p. 397). Eisner, op. cit., suggests that 'the dynamic and complex process of instruction yields outcomes far too numerous to be specified in behavioral and content terms in advance' (p. 254). It has been pointed out to us that this discussion does not do justice to the arguments for the use of objectives in education. This point is valid. We are, however, merely making some speculative comments about education conceived as a political and social process, and suggesting: (a) that the manner in which educational programmes are set up makes it difficult to find out much about the outcomes of such programmes; (b) that some people believe that educational processes, by their nature, cannot be evaluated in precise terms. We are not arguing against the use of objectives in teaching, learning, or in education in general. We would take the view that the *political* consequences of finding out what schools do to children, or what teacher training does to potential teachers (assuming that this could be done) would be so great as to make such research unlikely. Further, the central issue seems to us to be not can teaching be made more 'rational' through the use of objectives, but the *content* of what teachers have to offer. For those groups for whom teachers have little to offer it seems that teachers will have to (and perhaps ought to) learn *from* the children as well as teach them. For some of the arguments for objectives in education see E. Stones and D. Anderson, *Educational Objectives and the Teaching of Educational Psychology* (Methuen, 1972). See especially pp. 5–27, and for some of the literature see pp. 167–76.

[80] See Stenhouse, op. cit., p. 82, where he argues that the curriculum planners 'might aim to break the hypothesis: "The effects of any curriculum differ in important ways from those expected by planners, experimenters and teachers."'

[81] See p. 113, Volume II.

Such "perorations" have less influence on the course of educational development within technical institutions than the assumptions, interests and objectives of those agencies which exercise day-to-day control; the education service, local authorities, college principals, academic boards, examination councils, and so on.'[82] Burgess and Pratt, in their conclusions about the 1966 White Paper (on polytechnics), say that it had 'all the weaknesses of its predecessor, so it and ministerial speeches and pronouncements before and since remain declaratory only. They are not so much a plan as.a peroration. *It is not that no good will come of them, but that whatever comes, good or ill, will come by chance.*'[83]

These points do not imply that decisions ought not to be taken, but that the complexity of outcomes ought to be made explicit. Because it is difficult to find hard evidence about what education does or does not do, people can continue to believe in its great power to resolve social, political, and economic problems. Because we do not know much about what education can do (or does do) it is assumed that education is able to achieve anything.

The third issue about expectations in education concerns teachers. They may be encouraged to develop high expectations about what schools can do, even though it is not known whether these expectations can be fulfilled, and the goals associated with them achieved.[84] The reasons for this are likely to be complex: confusion about what the goals mean in practice; implicit value disputes, contained within an ambiguous vocabulary;[85] or confusion between the value and empirical issues involved. For example, what knowledge do we have about how to reduce race pre-

---

[82] D. Smith, p. 243, in E. Hopper, op. cit.

[83] T. Burgess and J. Pratt, *Policy and Practice: the Colleges of Advanced Technology* (Allen Lane, Penguin Press, 1970), p. 179, (Our italics.) For a review of the literature on politics and education see, Michael W. Kirst and Edith K. Mosher, 'Politics of education', *Review of Educational Research*, Vol. 39, No. 5 (1969), pp. 623–40. For an interesting discussion see Julia Evetts, *The Sociology of Educational Ideas*, op. cit., pp. 142–33. Unfortunately, this book came to our attention after our manuscript was nearly finished. For an analysis which is particularly relevant to the points made in this section see Rachel Elboim-Dror, 'Some characteristics of the education policy formation system', *Policy Sciences*, Vol. 1 (1970), pp. 231–53. For a case study see Raphaella Bilski, 'Ideology and the comprehensive schools', *The Political Quarterly*, Vol. 44, No. 2 (April–June 1973), pp. 197–211. Some of the issues raised in the last four references are covered in more detail in Anthony Hartnett and Michael Naish, eds., *Knowledge, Ideology and Educational Practice* (in preparation).

[84] As a result the teacher training process may be under pressure to achieve goals without knowing how to develop the skills in teachers which such goals require. The process might then come in for criticism. Cf. James Report, *Teacher Education and Training* (HMSO, 1972).

[85] See Volume II, p. 62, on this point. Stenhouse, op. cit., p. 79, makes the point that 'Groups of teachers who claim to have agreed on their objectives often demonstrate in the classroom that their agreement was illusory.' See also the later discussion on Gross p. 196.

judice in a school, or to make secondary schools more 'open' educationally,[86] and, more important, how do we know when these goals have been
achieved?

2. Innovation in education: the research of N. Gross, J. Giacquinta and M. Bernstein, *Implementing Organizational Innovations*, as a case study

Closely related to expectations about education are the views that are held
about the innovatory process in educational organizations, especially
schools. If education can achieve a great deal, then innovation (in terms of
curricula, organizational structure, teacher training, etc.) will be the
means through which expectations can be realized. It is therefore necessary
to ask what knowledge is there about interaction in schools which relates
to innovation, and which could be used to guide programmes of innovation; and what research has been undertaken into the process of innovation
itself, and into the diffusion of innovations in education?

The first general point that can be made is the shortage of *sociological*
work on what happens in schools. As Walker, in a review of the literature
argues, 'The classroom interaction of teacher and taught, which involves
a vital part of the teacher's role, has a central function in the organization
of the school, and provides a logical link between input and output, has
scarcely been considered by sociologists since Willard Waller wrote
The Sociology of Teaching forty years ago.'[87] Walker concludes, ' . . . we
British have not considered studying classroom events as a valid research
activity. Because our concepts lead us out of classroom, and school, and
into the home, and, ultimately, the social class structure, we have tended
to see schools as merely surface features of society.'[88]

The relative shortage of sociological research on interaction in schools

[86] B. Simon, *New Society* (17 October 1968), p. 580.

[87] Rob Walker, 'The sociology of education and life in school classrooms', *International Review of Education*, Vol. 18, No. 1, special number (1972), pp. 32–41. (Quotation from p. 32.) See, however, M. F. D. Young, op. cit. and the readings included in that book. Note Young's comment on page 15 'education is about the selection of knowledge, as well as of people, so comparative research which neglects the cultural content of education as a variable may end up . . . in not being about education at all.' See also Roy Nash, *Classrooms Observed* op. cit.; David Hargreaves, *Social Relations in a Secondary School* op. cit.; and Colin Lacey, *Hightown Grammar* op. cit.

[88] Ibid., p. 36. As an illustration of this Walker (p. 41, footnote 17) cites two textbooks in the sociology of education: one by Olive Banks and one by P. W. Musgrave. In the former Walker says that there are 218 'pages, 8 of which are about the classroom, 3 about the staffroom, 30 about teachers, and 29 about the school.' In the latter there are '270 pages, 13 of which are directly about the classroom, 18 about teachers, and 18 about the school'. Note also Walker's comment on page 38 that 'the longer you observe in a class-room the more complex become the interpretations.' This relates to our previous discussion on educational processes (p. 193).

has consequences for the quantity and quality of research findings about innovation in schools. In order to reinforce this point we have selected the Gross study for comment. We have done this rather than attempt a review of the literature on innovation,[89] because such a review would be beyond our competence, the space available, and our area of interest. The Gross study raises a number of issues which are central to the concerns of this book. These include: the lack of grounded knowledge about educational processes; the high expectations which exist about what schools can do, and ought to do, to cope with political, economic, and social problems; the lack of awareness among educational decision-makers of the intractable problems which programmes of educational innovation may give to classroom teachers; the complexity of the organizational factors which impinge upon the decision-making processes of classroom teachers; and the relationship between career pattern and involvement in educational innovation.

We do not wish to claim that the innovation, and the methods used in an attempt to implement it, which are reported in the Gross study are representative of innovations in schools either in Britain, or in the USA. The question we wish to raise is rather, what *evidence* do we have that 'grassroots' innovation in schools in Britain, or the USA, is any better thought out, or any different in its consequences, from what happened at Cambire school?[90]

Gross investigated an attempt to alter radically the professional role of a group of teachers who worked at the Cambire Elementary School.[91] The intention of the innovation was to enable the teachers at Cambire school to become catalysts for developing the students' talents rather than following the more traditional role.[92] The innovation was regarded as a

---

[89] For a bibliography see Robert B. Nicodemus, 'Annotated bibliography on change in education in England and America with an emphasis on science education', (Centre for Science Education, Chelsea College, London, December 1971). As *selected* examples of the literature see: M. D. Shipman, 'The role of the teacher in innovating schools', op. cit., M. D. Shipman, 'Innovation in schools' in J. Walton, ed., *Curriculum Organisation and Design* (Ward Lock, 1971); G. W. Bassett, *Innovation in Primary Education – a Study of Recent Developments in Primary Education in England and U.S.A.* (New York: Wiley Interscience, 1970); M. B. Miles, *Innovation in Education* (New York: Teachers College, 1964). For an empirical account of one aspect of school organization see Joan C. Barker Lunn, *Streaming in the Primary School* op. cit. especially Chapters 14 and 16. See also section 9 by Keith Cooper, 'Innovation and education', and section 6 by Brian Davies, 'The sociological study of educational organizations' in *The Sociology of Education: an Introductory Guide to the Literature*, ed. Anthony Hartnett, op. cit.

[90] A fictitious name. Gross, op. cit., p. 14.

[91] For details of the location of the school, and a history of the school, see Gross, pp. 65–89.

[92] See Gross, op. cit., p. 14. See also pp. 10–15, pp. 95–6, and appendix B, for full details of the innovation. Few of the behavioural traits outlined on pp. 95–6, appear to relate to learning.

solution to the problem of motivating lower-class children, and of improving their academic achievement.[93] The attempt to change the teacher's role from the traditional one to that of catalyst represented 'a radical redefinition of the role of the teacher and a fundamental change in her primary functions.'[94] The Gross study was not concerned with appraising the value presuppositions of the innovation, but with using it 'as a vehicle to study the *process* that unfolded after the innovation was presented to the teachers and to determine the degree to which it was implemented by them.'[95]

The study makes a number of important points relating to organizational theory, educational policy and classroom practice. We limit our discussion to: (*i*) an examination of one of the five barriers to organizational change at Cambire School which are discussed by Gross – lack of clarity about the innovation;[96] (*ii*) the relationship between the innovation and career prospects.

The documents outlining the innovation were vague and general, and Gross suggests that what was needed was to reduce the new role model to 'more specific actions',[97] that is, those which could be understood by the teachers and translated into classroom strategies. The Gross study demonstrates that the teachers' perceptions of the innovation did not become clearer as the process of change went on.'[98] Four reasons for lack of clarity are given; failure of the teachers to communicate their problems to the administration; the administration's lack of clarity about detailed specifications; the senior administrator's belief that 'creative teachers' could 'figure it out' for themselves what to do; and the fact that the assistant-director, who was in charge of the day-to-day running of the innovation, was not fully committed to the change.[99]

This raises some general issues about innovation in education. Firstly, about the importance of any documents which may be issued as part of an innovatory programme-these provide important data, and ought to be studied with care. This also applies to official reports on education (like

[93] Gross, op. cit., p. 10.
[94] Ibid., p. 14.
[95] Ibid., p. 15.
[96] See Chapters 6 and 7 of the Gross study for full details of the barriers to implementation at Cambire School.
[97] Gross, op. cit., p. 125. For example, how could children be 'subtly coerced' to do things that they did not want to do? See Gross, p. 133–4. It should also be noted that the third barrier to change was that the necessary instructional materials, which appeared to be central to the innovation, did not exist, and therefore could not be made available to the teachers. This may have accounted for some of the 'vagueness' about the innovation, see Gross pp. 135–9 and pp. 168–9. Even if a programme of educational innovation produces materials, it does not follow (*i*) that teachers will use them or (*ii*) that they will use them in the manner intended.
[98] Gross, op. cit., p. 127.
[99] Ibid., pp. 158–9.

the Plowden Report) which may be used to underwrite all kinds of changes within schools.[100]

Secondly, there may be those in education who regard innovation as little more than a new vocabulary with which to describe what goes on in schools. Altering how teachers talk about their work might, under this view, be regarded as a worth-while activity.[101]

---

[100] See the paper by Naish et al. in Volume II (pp. 55–117) which is concerned with the analysis of educational documents. See also Anne Gregory, Master of Education essay, University of Liverpool (1974) unpublished, which examines the documents in the Gross study (appendix B, pp. 245–84) through the critical apparatus reported in the paper by Naish et al.

[101] Until the James Report (and perhaps even after that) most in-service training for qualified teachers was of short duration, i.e. one term or less. Some courses appear to be for ten hours or so. Such courses could attempt little more than to provide partially new vocabularies. The slogan underlying such courses might be 'new vocabularies for old'. It is necessary to investigate the consequences, in classrooms and schools, of teachers talking about their work in different ways. The Gross study suggests that little changed at Cambire School. Note also the comments by Davies that 'teachers have a remarkable capacity for carrying on much as before under officially changed circumstances. The N.F.E.R. work on streaming in the junior school would seem to support this to some extent' W. B. Davies, op. cit., p. 21. The manner in which ambiguous vocabularies are used to cover a wide range of dissimilar activities is a further area of study. See Deanne Bealing, 'The organization of junior school classrooms', Educational Research Vol. 14, No. 3 (1971–72), pp. 231–5. Bealing concludes that, 'group work' meant different things to different teachers (and even the same teachers) p. 234; that children had less freedom of choice than might be supposed from the relatively informal classroom layouts; and that 'it is amazing to report that there have been virtually no systematic attempts to monitor or describe how a teacher's goals and organizational techniques influence what children say and do in the classroom and how these experiences affect their intellectual, social, emotional and moral development' (p. 235). See our discussion of the views of MacDonald and Rudduck (p. 201). Note also the comments of Bernice Martin, 'progressive education versus the working classes', Critical Quarterly, Vol. 13, No. 4 (Winter, 1971), pp. 297–320. 'Progressiveness is often the Linguistic Mystification of Failure' (p. 310), and on p. 315 where she suggests 'It would be tempting but perhaps over-simple to argue that teaching is simply a marginal profession. To compensate for its status ambiguity it over invests in the idea of change in order to prove that like any other profession it has techniques and a body of knowledge which are always being refined and improved .... The last thing that the specialist in education can afford is to be caught purveying the older received wisdom. He must be constantly discovering new truths which through nothing more cogent than the mere passage of time must automatically become invalid. Thus syllabuses, teaching methods, methods of assessment must constantly produce novelty and above all impact. One side-effect of this is to create a further vested interest in the perpetual round of educational change. Progress is no doubt very good for the publishers, manufacturers and distributors of the ever more expensive and diverse educational equipment which each new educational fashion requires.' See the comments of Webb, op. cit., p. 270; G. W. Bassett, op. cit., pp. 3–4. Note the description of a swimming club as 'an integral part of the recreational division of the co-curricular program whose major purpose should be the development of democratic principles of individuality and democratic practices of cooperation during leisure time activities', Marvin Bressler, 'The conventional wisdom of education and sociology', in Charles H. Page, ed., Sociology and Contemporary Education (New York: Random House, 1963), p. 89.

Thirdly, a lack of clarity about the detailed specifications of an educational innovation may make feedback difficult, if not impossible, to obtain.[102] Gross argues that the 'development and effective operation of workable systems of feedback are needed to ensure that difficulties will be pinpointed, analysed, and that steps will be taken to resolve them. At Cambire the lack of feedback mechanisms, for example, largely accounted for the failure to recognize and cope with the ambiguities teachers had about the new role model.'[103] It should be noted, however, that feedback procedures might also make explicit to those recommending the innovation that they are not clear about what they are doing, and that they have no reasonably good evidence upon which to base views about what teachers ought to do.[104] This might have consequences for status hierarchies in education.

In the Gross study comments are made about the career implications for the teachers of having taken part in the innovation.[105] As a result of the innovation at Cambire School most of the teachers were not reappointed to their positions at the school for the following year.[106] The

---

[102] For some British evidence on the importance of feedback see MacDonald and Rudduck, op. cit., 'In experiment, it would seem to be important for people involved to understand that the curriculum developers are the learners and that the school is the teacher' (p. 150); M. D. Shipman, 'The role of the teacher etc.', op. cit., pp. 10–11. Shipman notes that only in '2 of the 38 schools was feedback judged to have been sent regularly and promptly. In another 11 schools the total amount received was judged as negligible.' See also Joan Barker Lunn, op. cit., Chapter 14. Indifference, and even hostility to feedback, may be considered to be a feature of educational ideologies. See the paper by Naish et al., Volume II of this book, p. 55–117. See C. P. Ormell, 'Ideology and the reform of school mathematics', *Philosophy of Education Society of Great Britain, Proceedings of the Annual Conference* (January 1969), Volume III, pp. 37–54. Ormell takes the view that one of the characteristics of an ideology is that 'no channel of feedback from results or the experiences of individuals is permitted, so that the fallacy is protected *in perpetuum*' (p. 44). He also suggests that 'the theory on which the doctrine rests is protected from adverse results and difficulties which might seem, to the unprejudiced eye, to cast doubt on the promises implicit in the programme ... It is always possible to blame "lack of vigour in implementing the Cause" for any gap between promises and results' (p. 41). The education system may become committed to programmes such as nursery education for 'disadvantaged groups'; open plan primary schools; and comprehensive schools, etc. The considerable economic and ideological investments in these programmes may require that criticism of them (or even finding out what they achieve) has to be limited; and that any research which is allowed has to be carefully controlled by the Department of Education and Science, and the local education authorities. See Volume II, page 172 on this point.
[103] Gross, op. cit., p. 210.
[104] This may make teachers aggressive towards people 'selling' what they regard as inadequately worked out ideas. See Gross, Chapter 7, pp. 178–80, and pp. 187–90 on this point.
[105] Gross, op. cit., pp. 171–94.
[106] Ibid., p. 188.

director came to be seen by the teachers as 'after a big job somewhere else.'[107] These career factors contributed greatly to the decline in staff motivation.

Career factors may affect innovation in other ways too. For example, activities which can be talked about at interviews for new posts, filmed, or shown to visitors, might come to structure the innovatory process.[108] Innovations, in short, may be 'packaged'. This could result in particular innovations being regarded as generally desirable, rather than being only relevant to certain sorts of school context. An innovation which was successful in one social context, with its special 'mix of factors,'[109] might be a complete failure in another context. In all cases the important variables are: which teachers are using which methods, with which children, in which schools, and in what sort of social context.[110]

MacDonald and Rudduck provide further insight into this area. Commenting on their experience of three years involvement with the Humanities Curriculum Project, they call attention to: 'a phenomenon which could be described as innovation without change. A head or principal may be beguiled by the cachet of innovation and become involved in a development project without its being esteemed by the power nucleus of the school. The school may try to protect itself from real change by immuring the curriculum development within a small area of the timetable, by involving only one or a few low-status teachers and by providing little opportunity for communication with the rest of the school. Such a phenomenon is consistent with the growing concern of schools – and particularly English secondary modern schools – to improve their 'brand image' through external appearances such as school uniform. On this analogy, innovation without change involves merely a modification in the packaging of the curriculum and does not necessarily involve the school in any concern with modification of content.'[111]

---

[107]Ibid., p. 187.

[108]This may also have implications for how teachers and students are evaluated. They may be judged in terms of what can be photographed, or in terms of visual displays, rather than as a result of factors which are complex and implicit in the social processes which take place in classrooms. There may even be an element of 'impression management' which some teachers have to learn to apply. On this see E. Goffman, *Presentation of Self in Everyday Life* (Allen Lane, 1969). See also the photographs in the Plowden Report, especially plates 2, 3, 19 and 20, and our discussion of these matters in Volume II, p. 110–11. See also Gross, op. cit., pp. 184–7.

[109]Stenhouse, op. cit., p. 81. Also important is how 'the package' of the school, or educational practice, relates to what in fact goes on. The way, for example, television producers select from a school might make a useful area of study.

[110]Ibid., p. 82.

[111]B. MacDonald and J. Rudduck, op. cit., p. 151. See also M. D. Shipman, 'The role of the teacher in innovating schools', op. cit., particularly pp. 14–16.

The Gross study therefore supports the view that the outcomes of educational practices, policies and innovations can only be investigated empirically in schools. It demonstrates that one innovation, at least, remained a series of confused and vague ideas in the minds of those who believed in it, because few of the teachers could understand what the innovation involved, how it was to be implemented, or what precisely it committed them to. The study also supports the view that innovations have to be introduced into schools where there is a unique 'mix of factors'[112] which may have a crucial bearing on the outcome of the innovation.

What now needs to be done is to look at the considerable organizational, curricular, and structural changes, which have apparently characterized all levels of the education system in the UK during recent decades, and to ask:

(i) Have these changes really taken place? If so, to what extent? What is meant, for example, by 'modern primary school methods' and how many schools use them?[113]

(ii) What have been the consequences of those innovations which have been implemented?

(iii) Why does there appear to be so little research evidence about consequences, which can compare with that contained in the Gross study?

3. Expectations and innovation in education: some possible consequences for classroom teachers

Riesman[114] found that the teachers in his research sample appeared to have accepted many of the demands made upon them and, 'underneath the protective coating of cynicism and careerism . . . they harbor the most idealistic but impossible expectations of omnicompetence in the classroom. They expect themselves to respond sympathetically to individual problem children, even psychotic ones that would baffle an experienced psychiatrist. What with the current emphasis on psychology, they can no longer simply reject a child as a trouble-maker, or if they do they will feel guilty about it. Overtly, they may resist the expectation that there is no

---

[112] See this section, p. 193.

[113] Cf. Plowden Report, p. 51, paragraph 136. Note the list of 'danger signs' p. 187, paragraph 503, one of which is 'much time spent on teaching'. One point may be that some teachers have what might be described as a general ideological commitment to innovation, rather than a concern for concrete, specific examples of innovation. Sometimes the former is expressed in a generally accepted 'progressive vocabulary' whose relationship to social and educational processes (and to individual personality factors) is obscure. See also N. Bennett 'Plowden's progress', *Times Educational Supplement* (18 October 1974), p. 21.

[114] D. Riesman, 'Teachers amid changing expectations', *Harvard Educational Review*, Vol. 24, No. 2 (Spring 1954), pp. 106–17; see also D. Riesman, 'Notes on educational reform', *Journal of General Education*, Vol. 23, No. 2 (July 1971), pp. 81–110.